# WITH GOD'S SONG IN MY HEART

ॐ

## A STORY OF FAITH

*To Gloria,
my cousin! Enjoy!
Love + blessings,
Faith*

## by Faith Skepstad Bradley

Editing and interior design by: Betsy Goldthwait Atkinson

Jacket Design by Kudzu Branding Co., 2015

ISBN: 978-0-692-41120-9

Printed in the United States of America

## Dedication

I dedicate this book,

"With God's Song in my Heart:
A Story of Faith"

To my four children

Karen Elizabeth Bradley Nelson

John Hugh Bradley

Anne Sharon Bradley Wilbanks

David Mark Bradley


Who have been through many of these days of my life with me.

# Contents

# Preface

The thought of writing a story of my life began during my college days when I thought about how different it had been from most teenagers in the United States, living in China as a daughter of Lutheran missionaries during the days of the Japanese bombings, occupation, and many needed evacuations, both before and after World War II. Verses from Scripture came alive, as we experienced the Lord's protection on many occasions.

The thought continued in later years after I went to Taiwan as a missionary nurse, to a boarding school for missionaries' children. There I was dorm mom to seventeen girls in grades one through high school, and nurse for the entire school community. It was a real mission opportunity – and I loved it.

Marriage to a Presbyterian minister and living in the mountain area among the Bunun people, raising a family, three children at that time, and occasional trips into the high mountains as nurse were challenging. We saw God at work, as individuals accepted Christ into their lives, and their lives were changed, as they knew they were loved and accepted by God.

There were many adjustments to make when we had to return to the United States permanently. A fourth child was born. Later, I had the loss of my husband, then returning to nursing after twenty years of being away from hospital duty, and also life beyond, with its adjustments and opportunities. Then, years of travel to many countries abroad was fascinating, and my worldview of life expanded. God's world!

During all this time, the Lord was the one to whom I looked for guidance and direction, and His Word sustained me through each day.

In my church this year our minister told us that we each have a story to tell. "Tell your story!" I felt that she was speaking directly to me. So now was the time to write "With God's Song in my Heart: A Story of Faith"

## FAITH BRADLEY FAMILY TREE

### FIVE GENERATION

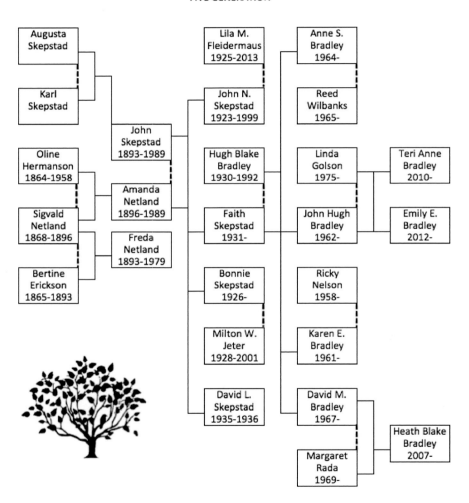

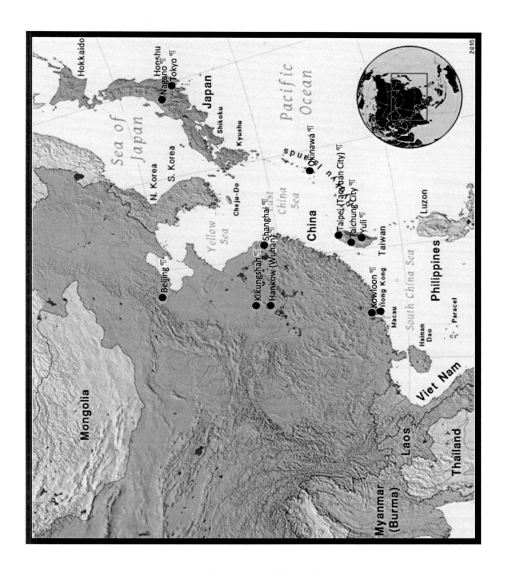

PAT map copyright © 2010, 2013 Ian Macky

# CHAPTER 1

## On Both Sides of the Ocean

My dad's first call to serve as pastor of a church in the United States was in 1929, to the Lutheran Church in Stephen, Minnesota, close to the Canadian border. In the wintertime, that part of the country was a flat, barren land with frigid temperatures and howling blizzards – but in the summertime it was potato country!

There, my dad Rev. John Skepstad, mom Amanda, son John and daughter Borghild settled into a large two-story parsonage with electricity – but no running water at that time. Water had to be carried in pails from a town pump a block away. Cooking was done on a wood stove, and a large pan of water was kept heating on the side of the stove for washing dishes. There was no refrigerator, so blocks of ice were kept in the garage to replenish the ice in their icebox to keep food cold.

On June 11, 1931, during the days of the Depression, I, Faith Evangeline, was born in the nearest hospital in Warren, the county seat. As an infant I had colic. Many were the nights my parents walked me back and forth, trying to comfort and quiet me. They were uncertain of my survival, and after a bad spell of croup, Rev. Lawrence Halvorson baptized me on July 2, though I was only three weeks of age.

Memories of my early days in Stephen include walking to Sunday School with a penny for offering tied in the corner of my handkerchief. I remember that my maternal Grandma Netland lived with us part of the time, and as a three year old, I used to dust her room for her. One day she noticed that her clock had stopped running, and she asked me if I had touched it. "Oh, no, Grandma, I only put a toothpick in it!"

In the winter, with the heavy snowfalls and cold weather, we kids had to be bundled up in our snowsuits and boots, but we had a wonderful time building snowmen, throwing snowballs, and sledding. Some storms left snowdrifts that reached up to the second story of our house. One year I had bronchitis (perhaps from sitting on the ice in the garage!) and had to stay inside for three months, much to my dismay!

In 1935, a little brother, David Lowell Theodore, was born. When he was brought home from the hospital, several of us had a communicable disease – was it measles? – and we had to stay at the home of a neighbor, whom we called Grandma Peterson, until we recovered. David was a Down's Syndrome baby, but none of us children were aware of this at the time. Just before his first birthday, he developed "double pneumonia," which claimed his life. Penicillin had not yet been discovered. As Heaven's new little boy, he had already gone on to his eternal home, and I thought Heaven must be a very special place.

In the summer we used to go to Ottertail Lake for several weeks of vacation. Dad had a Whippet car with a running board. He bought the car from a member of the congregation when our family first moved to Stephen, and at 35 years of age had to learn how to drive. One day as we were riding in the car, and going a little faster than usual, John Jr. piped up from the back seat and said, "45 miles per hour! 50 miles per hour!" Dad wasn't too happy with his back seat driver!

Depression days were difficult for everyone, and while we were in Stephen Dad had to take a cut in salary. However, folks in nearby Happy Corner supplied us with meat and potatoes and made it possible for Dad to continue his work.

During our days in Stephen, Grandma Netland moved to Minneapolis where her brother had an apartment building. One wintry day, while she was out to buy groceries, she slipped on the ice and broke her hip. An ambulance arrived and she was put onto a stretcher. The attendant at the head of the stretcher carrying her to the ambulance slipped and fell, throwing her out onto the ice again. In the hospital, the hip was set incorrectly and had to be reset a second time, but the condition was never fully corrected. From that time on one of her legs was shorter than the other, and she had to use crutches.

Dad used to take my brother John to a farm for a few weeks' stay in the summertime. One such time while at the farm, Dad told John that we were going to leave Stephen and go back to China. John's reaction was, "Leave Stephen?! Where I was confirmed?! Where I play clarinet in the band?! Where all my friends are?!" John's world fell apart for him at that moment, and he felt like he was about to walk off the end of the earth.

We left Stephen just before Christmas in 1936. During our last visit with Grandma in the Pioneer Home in Fergus Falls, Minnesota, we three children sang Christmas carols for the elderly folk there…"Away in a Manger"… "Joy to the World"… "Silent Night." It was difficult to say goodbye to Grandma Netland.

Early in January our family took a train to Seattle. A longshoreman's strike was in progress, and we weren't able to sail for another two months. At last, in March, we were able to secure passage on the ocean liner the *Empress of Russia*, out of Vancouver, and began on the voyage to China.

The *Empress of Russia* pulled away from the docks of Vancouver, Canada, that March day in 1937, as the ship's whistle sounded, and the colored streamers bonding

The Rev. John Skepstad
Family 1936

passengers with friends on shore tore apart and waved wildly in the wind. The voyage was by the northern route across the Pacific Ocean to the Orient, and choppy seas whipped up by those northerly winds made for rough sailing for passengers and crew alike.

As passengers, my parents were returning to China as Lutheran missionaries with their three children: John, Borghild, and Faith. I, the youngest, was only five years old, yet remember parts of the journey quite vividly. We struggled to gain our "sea legs." I turned out to be a pretty good sailor – with a few exceptions!

A young missionary couple on board ship held a children's story time in the mornings, when we would sing choruses and praise-songs and hear stories from the Bible. I remember so well singing...

"Climb, Climb up Sunshine Mountain"
"Every Burden of My Heart Rolled Away"
"Safe Am I in the Hollow of His Hand."

As we came closer to Japan after a stormy trip, we hoped that calmer seas were ahead. However, the worst was yet to come! The ship encountered the tail end of a typhoon off the Japan Sea enroute to Shanghai. Gale winds blew the ship off course. Huge waves swept over the deck, taking with them a

4

side rail and one of the stairways up to the next deck. Only essential crewmembers were allowed out on deck, and they had ropes tied around them in the event they were swept overboard. Inside, the piano in the lounge was chained to the floor. In the dining room, those who were able to come to meals found their dishes sliding off the table and crashing down to the floor. The Captain's party for the children on the final day of the voyage was complete with hats, noisemakers, cookies and punch, but somehow it wasn't so festive when the cookies and punch ended up in our laps!

During this winter trip on the ocean, it was good to remember that we were "safe in the hollow of God's hand."

Disembarking in Shanghai, I knew we were in a foreign country for sure! We blond, blue-eyed children of Scandinavian descent were a curiosity in this land, and the people with dark, straight hair and dark eyes turned to stare at us as we walked by. "Big nosed people!" they called us. The Chinese spoke a language I didn't understand. It was reassuring to me that my parents were able to comprehend and communicate with them.

Our brief stay in Shanghai was at the China Inland Mission Home while preparations were made for us to continue our journey inland. Then we sailed on the Yangtze River on a riverboat, arriving in Hankow, a large city in the interior of China, a number of days later. Our final destination was Kikungshan ("Rooster Mountain"), and we boarded a train headed north on the Peking-Hankow railroad to the station closest to this mountain retreat, where many of the missionaries, including our family, had a home. Our home had been built for my Grandma Netland, who had been one of the pioneers in the Lutheran Mission Society. She had arrived in China in 1893. So you see that the trip my brother, sister, and I were making

Rev. Sigvald Netland
1890

with our parents was just the newest link in my family's connection with China.

Our connection to China starts with my grandfather, Sigvald Netland, who was the first one in the family to have the call to China. He was born on October 11, 1868, in Ladestedet Sogndal i Dalerne, Norway. His parents were both believers. As a small boy he was taught Bible verses, hymns, and prayers. As he was growing up, he could not remember that he experienced any close relationship with the Lord. While he did not sin willingly or openly, he felt his sinful nature was a heavy burden. One cold winter night, as a teenager, Sigvald attended revival services and heard the preacher speak about Zacchaeus, and how if he wanted to see Jesus, he had but to climb up into the tree of promise. That night under an open Heaven, kneeling alone on a stone, Sigvald found his peace with God.

As an apprentice to a shoemaker, Sigvald now kept his Bible and hymnbook beside his tools, and his singing accompanied the blows of the hammer. Whenever it was possible for him to be away from work, he traveled to many places around Stavanger, Norway, holding revival meetings and organizing mission societies. He was deeply touched when he read Hudson Taylor's booklet, "China's Spiritual Needs and Claims," and his zeal and enthusiasm for missions continued to grow.

Sigvald had intended to enter the Bergen Inner Mission School on the west coast of Norway in the fall of 1889, but the call from foreign lands had become too strong. Instead he applied to Baxter's Training Home in London, and in three weeks time, after paying his last visit home, he was ready to leave for London. Friends in Stavanger arranged a farewell party, and on October 12, 1889, just one day after his 21st birthday, he sailed out of Stavanger Fjord, with a gift of one hundred crowns in his pocket, and with the blessing of God and his friends. At the mission school he met Mr. Nestegaard, Jr., who was also preparing for work in China. Four months later, Mr. Nestegaard loaned Sigvald enough money for a third class ticket, and the two of them sailed to America enroute to China.

In Minnesota and the surrounding states, the two men had opportunities to speak for China missions. In those six months, a deep interest was awakened in the congregations. One pastor reported, "The fire which they succeeded in starting will not soon be quenched. This fire has spread far and wide, and the Lord has clearly shown us that He has a work for us in China." Two thousand dollars was raised, most of which was divided between the two men. Sigvald had hoped to attend Red Wing Seminary in Minnesota, but Mr. Nestegaard's older brother, who had just arrived from three years in China, urged the two men to leave for the field that fall. With the money raised, Sigvald could pay his debt, buy a steerage ticket to China, and still have some money to spare. God was good!

Leaving San Francisco on September 4, 1890, they sailed on the *S.S. Oceanic* across the Pacific Ocean to Shanghai. Continuing on by riverboat they traveled inland on the Yangtze River, landing in Hankow on October 7. Here a pioneer missionary, of another mission, Dr. Griffith John, was most helpful in assisting them to rent a native house in

Wuchang, across the river from Hankow, and to secure a Chinese language teacher. This house, the first home in China for missionaries of the Norwegian Lutheran Church, became known as "Place of Many Blessings." In June 1891, the Norwegian Evangelical Lutheran China Mission Society was formally organized in the United States, and Sigvald was accepted as a worker of the Society.

A year after Sigvald arrived in China, his fiancée, Bertine Erickson, joined him in China. Six days later they were married in the Cathedral in Shanghai. In time a baby girl was born to them, Siegfred, or "Freda" as she was called. Just six weeks later, Bertine died of cholera. Sigvald wrote, "We have sorrow upon sorrow out here. One witness after another is laid in the ground. Just think, He did not spare my beloved wife, but took her from me. Oh God, how are your ways unsearchable. Teach me Thy way, and let my soul once more have peace and rest."

Grandmother Oline
Hermanson Netland

My maternal grandmother, Oline Hermanson, arrived in China in January, 1893, from Nicollet, Minnesota, in response to God's call to her for missionary service. She had grown up in Minnesota and supported those who went as missionaries to China, financially and in prayer. When a pastor asked her if she would go to China if asked, she replied, "I would like to, but I am not fit to be a missionary."

He replied, "You better speak to God about it. I think God wants you to go to China."

She later writes, "I asked the Lord to let me know for sure. He answered my prayer in a wonderful way. I was away from home teaching in a school held in a home. One day I had a bad cold, and the man of the house gave me some medicine and said, 'I am going away, but at noon, you take another spoonful.' So when school closed at noon, I took a full spoonful out of a bottle from the cupboard. It had a horrid taste! It wasn't the same as I'd had before. In looking at the bottle again, I saw it was apart from the others and on one side of the bottle 'Poison' was written. The poison did not hurt me at all. When the man returned and heard what had happened, he said, 'It is nothing short of a miracle, strong poison as it was. God wants you to go to China as a missionary.'"

She then applied to the Mission Board to be accepted as a missionary to China and was approved. On her trip to the Orient, she experienced a train wreck on the way to the west coast, a typhoon on the ocean, and an earthquake in Japan, but finally arrived in Hankow, China, on January 25, 1893, where she began to study the language. The next year, she met and married Sigvald. They left for the new station in Fancheng, Hupeh, a ten-day trip up the Han River by riverboat. There she took on the added responsibilities of wife – and mother to Freda, now six months of age.

In spite of an initially hostile reception by government officials, with many of the people calling out, "The foreign devils have come! Kill them! Kill them!," the missionaries gradually won the confidence of the people through their friendly contacts and treatment of the sick. Sigvald had taken some medical training in London, and in Hankow he had helped out at the Catholic Hospital, and that training was invaluable from the beginning. The coolies who carried passengers' luggage from the boat had sores on their legs, and he cleaned and treated them. They in turn brought others to him for treatment.

Services presenting the "Good News of the Great Physician" were held and were well attended. Sigvald bought a horse, which he used when he made trips into the countryside, preaching, selling books, and helping the sick. After several years of ministry in Fancheng, he had the joy of seeing five men baptized.

During this time, the strenuous work from morning till night – and the unhealthy living conditions – undermined Sigvald's health. A two months' vacation did not restore his health.

Joys and sorrows were often intermingled in those early days on the mission field. There was joy in the Netland home when a daughter, Amanda Borghild, was born on March 29, 1896. Four-and-a-half months later, Sigvald and family traveled to Hankow to welcome a new missionary, Rev. K. S. Stokke. An epidemic of cholera was raging in the city. At 4 p.m. one afternoon, while working at translating some textbooks into Chinese, Sigvald became ill with cholera, was taken to the Catholic Hospital and treated by missionary doctors, but to no avail. Ten hours later, on August 9, he was called to his Eternal Home. The following day a letter arrived from the Mission Board asking Sigvald to return to the United States to take up medical training for future work in China. He, however, had already received his summons to higher service.

Oline Netland was now left with a three-and-a-half-year-old as well as her four-and-a-half-month-old infant. She was run down in health and had to return to the United States to recuperate. The two children were ill on the way home, and it was a very difficult trip for them all with no one else along to help. Once she arrived in the United States, she sent a telegram to her farm home as to when she was to arrive by train in Minneapolis, hoping someone could help her. Concerning this incident she has written: "My folks lived out in the country, with no telephones or autos at that time. The telegram was put in the newspaper, and it happened that someone at home picked up the paper just as it came. It was a busy time in the threshing season. My brother saw the telegram at once and said, 'I wonder if I can make it.' He got ready in a hurry, took his bike as fast as he could go to the local train station. He came just as the train pulled in, so he had no time to buy a ticket, but he jumped on. As the train pulled in at Minneapolis from one side, ours came from another direction. Again we saw God's wonderful answer to prayer."

After several months of rest, fresh air, and good food, Oline still had not regained her strength. Before her husband died, he had requested that if anything should happen to him, she would take Freda to his family in Norway and leave her with them. At this time, Oline's parents paid for her, Freda and Amanda to travel to Norway to meet her husband's family. Oline was to make the arrangements for Freda to stay with the Netlands in Norway. Oline and the girls stayed with the Netlands for three months in a beautiful part of that country. When it was time to leave, Freda cried and cried about Oline and Amanda going to leave without her, for they were the only family she knew. Finally Oline made the decision to take Freda back with them to Minnesota, and she raised her as her own daughter. During their home stay, Oline took in sewing to support her family and also traveled to various churches, sharing her experiences in mission work in China.

In 1901, after the Boxer Rebellion in China was over, Oline returned to the field with the two girls and was stationed in Hankow. A gift from a man in Wisconsin whom she had never met, but who had learned of her situation on the field as a widow, made it possible to have a house built for her use on Kikungshan, the mountain retreat for missionaries in this area of China. There on the mountain, at more than 2,400 feet above sea level, the air was fresh and folks found relief from the heat on the plains.

Because one of the missionaries had to return to America with his sick wife, Oline had to temporarily relocate in the large city of Hankow. From here she had to send building materials by wheelbarrows to the stations inland where they were needed, as the railroad had not yet been completed. About one experience she writes, "The evangelist took a whole day to get 30 wheelbarrows, as they put prices so high that you needed a long time to argue. At last the wheelbarrows came, and we were to load up. Each barrow was to carry a certain weight, so everything was weighed. As some barrows were loaded, we turned to some other barrows to load. Then the first coolies would use this opportunity to take off some of their load and put it back on the pile. So it took all day, and glad we were when we heard the music of the wheelbarrows going on their long journey."

Each spring and fall the family would send in an order to Montgomery Wards for groceries and clothing. It was a red-letter day when the shipment arrived – if duty wasn't too high!

Furlough time arrived, but Oline became ill with pneumonia. After three weeks, the crisis seemed to pass, but the fever did not abate, and her heart was failing. The doctor felt the end might come at any time. She was in a coma. When people spoke to her, she could hear and answer, but then she would be "away" again. Her daughters stood by her bed weeping. Amanda had written some Bible verses on paper and rolled them up and called them pills. She asked her mother, "Do you want a pill, Mama?"

"Yes."

She picked one, Psalm 4:8, "I will both lay me down in peace and sleep, for thou, Lord, only makest me dwell in safety." As soon as she heard it she was in a coma again. She later wrote, "I saw two angels dressed in long white dresses and beautiful wings, who took that verse and made a little bench of it, and lifted me on top. One angel on each side took hold of my hands, and up we went … and what beautiful things I saw! I asked if this was heaven and was told that this was the valley of death. The higher we came, the more beautiful it was. She said again, 'This must be heaven,' and again they said, 'No.' They pointed up higher and said the portals of heaven were there but, 'You cannot enter this time. We must take you down again as there is some work for you to do yet. But your mother and father are soon to be taken up here.'" When she woke up, the fever was gone. Several days later her mother fell dead, and her father followed soon afterward. It was a sad home going to Minnesota for Oline.

Terms of missionary service were seven years at that time, and after the next furlough, Freda, sixteen years of age, was left at home with relatives, for there was no adequate schooling for her (high school) on the field. This term Oline was stationed inland in Kioshan, and a teacher was secured to teach Amanda and two other missionary children. As more missionary children arrived, the school was moved to the mountain resort of Kikungshan.

In the spring of 1915, ground breaking took place at Kikungshan for a school building, and on June 20, Amanda and Nora Nelson became the first two graduates of the American School of Kikungshan, known as ASK. After graduation Amanda returned to the United States and attended St. Olaf College in Northfield, Minnesota. Oline returned to Minnesota in 1916 and rented a house in Northfield so that Amanda could stay at home while attending college. Oline did not return to China until 1920.

During Amanda's junior year in college, she began dating a senior, John Skepstad, who was headed for Luther Theological Seminary in St. Paul, Minnesota, and mission service following graduation from seminary. John had been born in Lillehammer, Norway, in 1893, and had come to America when fourteen years of age. Knowing very little English, he was put in a second grade class until he learned English, and then advanced to his appropriate grade rapidly. At graduation he was salutatorian of his class of 100 students. In order to make money for college, he worked in a department store for two years and then applied to St. Olaf College. Before he left Norway, he had heard the St. Olaf Concert band on tour, but he never dreamed that he would one day attend that school!

When Amanda graduated from college in 1920, she enrolled in a short medical course at Deaconess Hospital in Chicago and then attended Moody Bible Institute for a term. After Christmas of 1921, she taught school in Donnybrook, North Dakota, till the end of the year. Prior to her engagement to John, she had applied for missionary service in China, and she returned there and served as a single worker before he graduated from seminary and joined her there. On September 6, 1922, Amanda and John were married by Rev. Landahl in the little stone church on Kikungshan.

During this term, the couple was assigned to work in Suiping, the northernmost station on the field. In addition to their work in evangelism, church growth, and leadership training conferences, John would also bicycle out into the countryside to do visitation and assist in the work at several outstations. There was good response among the people there, and the work brought forth much fruit.

Their personal lives were blessed with a son, John Netland, born to them at the hospital in Kioshan, Honan, on December 17, 1923. To avoid confusion in the home, he was called "Sonny."

Times in China were very often unsettled due to bandits, soldiers, warlords, and uprisings among the people. 1926 was no exception. Sun Yat Sen's forces were attempting to unify the country under the influence of the Bolsheviks, and civil war flared up. Americans were urged by the American consulate to evacuate. As a result, John and Amanda, who were expecting their second child, had to flee. It was while they were temporarily in the mountains at Kikungshan that Borghild Arlene chose to put in her appearance. Thankfully, a missionary doctor was also at Kikungshan at that moment and was called into service. Because of the continued prospect of war, John, Amanda, and their two young children, along with Oline, returned to the United States, and John accepted a call to serve a Lutheran congregation in Stephen, Minnesota.

# CHAPTER 2

## Japan Invades China

When my parents, siblings and I spent our initial months in China in 1937, we stayed in Grandma Netland's home on Kikungshan, "Rooster Mountain," where many missionaries had homes to use in the summer. The summer heat on the plains made it necessary for the missionaries to get to a higher elevation for vacation and renewal. The boarding school for missionaries' children, known as the American School of Kikungshan, or "ASK," was located there.

That fall, when the summer heat had lifted, John remained at the school while Mother, Borghild, and I joined my dad at his station of work in Suiping, north of Kikungshan on the rail line. Like many Chinese cities, Suiping, with a population of around 300,000 people, was a walled city, for protection from roving gangs of bandits and warlords. A new danger had arisen in July when Japan invaded northern China and war was declared.

Our family and one older single lady worker, Sister Inga Dvergsness, a Deaconess, were the only foreigners in the city, and we lived in a mission compound. Over the gate to the compound were the large characters for "Gospel Hall." Within the compound was a brick church that seated about 250 people, with plain glass windows, cement floors, hard rough benches, and no heat. There was also a boys' school and a girls' school, and other quarters used in women's work. One could always tell when school was in session, for primary students learned their lessons by singing them out loud in singsong fashion!

In an inner courtyard was the residence for the foreign missionaries. Outside the house some lovely roses were growing, and there were persimmon trees – and I loved persimmons!

That fall, Mother home schooled Borghild and me. Just living in a foreign country and learning about life among the people there enhanced our education. At Christmastime, my brother John joined us for the holidays.

There was no snow on the ground, but it was cold, and we dressed warmly. We heated only two rooms in the house, for coal was at a premium. The coalfields were flooded, and available coal was needed for the war effort.

Around 4 a.m. on Christmas morning, before it was light, carolers from the school awakened us singing of Christ's birth! Later at the morning service, the school children marched in and sat in the front pews, boys on one side and girls on the other. They led the singing along with a pump organ, and they loved to do it. The church was festively decorated with gaily-colored streamers, paper lanterns, lovely paper flowers, and wreaths of green hung over the doorways.

Because of the Japanese invasion, the church bell was no longer used to call people to worship. It now had another purpose – to sound air alarms over the city and countryside. We knew what it was like to run and hide in ditches or corners of the yard, listening to that never-to-be-forgotten sound of heavily loaded bombers approaching.

Dad led the service in his Chinese padded coat and cap – and even fingerless half-mitts – because of the cold. We had brought heated bricks to church wrapped in paper to keep our feet warm. The Chinese evangelist was in the middle of his message when there was a scuffling in the church tower, and the quick, sharp ringing of the bell sent everyone scurrying out of doors. By government orders, any large group of people had to disperse and scatter outside into yards, lanes, and alleys. We watched, trembling, as the bright shiny bombers drew ever closer, and wondered where their bombs would fall. We almost held our breath when they were right overhead – and we heaved a sigh of relief as they passed on. The neighboring city was not so fortunate; we could hear the explosions that followed the bombing. Then our church bell rang again, sounding the "all clear," as the bombers headed back to their base.

In the late afternoon, we gathered again for the children's program. The church was packed to hear the girls and boys recite portions of Scripture and sing carols and hymns. They have marvelous memories! A skit written by the Chinese teachers was presented, followed by the giving of gifts from under the small tree. There were peanuts and candy for all the children, and a pencil, bar of soap, or a washrag for the school children, gifts given by friends back home in the United States. It didn't take much to make the children happy!

Back in our home, where we had a small tree decorated with ornaments and tinsel, we sat down to our Christmas meal. Canned fish balls with locally made flatbread took the place of lutefisk and lefse. There were sweet potatoes and rice, Jell-O with whipped cream made from evaporated canned milk, and even homemade ice cream.

Because of the war with Japan, parcel post was not able to deliver packages to inland cities, so we didn't have our gifts from loved ones in America to put under the tree. However, Mother and Dad had some ideas of their own. By hiring a local carpenter, and showing him pictures from a Montgomery Wards catalog, our parents were able to present Borghild and me with doll beds for our dolls. John received a set of bookends. Also, Mother opened the trunk of reserved clothing brought from the United States and took out and wrapped something for each one of us, so we all had several gifts. Our Chinese cook joined us and received his gift.

There was a knock on the door, and old Mrs. Wang came in carrying something in her warn handkerchief. She was the gatekeeper of the women's court. She had a tiny little room, and she cooked her simple food in a pot on an open fireplace in the yard. Her garments were old and shabby, and she earned just enough to get by. Yet there was a light in her eyes. She was a Christian, and she wanted to share what little she had. She unfolded her handkerchief on the table, revealing a few eggs and some Chinese candy. "The children must have some good things to eat. They mustn't suffer because you are here working with us," she said. She had learned the gift of sharing, and we were touched!

As the day drew to a close, we sat around the fireplace. As a special treat we had a charcoal fire and roasted chestnuts in the coals. We enjoyed tangerines, Chinese dates and figs, and Chinese candy. Delicious! We gathered around the baby organ, and Mother led us in singing our favorite carols. Then, as he did each year, Dad read the Christmas story from the Bible. We thought of our loved ones in America, and closed the evening with prayer.

A week later my dad accompanied my brother John back to school on Kikungshan. While he was gone, we heard that 10,000 bandits had joined together with plans to attack our walled city. My sister and I were not told of the danger at first, but we thought it strange when Mother told us not to undress when we went to bed at night. Then a prayer meeting was called by the Christians and held at our home, asking for Dad's safe return, our escape (for foreigners were targets for kidnapping), and for sparing the city and its people from killing and destruction. When the prayer meeting was over and our Chinese Christian friends surrounded us, I had a deep sense of peace in my heart and trusted the Lord to take care of us through whatever might happen.

Dad did arrive safely and made immediate plans for our escape. Not even our servants were told of our plan to leave in the middle of the night, under cover of darkness. Disguised in Chinese clothes and with our blond hair covered up, we left home in two rickshaws, with Dad walking behind. At the city gate, the soldiers were adamant that they would not open up the gate for us to pass through to head to the train station a mile out into the countryside. We began to think that it would be necessary to be let down over the wall in a basket. At the last minute, the soldiers relented and opened the gates cautiously, saying that we would be on our own and for no reason would they again open the gates if we ran into trouble. We passed through the gates and into the darkness outside, as there were no lights along the way. We were alert for any sounds around us, praying all the way.

When we reached the train station, the stationmaster told us that the next train was an express that didn't stop at this station. But he promised to try to flag it down. He was successful! The train stopped just long enough for us to climb aboard, and we were off into the night. We were able to travel to the station where we could get off the train and head to our house on Kikungshan. The Lord had made a way for us to escape! We heard later that the bandits had attacked the city next to ours and had caused much destruction and suffering there.

With the dangerous conditions brought about by the invasion of Japanese forces, and the mountains mostly unprotected, the decision was made to temporarily evacuate the American School of Kikungshan from Kikungshan to the large city of Hankow on the Yangtze River. My older brother John was attending this boarding school. In Hankow, the American Consul recommended further evacuation to a port city for the school and other Americans as well, including my family that was also in Hankow at that time. On February 1, 1938, the school and missionary families, including ours, numbering approximately 70 people, boarded two third-class coaches on the *International Express*, bound for Hong Kong. Tied across the top of those two coaches was a large American flag, to alert the Japanese bombers that American citizens were aboard.

The trip normally takes from two to three days, but this trip took twice as long. As the train pulled into the station at Canton (Guangxhou), where we needed to change trains, an air alarm sounded. A representative of the American Consulate met the train and evacuated us by bus to a safer place until we could return several hours later.

It was 10:30 at night when we finally arrived in Kowloon, the mainland across the bay from Hong Kong. The Consul had arranged for us to stay at the elegant Peninsula Hotel! Cot beds had been set up in a large room for us travel-weary folk to spend the night.

The teachers found quarters for the school to locate on Cheung Chau Island, an hour's ferry ride from Kowloon, in a hospital partly unoccupied at the time. My brother John went with them. The rest of the family was able to stay in several rooms at a private Chinese school, at 3 Duke Street in Kowloon. I remember having to be quiet during their classes, but we had more freedom after the children had gone home for the day. After Mother, Borghild, and I were settled, Dad returned to his station to resume his mission work in north China.

Mother again taught Borghild and me using the Calvert System (a curriculum available to American parents teaching their children overseas). Living in this big, bustling city and seaport was an education in itself! It was much different from inland China! There were people from many different countries living here in the British colony, and many different languages were spoken. Cantonese was the language of most of the Chinese living here, rather than Mandarin, spoken in the north.

Hong Kong was on the South China Sea, and steamers, freighters, and warships could be found in the harbor along with the Chinese junks and sampans. The Star Ferries transported people back and forth between Kowloon and Hong Kong. There were signs on the ferry telling people to beware of pickpockets! Good advice! At night the harbor was a beautiful sight with the boats weaving a pattern of lights across the waters.

The Star Ferry in
Hong Kong Harbor

Double-decker buses, taxis, cars, bicycles, and rickshaws were all a part of the busy traffic on the streets. Shops were selling merchandise from all over the world at good prices. Watches, cameras, carved chests, embroidered jackets, silver, jade, and pearl jewelry, linen tablecloths, and much, much more! My mother loved to shop and knew how to bargain with the shopkeepers to get a good price!

Our stay in Kowloon lasted about four months. It then seemed possible for us to return to Honan. While we returned to Kikungshan, Dad went back to Suiping. John remained in Hong Kong with the school.

The Netland Home in Kikungshan

The summer of 1937 was drawing to a close. We had enjoyed fellowship with other missionary families on the mountain, picnics, and the cool breezes. On Sunday evenings, we had hymn sings out of doors in the courtyard while we watched the colors of the sunset spread across the sky.

Always we were aware that China was a country at war, and we didn't know when the Japanese troops would be heading our way. As we prepared to leave Kikungshan, we packed our belongings to travel back to Suiping, my father's station of mission work. Before we could leave, it began raining, and it rained for ten continuous days, making the mud paths down the mountain impassable. Before the ten days were over, we received a telegram from our mission superintendent telling us not to go north to Suiping, but to head south immediately to Hankow, for the Japanese were about to cut off the railroad!

As soon as the weather permitted, we began the hike down the mountain with several coolies carrying our heavier luggage, using bamboo poles over their shoulders. "Hey-a-ho, hey-a-ho," they chanted in a singsong fashion as they walked down the mud paths. We all carried what we could.

Down at the train station on the plains, in Sintien, we waited for the train to arrive. We watched as many troop trains came along from the south and headed north to the war front. Several times Japanese warplanes flew overhead. Everyone scattered to find shelter under the trees. Mother had only one warm wrap along, a red knit sweater. The Chinese soldiers kept pointing to her sweater and told her to hide it, for it could easily be spotted from the air. She would be an easy target. It wasn't easy to hide — but it was cold outside!

As the night shadows deepened, and no southbound train had come, Mother found two bamboo chairs, which she put together for a makeshift bed for Borghild and me. It was difficult to sleep in those circumstances, but we slept more than our parents did, I'm sure.

The next morning the train did arrive, and we were able to board it and get a compartment for four. The 100-mile ride to Hankow usually took five to six hours. However, this was no ordinary trip! It took us four days and nights from the time we left Kikungshan until we arrived in Hankow. Japanese bombers were determined to keep our train from reaching its destination. Because of frequent air alarms, we didn't make much progress. When the train had just left Sintien and had rounded a bend, another of our missionary families, the Dan Nelsons, made it to Sintien. The train was gone! Dan, a very resourceful person, hired a locomotive to catch up to our train. Then we heard a knock on the door of our compartment. Opening our door, we found Dan and Esther Nelson with their two children, Rita and Danny. Rita was a year younger than I, and we had become good friends on Kikungshan. We shared our compartment with them the rest of the way. (A note of interest: Rita's grandparents and my grandfather, Sigvald Netland, had been the earliest pioneer missionaries in our mission, both arriving in China in 1890.)

The bombers' targets, we found out later, were two towns along the rail line. By consistently bombing them, the Japanese planned to keep our train from reaching its destination. When an air alarm sounded, the train would stop, and the engine detached itself from the train and went on to find a place with tree shade overhead. The passengers would all hurry off the train to find shelter anywhere they could. Then the engine would return and all would board the train again. Mother hoped that we would pass through those towns at night so we children wouldn't see the carnage. However, it was broad daylight when we came to Gwangshui, and our eyes were glued to the window. Dead bodies of people and animals were strewn on the ground. An ammunition train on a track near ours was burning furiously as we passed by. There was a large crater in the ground in front of us, and new tracks had been laid across it. I held my breath as we passed over it slowly, and it worked! We made it across! The train stopped in the town for only a few brief moments. In that time Dad and Dan Nelson stepped off the train to retrieve some shells on the ground. Clearly marked on the shells were the initials "USA."

Our train was the last train to complete this journey before the Japanese severed the rail line. We were so thankful to arrive in Hankow safely after our harrowing trip! It was a short time after we arrived that Mother dyed her sweater *black*!

Our family was most thankful to have arrived safely in Hankow. We lived in the Lutheran Home & Agency, a six-story concrete building with rooms for missionaries to stay in while in the city. A central kitchen provided meals for us in the dining hall.

At that time Hankow was the "acting capital" of China. The Japanese forces grew closer, and the Chinese government decided at the last minute to evacuate their forces. Generalissimo Chiang Kai Shek's secret underground shelter, a few blocks away from the Home, was blown up, and the explosion rocked our building, shattering the glass in our windows. After the Chinese government officials left, the Japanese began bombing the city in earnest, many times a day.

The night before the Japanese took over the city, we stood on the flat roof of the six-story building and counted 19 major fires blazing in different sections of the city. Many were from bombings by Japanese planes; some were the result of China's "scorched earth policy," of not allowing the Japanese to take over buildings and equipment beneficial to them. The railway station had the whole inside of it blown out. We heard that American newspapers had headlines saying, "Hankow entirely surrounded by fire."

On October 25, 1938, the city of Hankow fell to the Japanese. It was easy to tell when the Japanese troops took over. Having embarked from Japanese ships in the Yangtze

River a block away, the soldiers marched down the street, their leather boots scuffing the pavement, in contrast to the soft padded shoes of the Chinese soldiers. We were under occupation. All persons were required to get a permit with picture identification in order to be out on the street. At each intersection there were soldiers in sentry boxes who checked our permits before we were allowed to proceed.

As one can imagine, the government functions of the city were severely disrupted, and the missionaries were called on to assist temporarily. Dad was put in charge of sanitation. You can imagine the scene – babies were born on the streets, people died on the streets, garbage was strewn everywhere. With Chinese soldiers having dug and occupied trenches in the city, lice were alive and well. Soon I became ill with typhus fever and had to be hospitalized. Night sweats and high fever required many changes of bedding and gowns. My folks, who walked from the Home & Agency to the hospital, passing many sentries, tried to provide me with the food I craved. "I want mashed potatoes! Mashed potatoes!" From somewhere my folks managed to bring me those mashed potatoes. As the fever finally broke, with the characteristic rapid drop to sub-normal temperature, it was a critical time, but the Lord answered our prayers and restored me to health.

When the situation returned to some semblance of order, Dad and other missionaries headed north – through the lines of fighting, back to their mission stations in unoccupied territory – while the families stayed in Hankow. My older brother John was still in Hong Kong at the American School of Kikungshan, and our letters to him were not getting through. There were many times when John didn't know whether his family was dead or alive – quite emotional for a fourteen-year-old in a foreign land.

In anticipation of the coming occupation of Hankow, the cooks at the Home & Agency went out and bought up chickens and rice, but they neglected to buy any feed for the chickens. So meals were less than adequate, often including skin and bones rather than the chicken itself. There was rice, also homemade peanut butter, and a few vegetables as they were available.

Christmas came during our days in Hankow. We tried to have some festivities, and we sang the Christmas carols. The one thing that I remember most about that Christmas was that each child in the Home received a shiny red apple! Never before, or after, had an apple tasted so good!

The American Consulate in Hankow felt that missionary families with children should leave for Shanghai where there was a larger foreign population, including American marines and sailors who were based there. It seemed that the only transportation available was the river steamers, and they were exceptionally crowded. Passengers slept on the floor of the decks, side-by-side with other passengers, and sanitation was a problem.

However, a communication from the American Consulate had word that a solution had been found. Admiral Yarnell, Commander of the American Asiatic Fleet, offered to sail up the Yangtze River from Shanghai on his flagship, the *USS Isabel*, with gunboat escort, and take our two mission families with children (the Dan Nelson family and us) back out to Shanghai. Mother was able to send word to Dad at his station regarding this development, and he agreed we should leave.

On April 23, with a few suitcases in hand, we gratefully – and with excitement – boarded the *USS Isabel*! Our first meal on board was a turkey dinner with all its trimmings! What a feast after our meals at the Home & Agency in Hankow. Admiral Yarnell apologized that we were served the seamen's fare rather than officer's fare.

That evening as we children prepared for the night, I remember Admiral Yarnell coming by to tuck us into bed and to see if everything was all right. He asked us children if we would like some candy. "Candy? What's candy?" He then had his chef stir up a batch of fudge for us! I won't forget Admiral Yarnell!

One of the sailors on board became a special buddy of mine. When we neared Shanghai, he asked for my address there. Mother gave me the address but never expected that Michael Vallone would show for a visit! On the contrary, Michael would visit us whenever he had leave. He became like a member of the family and was my very special friend! He helped me learn how to ride a bike, and we spent many happy times together.

Michael and me in Tsingtao, China

During our first year in Shanghai, my mother, Borghild, and I lived in a Russian boarding House off Bubbling Well Road. Meals were served in a central dining room. I remember we were frequently served mutton, mutton, *mutton* – till I was sick of it! We attended a private school, Asbury Academy, and we hired a rickshaw coolie to take the two of us children to and from school every day. Borghild was in eighth grade and I was in third grade. This was the school that Pearl Buck had attended in her day.

A U.S. marine couple living in the boarding house gave me two canaries in a cage, "Marge" and "Pete." I liked them but soon felt sorry for them being cooped up in a cage. One day I opened the cage and let them fly away, not realizing that they would probably not survive "out there."

In the summer, Dad came through the war lines and traveled to Hong Kong to bring John from Hong Kong to spend time with the family. We took a boat up the coast to Tsingtao for our vacation time. At the nearby peninsula, Iltus Hook, there was quite a missionary community, and we were refreshed by our time together. While in Tsingtao, we heard about a Presbyterian mission boarding school for missionaries' children in Pyongyang, Korea, and John transferred there for his senior year. When he graduated in 1940, he was salutatorian of his class. Then as a sixteen-year-old, he sailed back to the United States to attend St. Olaf College in Northfield, Minnesota. Soon he made the headlines in the college newspaper: "Frosh is fresh from the war-torn fields of China."

The second year in Shanghai, Mother and I moved to the French Concession (controlled section) and lived in Elim House on Avenue Joffre. Borghild traveled to Korea to attend Pyongyang Foreign School as a freshman in high school. The Presbyterian students there, unaccustomed to her Norwegian name "Borghild," called her "Bonnie," and she has been Bonnie ever since!

Two months into the school year, on October 12, 1940, the American Consul notified the school in Korea that due to the deterioration of the international situation, the school would have to close or move to another location. While the school with many of its students sailed to America, Bonnie returned to us in Shanghai. Mother was her teacher, as well as mine, using the Calvert Course.

In the summer, when Dad left his station in Suiping, he was traveling with two lady missionaries. Travel was uncertain, round about, and very dangerous. Rivers were swollen from the rains. At one point, after they had just crossed a river in a rented boat, river bandits accosted them. They took all their luggage and strewed the contents over the wet grounds, plundering whatever items they wanted. Then one of them led Dad away up a hill. He felt a pistol in his back. Looking at the women, he saw them pointing up to heaven, as they faced the bandits. He thought they were giving him encouragement, indicating that he would soon be in heaven. However, the ladies were warning the bandits that if they shot him, *they would be responsible to God in Heaven!* They apparently heeded the women and released my dad. It had been a close call!

When Dad arrived in Shanghai, we received a cable from our mission superintendent. Since the world situation was becoming more critical, he recommended that our family return to America for furlough and be ready to return after a year if possible. We booked passage to the United States on the *President Coolidge*. On June 19, 1941, we sailed back home, our trip including a short stop in Hawaii on the way.

# CHAPTER 3

## Move and Move Again!

Arriving in Minneapolis the summer of 1941, our family settled into the Gethsemane Lutheran Church parsonage, which was vacant that year. On Sunday morning, December 7, we were listening to the radio as we ate our noon meal. What shocking news we heard! Japan had bombed Pearl Harbor; many warships in the US fleet had been sunk and countless servicemen and women had lost their lives. It was the beginning of World War II. Then we realized that had we remained in China at that time we would have been interned in a Japanese concentration camp.

My brother John, who had been attending St. Olaf College, transferred to Augsburg College in Minneapolis so that he could live at home with the family once again. Dad was itinerating for missions, so he was frequently gone on speaking engagements.

There were a lot of things to get used to, being back in America. One was learning to use the telephone! A younger cousin showed me how to dial their number, CH(erry) 0794, and to this day, that number remains in my memory.

I enrolled in fifth grade at Hamilton Elementary School and was happy to find out that, despite my unusual schooling situations in China, I had no problems in keeping up with my class. Recess was another story: when a game my classmates liked to play involved knowing the names of the current movie stars, I hadn't a clue!

After a year we moved, this time to south Minneapolis into a vacant home belonging to relatives. In sixth grade I was at

Cooper School. We students all walked to school and came home for lunch, as I remember. What I especially liked about my class there was learning geography through map drills. Our teacher would call us students to the map, one by one, give us a category – such as rivers, capitals, countries or lakes – and in one minute's time would have to name and locate all the places for that category we could remember. It was amazing how quickly we learned!

After school I was allowed to listen to one program on the radio at home, and I chose "Captain Midnight," with its thrilling adventures continued from day to day. I sent in for a Captain Midnight's ring, with special "code detecting" capabilities.

While living there I came down with a bad case of chickenpox. I was feeling miserable, the skin lesions and scabs itched dreadfully, and I finally had had it! "Call the doctor! Call the doctor!" I moaned to mother. In those days doctors made house calls. When the doctor arrived, I had finally fallen asleep, but he left suggestions for coping with the itching until I recovered.

Bonnie and I both took piano lessons and practiced faithfully. Learning that our teacher held her recitals in the Leamington Hotel in Minneapolis made us a bit anxious, but we managed to perform in a presentable manner.

With World War II being fought in the Pacific as well as the Atlantic Ocean, there was no possibility of our family returning to China, and Dad accepted a temporary call to Bethlehem Lutheran Church in Fergus Falls. So we moved from south Minneapolis. The church's minister had joined the military chaplaincy for the duration, with arrangements to return when the war was over. For two-and-a-half years our family would be in one location!

Fergus Falls was a lovely town of around 12,000 people, with one junior high school and one senior high school. While we were there, John graduated from St. Olaf College and Bonnie graduated from high school. Grandma Netland, who had served as a missionary in China for about 33 years, now lived in a nursing home in town. She had fallen and broken her hip years before, and it had never been set straight, so she always walked with crutches. She would often be in our home, keeping busy crocheting tablecloths, bedspreads, and smaller items, or knitting shawls and mittens. I would be her helper by packing the items in a bag before visiting people we knew, displaying items for sale. This was Grandma Netland's way of earning money so she could send money to missions overseas. She had a wonderful spirit, never complained, and she made a great impression on my life.

It was here in Fergus Falls that I learned about homecoming parades, football and basketball games, and sleigh rides in the winter. I attended the youth Luther League meetings at church on Sunday evenings. It was great to make friendships that lasted for two-and-a-half years, with memories lasting long after our family left.

It was during this time that the family listened faithfully to the radio every night at 7 p.m. to hear H. V. Kaltenborn report on the latest developments of the war. In August 1945, after atomic bombs had been dropped on Hiroshima and Nagasaki, Japan surrendered and the war was over.

At Christmastime we moved out of the parsonage, because the minister of the church had returned, and into a hotel so that I could complete the first semester of my freshman year in high school before moving to a new school in another city. At the end of the semester, my homeroom class had a going away party for me. It was wintertime in

Minnesota, and our skating party on Lake Alice was well attended in spite of minus 20-degree temperatures that evening! We skaters spent much time in the warming house, to be sure. I stood so close to the stove that it burned a hole in my coat. Fortunately it was my old coat! After braving the cold, my classmates gathered at Skogmo's Café for hot chocolate, and they presented me with several gifts. I have fond memories of my time in Fergus Falls.

Since World War II was over, Dad began making plans to return to China. However, women and children were not yet allowed to return, so Mother, Dad and I moved from Fergus Falls to Northfield, Minnesota into a home owned by a missionary family, at 319 Plum Street. Bonnie, who was attending St. Olaf College, moved back home with us.

Two things I especially remember about living there. At Northfield High School I played a clarinet in the band and sang in the chorus. In the spring we presented a musical, "Without A Song, the Day Will Never End." Music invigorated me!

It was at St. John's Lutheran Church in Northfield that I was confirmed. I had been in Dad's confirmation classes for several years in Fergus Falls, but he was not able to be with me on my special day, May 12, 1946, because on that day he sailed from San Francisco to return to China.

That summer we moved once again, this time into one of the four mission cottages located behind Luther Theological Seminary in St. Paul. This was the seminary from which my Dad had graduated and that my brother was now attending. So John was able to live at home with us. The years that we had been together as a family since going to China were few and far between.

I attended Murray High School, a large school in the state capital city, St. Paul. Here, as a sophomore, it was more difficult for me to make friends, especially as my values and standards were different from many of the other students at the high school level. Social events were often dances, and my parents did not approve of dancing. Band was again a redeeming factor, and our marching band won first place among the high school bands in St. Paul that year.

The following year I enrolled at Minnehaha Academy, a Christian school in Minneapolis. We carpooled with several other families in the area. A friend for many years, Anna Marie Burgess, had been attending the Academy and introduced me to many of her friends there.

In October, Dad sent us word that the situation in China had calmed down, and Mother and I would be able to join him there. On October 31, 1947, our journey began as we went to the train station. To my surprise, Anna Marie and a group of her friends had skipped school and come down to the train station to "soong" me, as the Chinese would say. They sang hymns, ending with "God Be With You Till We Meet Again." To this day, I can't sing this song without my eyes filling with tears. As the train moved slowly out of the station that evening, I looked out the window and watched the ghosts and goblins going from door to door for "Tricks or Treats" on Halloween.

Our ship, the *General Gordon*, sailed out of San Francisco Bay on November 7, headed for Japan and the China coast. Mrs. Tvedt, another of our China missionary wives, traveled with Mother and me. Needing to keep up with my classes, I studied from schoolbooks I had brought along, especially Geometry and German. This trip was fairly uneventful, and we arrived in Hong Kong on schedule.

Dad had traveled south from his mission station of work at Suiping in central China to meet us. In anticipation of our coming, he had arranged for the house on the mission station to be repaired after it had been torn up by the Japanese troops through the war years. During the few days that we had in Hong Kong before heading north, Dad received a cable from our mission superintendent that the Communists had already occupied the city of Suiping. Nevertheless, we did proceed by train as far as Hankow, on the Yangtze River, a three-day trip.

There were adjustments to be made in living in China again. On the first lap of the journey, one of the family members had to sit with our luggage in the baggage car to keep our luggage from being stolen. It was late November and the weather was getting cold. We had to wear long cotton stockings to keep warm. I recall trying to get used to powdered milk again by adding Ovaltine, which we had brought along from the States.

The school I was to attend, ASK, had relocated to Sinyang as it was dangerous to be on Kikungshan in the mountains. Sinyang was on the rail line north of Hankow. Just before Christmas vacation, the fighting between the Chinese Nationalists and the Communists was so close that from ASK's temporary quarters, one could see flares in the sky at night and hear the report of the cannon. Troop trains kept moving north through Sinyang toward the front, so it was determined that the school must evacuate to Hankow as they let out for Christmas vacation. For three days they tried to get a train before they could get to Hankow. One of the teachers accompanied the students, and three of the faculty members stayed behind to pack up the school's beds, books, tables, and food supply and to get them moved to Hankow.

Students and staff were housed on the sixth floor of the Lutheran Home & Agency. The elevator had been removed by the Japanese during the war and not replaced, so we had plenty of exercise walking up and down the stairs many times a day. We ate meals in the large dining room on the main floor. Classes were held in teachers' bedrooms, hallways, or wherever a site was available. With no central heating at that time, we wore layers of clothes. Washcloths hung up to dry were often frozen in the morning. But we were hardy souls! And we enjoyed eating tropical Hershey bars when available.

Two months later, after three Swedish Covenant missionaries had been killed by the Communists not too far away, the American Consul strongly advised the school to move to a port city. All the older students helped with preparations, packing supplies, making sandwiches, and numbering all the pieces of luggage.

My dad seeing off the ASK students
on the train enroute to Hong Kong

Twenty-seven students and five faculty members made the trip heading south to Hong Kong. To catch the train we had to cross the Yangtze River on a ferry to Wuchang – for there were no bridges across the river then! At the train station, we said goodbye to parents who were staying behind as we headed south. Three days later, on the evening of March 9, as we rounded the final curve into Kowloon, we saw the spectacular lights of the island of Hong Kong, and of the boats plying back and forth across the harbor from Kowloon to Hong Kong. A dazzling sight to our eyes! We spent the night on the floor at the YMCA in Kowloon, and in the morning we saw that our school evacuation had made the front-page headlines in the English paper!

(Unser Blindenheim Eben-Ezer, Hong-Kong)

Ebenezer Home for Blind Girls at Pokfulam

Our final destination was the Ebenezer Home for Blind Girls at Pokfulam on the far side of the island of Hong Kong. The Home was using only half of their building at that time and willingly rented the other half to our school. One large room housed all the boys, and adjacent to it was a large room for all the girls. Teachers had smaller rooms, and downstairs were a parlor, dining room, and classrooms. A porch off each of the dormitory rooms provided a magnificent westward view of the small islands and the ocean beyond. The color of the ocean varied, depending on its mood!

Every evening during the week we had supervised study hall. Piano students practiced in "Albatross," a two-story garage across the street from the school. Our teachers not only taught our classes well but were also responsible for the students 24 hours of the day! They surely were to be commended! Pastor Earl Dahlstrom was our principal; Miss Ruth Gilbertson, Miss Gertrude Sovik, and Miss Lillian Landahl, our junior and senior high teachers; and Miss Hannah Hanson taught the elementary classes, with Mrs. Selma Lindell as our matron.

In 1948 the student body began publishing the monthly school newspaper, "The Chanticleer," for the first time since World War II.

In our free time, we students played a lot of Ping-Pong with ladder tournaments and constant challenges. Anyone able to stay on the top of the ladder for eight straight days was rewarded with a free Chinese meal! We would have game nights on the weekends, including dancing the Virginia reel and swimming in the ocean on the rocky shores down the hill from the school. There were hymn sings outside on Sunday evenings as we watched the colors of the sunset fade into the west over the ocean.

When school was out following my junior year, Dad came south to accompany all the students who were heading north to join their parents for the summer.

This summer, 1948, was spent on the mountains of Kuling, where there was a missionary summer retreat area. From Hankow it was a day's journey east on the Yangtze

River toward Shanghai. Disembarking at Kiukiang, we had to ascend a 4,000-foot mountain, either by climbing (as Dad did) or riding in a sedan chair carried by two coolies (as Mother and I did). From the top of the mountain we had a wonderful view of the surrounding mountain ranges and the winding river below. The house we lived in was high up the mountain even from the town, and we had a glassed-in front porch. Each evening we would move our chairs to the porch, which faced west, and watch God's spectacular sunsets spread across the sky. As their colors faded behind range after range, and it became dark, we lit the Aladdin lamp, which gave quite a bright glow, and finished whatever tasks remained before retiring for the night. Those sunsets are memories that I cherish to this day.

The Harold Martinson family of our Lutheran Mission was also spending the summer at Kuling. One day my schoolmate Char Martinson and I decided to go for a hike on one of the mountain trails. As we reached the peak of one range, we saw higher peaks that beckoned us onward! We were having such a great time exploring that we had not paid attention to the dark threatening clouds gathering about us. Suddenly a loud clap of thunder got our attention, and as the rain descended, we turned back and "flew" homeward, with our open umbrellas acting more like parachutes than umbrellas to keep us dry!

Kuling was China's summer capital. Generalissimo and Madame Chiang Kai Shek worshipped with us one Sunday at the English speaking service we attended.

Other memories of Kuling were: listening to the high pitched droning sound of cicadas outside, drinking from a spring above our house, enjoying the Easter lilies in bloom, and watching the mists rolling in and obscuring the view of the river and fields below. There was a natural swimming pool, which we frequently enjoyed.

One day we received a telegram that the Dan Nelson family of our mission had all been killed in a plane crash between Macao and Hong Kong. It was the first case of air piracy that we had ever heard of. The only survivor was one of the pirates who was sitting in the back of the plane and had both of his arms and legs broken. Rita Nelson was the first friend I had had in China when we first met on Kikungshan when I was five years old. Rita and brother Danny had been planning to attend ASK in Hong Kong in the fall. The mission community held a memorial service for them, and we students from school sang:

"Around the throne of God in heaven great hosts of children stand,
Children whose sins are all forgiven, a holy, happy band, singing
Glory, glory, glory be to God on high."

We all felt the loss keenly.

In the fall the school opened again in Hong Kong at Pokfulam. It was my senior year! There were three of us in my class, Dave Lee, Bob Bartel, and me. Some of last year's students had gone back to the States, and other students had newly joined the student body. There were some additional faculty members as well. I especially remember German classes taught by Miss Sovik, for though she was a hard teacher, her classes were stimulating and challenging and we learned a lot!

The high school girls had a club, the JSK – the Jolly Sunshine Klub. We looked for a secret place to hold our meetings. One day, walking on the trails of a mountainside above our school, we found an underground fort, or pillbox, used by soldiers during the war. We were elated and spent much time in cleaning it and preparing for our meetings. The big iron door was lying on the ground to the side of the doorway. With great effort we managed to get it back on its hinges.

**Four-ever:**
**High school pals at ASK**

For weeks the boys tried to find our secret meeting place but could not find it. Later, when they did, and I was in the fort with one of the high school boys, he looked up and saw the ventilation shafts angling up through the ceiling and reached his hand up into the shaft. With an amazed look on his face, he pulled out, from several shafts, belts of ammunition, shells, then two mortar shells, and a hand grenade. He told me he knew a safe way to carry the ammunition, so we carried it back to the school. When Orvis Hanson, our new principal, saw what we were carrying, his face turned white as a sheet, and we quickly deposited the items outside. Supper was temporarily forgotten while he called the chief of police in Hong Kong who promptly sent an officer out to the school. The officer maintained that each of the many pillboxes on this side of the mountain had been searched after the war and cleared of all weapons. He surmised that smugglers were using the fort. From then on we could use the fort only if we were a large group together.

Generally anyone late for meals received only bread and water, but that night we were allowed to have full fare, for Rev. Hanson was so relieved that we were alive and uninjured by our episode.

From time to time American warships would sail into Hong Kong harbor for "R and R." For us students there were moments of pride as we saw the American flag flying on the ships. When tours were permitted on board, we made use of the opportunity! The cruiser, *St. Paul*, was one of the ships. I especially remember an aircraft carrier, the *Tarawa*, and the sailors who showed us around!

Later that year my parents went from Hankow to Kowloon to find a place for the Lutheran Mission to relocate to and use as a Center. Although they did relocate, I remained at the school. However, sometimes, I went home on the weekends, taking the bus, then the ferry across the harbor to Kowloon.

On May 22, 1949, our class of three graduated from high school. Due to Generalissimo Chiang Kai Shek's steady retreat southward from the "Liberation Army," most of the students returned to the United States. My parents were asked to take an early furlough but be prepared to return to China if the way should open up again, so we sailed back to America together on the *S. S. President Wilson*.

Life on board ship was great! With plenty of practice in Ping-Pong at school, I managed to win the women's Ping-Pong tournament, and I still have the trophy I received! The meals were wonderful, with our choices made from a variety of selections on the ship's colorful menus. When our waiter found out that I love fresh strawberries, he would bring me a double portion. The "bath steward" would come by daily at a specified time to notify me that my bath water had been drawn. Soaking in a tub of hot water was so relaxing … a treat we had not experienced in the Orient.

One of the passengers was Guillermo F. Pablo, one of the Justices on the Supreme Court in the Philippine Islands, and he gave me some Spanish lessons in the mornings. I had also been interested in Morse code and struck up a friendship with the radio operators on the ship. They were helpful in instructing me about their work. The chief operator, a Lieutenant Commander, corresponded with me for several years following our trip.

As our ship sailed under the Golden Gate Bridge, we said goodbye to our new on-board friends – and hello to America!

# CHAPTER 4

## Preparation for my Life's Work

Where would I attend college? There was no doubt! My parents and my brother had all graduated from St. Olaf College in Northfield, Minnesota, and my sister was entering her senior year there, so I looked forward to being a part of this student body! My parents were able to rent a mission home in Northfield, so Bonnie moved home with us. Daily Bonnie and I walked along the path up the hill to the beautiful campus of "The College on the Hill" for classes.

The combined five-year St. Olaf/Fairview Hospital Nursing Degree program was my vocational choice. However, during my freshman year the program was phased out in favor of a four-year combination program, which was not yet in place. I spent two years at St. Olaf and have many memories of good times – and I learned much! It was natural for me to gravitate to the Mission Study organization, with regular weekly meetings and weekend deputation trips to nearby churches, and I enjoyed singing in a mixed quartet on these trips. The Mission Study Group also visited a nursing home regularly. One time we put on a special fun event for them and sang numbers like, "Put on Your Old Gray Bonnet," that brought out many a smile.

In my sophomore year I advanced to a second tryout to the St. Olaf Choir! Those of us recalled were nervous, of course, and stood around in a circle holding hands as Dr. Olaf C. Christiansen played various musical patterns on the piano and asked us one by one to sing them. During my turn, he asked me to sing above my range, and I said, "I can't get up that high!"

He replied, "Don't ever say can't. You try!"

So I did. I was the last alto that did not make the choir that year. I did sing in the chapel choir and took voice lessons. I recall one of my practice songs was "Oh, My Lover Is a Fisherman." I also enjoyed singing in a girl's trio for events on campus. A favorite song we sang was "Walking in a Winter Wonderland." The campus was truly a winter wonderland after a snowfall.

As a sophomore I chaired the Mission Emphasis Week Committee that brought a missionary speaker to campus for a week of special chapel services once a year. The speaker that year, Rev. Herb Loddings, certainly held the audience's attention as he focused on the verse, "My son, go work today in my vineyard," from Matthew 21:28. Each day he emphasized a different word or phrase in that verse.

I recall taking a course in creative writing from Dr. Art Paulson, who gave us some unusual assignments. One class period was spent in impromptu writing on the topic, "The Most Interesting Person I've Ever Met − Myself." Somehow I managed to get an "A" in the assignment and in the course, not because I was such a good writer, but because Dr. Paulson thought I was working up to my capacity.

At Homecoming, students would lay a huge stack of firewood for a bonfire. It would have to be guarded at night so our archrival, Carleton College, across the river in Northfield, would not be able to burn it prematurely. I'm sure there were some Oles trying to do likewise on their campus. Sounds of "Um yah yah, tonight Carleton College will sure meet its fate" were sung often at school athletic events.

Girls Date Night was an annual event, and it took courage to ask the boy we really wanted to date that night! I thought long and hard before asking someone. He accepted. The event was a program on "The Hill," and afterwards we were walking down on the mountain trail to my home when it happened. In the dark I tripped over a stone on the path and started rolling down the path, unable to stop. With my nylons torn and knees skinned, I was grateful it was dark as we continued on our way home. It was not exactly as I had planned it. Girls Date Night had become my most embarrassing moment. But there was always tomorrow.

The highlight of the year was the Christmas Concert with all the many choirs, band, and orchestra participating in a magnificent event honoring Christ's birth. "Lullaby on Christmas Eve," that beautiful lullaby written in Norway by Dr. F. Melius Christiansen, founder of the St. Olaf Choir, is a song that I will always fondly remember from the St. Olaf Christmas Concert.

In the summertime, after my freshman year in college, I worked for a dentist, Dr. Ned Brown, in Northfield. He invited me to work for him, saying, "If you come and work with me, I'll teach you everything you need to know to be my dental assistant." We always opened the day with prayer together before seeing patients. He had Christian music playing softly as he worked. I very much enjoyed working with him that summer.

The next year, at Christmas time, I traveled with several busloads of students from Minnesota to Urbana, Illinois, for the Urbana Missionary Conference for students, which was held every three years. Several thousand students from all over the nation and many missionary organizations were present and shared opportunities to go overseas to share the Good News of Jesus Christ to all the world. The music and hymns sung by all resounded throughout the whole auditorium! It was there that I learned the hymn, "And Can It Be That I Should Gain," and it has become one of my most loved hymns.

The summer following my sophomore year, I joined five other Oles in working at a resort in Door County, Wisconsin, in the town of Ephraim, situated on the coast of Lake Superior. Three of us were waitresses, and the other three were chambermaids. It was interesting work, and the beauty of the area along the shoreline enhanced our summer experience. This area was "cherry country," and the local cherry pies were delicious!

One event I remember was a boat trip that two of us took. We were out rowing on the lake, enjoying our free afternoon. We had traveled quite a ways from the resort when a sudden squall came up, making it very difficult to maneuver the boat. With the wind and the rain, it was with great difficulty that we managed to get to shore. Finding an inhabited cabin, we knocked at the door and were invited in. By telephone we contacted our resort to let them know where we were and learned that they had already sent out a search team to find us. They were relieved to learn that we were safe!

Before entering nursing school, I spent one year at the Lutheran Bible Institute on Portland Avenue in Minneapolis. I felt that this concentrated study of the Bible would better prepare me for the work ahead. Dr. Oscar Hanson and Dr. Reuben Gornitzka were two of my favorite, excellent teachers, who well exemplified the Christian life for me.

Nursing had been one of my goals for years, since it was one of the ways women could serve on the mission field at that time. On the day I turned sixteen, June 11, 1947, I applied to Fairview Hospital to be a nurse's aide. I was accepted and served throughout the summer until school resumed.

Now that I had finished two years of college at St. Olaf College in Northfield, Minnesota, and a year at the Lutheran Bible Institute in Minneapolis, I began my three-year nursing program. My good friend Grace Anderson, who had attended Concordia College while I was at St. Olaf College, and who was my roommate at the Lutheran Bible Institute, was again my roommate. Her parents were missionaries to China in the same mission as my parents, and they had known one another from the time both couples had been married. Long-time friends!

Because Grace and I had had two years of college, we were exempt from some of the science courses, much to the chagrin of many of our classmates! Classes occupied much of our time at the beginning of our first year, and then came the Capping Ceremony!

My capping picture from Fairview Hospital School of Nursing

Our class chose as our Scripture verse:

"In all things I have shown you that by so toiling one must help the weak, remembering the words of our Lord Jesus, how he said, 'It is more blessed to give than to receive.'" Acts 20:35.

And the hymn selected...

"Thy life was given for me, Thy precious blood was shed,

That I might ransomed be, and quickened from the dead.

Thy life was given for me. What have I given for Thee?"

51

We learned the basics such as bed making and giving baths. One day, being a first-year student, I watched a second-year student making a bed and wondered how many beds she had made since entering training!

Time in special nursing departments such as surgery, obstetrics, and care of delivered mothers was part of our training at Fairview. However, for other parts of training we went on affiliation to other hospitals. For instance, for pediatric nursing we went to General Hospital, for psychiatric nursing to the State Hospital in Fergus Falls, and for Rural Nursing to a hospital in Grand Rapids in northern Minnesota. Not all nurses went to the same place.

There is a lot of responsibility that nurses shoulder in caring for patients who are ill. For part of our time in training, we had classes in the daytime and worked the night shift as well! That is where I learned to drink coffee!

We had our fun times as well. Our classmates lived on the second and fourth floors of the dormitory, and we sometimes had hall parties in the evening when we were off duty. I remember a Halloween party for all with folks coming in costume. Because of our unusual costumes, our classmates seemed to remember what Grace and I were dressed as, for we came as a pair of dice, holding hands, and wearing big boxes around us!

In order to make spending money, we nurses would take on house cleaning opportunities. There was a phone number for folks to call in to request one of the nurses to help with their cleaning.

Luther Theological Seminary was located nearby in St. Paul, and there was much dating between our two student bodies!

We had a nurse's chorus, and some of us sang together in a trio or quartet. Occasionally we had the opportunity to attend the Minneapolis Symphony. I remember hearing a concert by the Vienna Boys Choir.

Fairview Hospital had a cottage on Lake Minnetonka, and as students we were occasionally allowed to go out there for the weekend as a group when not working. We were given an allowance to buy food and had some good homemade meals! There were rollaway beds to sleep on. We had a grand view out the large windows of the grounds and of the lake. We didn't go swimming, but there was a dock, and occasionally we would have a boat ride. In the winter, when the snow lay on the ground, we had toboggans to use. One time I remember, when some of my friends were tobogganing, they hit a tree, and Grace, for one, had to be taken to the hospital for treatment and was out of commission for a few days.

Fairview Hospital was a Lutheran facility. My first year I was elected class representative to the student council and my second year I served as treasurer. My senior year I was a write-in candidate for president and was elected! That year the student body was asked if we would like to have one of the dormitory rooms converted into a chapel for us to use. This would mean two fewer students would be accepted into each new class. We voted to have the small chapel; the school built it and it even included stained glass windows. Students would drop by there for times of quiet meditation and prayer.

Commencement and graduation of our Fairview graduating class was held at Central Lutheran Church in Minneapolis on Sunday evening, May 15, 1955 at 8 o'clock. Chaplain Elmer Laursen read Scripture and led in prayer; Nina H. Denklau, R.N., Director of Nurses, presented the graduating class; and Carl F. Granrud, President, Board of Trustees, presented the diplomas. A total of 53 nurses received their diplomas that night, with 13 of them in the Spring

Division, and 40 of them being in our Fall Division. The experiences that we as nursing classmates went through together have fostered a bond that will go with us through the years. May it be so!

The year after I graduated from Fairview Hospital, I moved to a house on Franklin Terrace in Minneapolis and lived there with three other girls, Ruth Pedersen, a classmate, Joan Larson, a teacher, and Shirley Dahlen, who was involved in other type of work. That year I attended the University of Minnesota, taking courses in Public Health. I had no car, so to get to school I walked across the bridge spanning the Mississippi River. In the winter with the icy winds blowing, my cheeks would be cherry red by the time I got to class!

Inter-Varsity Christian Fellowship was active at the University, and I appreciated the Bible studies and fellowship there.

After a year of study, I still had three months of public health affiliation to do. Effie Koenig and I were assigned to go to Santa Fe, New Mexico! She had a little car, and we hoped that it would be travel worthy enough to get us to Santa Fe and back. Being short of money, we slept in a park the first night on the road, and the next in a lumberyard. The night before reaching my Aunt Marie's home in Encampment, Wyoming, we slept out on the North Platt River. My aunt, on hearing this information, said, "Land sakes, girls, didn't you know that there are lots of rattle snakes out there?!" The Lord must have been looking out for us!

The night we spent with my aunt, we listened to the radio as we settled down for the night. For the first time I heard the song, "How Great Thou Art," sung by George Beverly Shea. That hymn spoke to my heart. I had felt a call to the mission field for many years, but I hadn't planned to go out as a single missionary! It was then the thought came to me, "If God is that great, why couldn't I trust Him."

Arriving in Santa Fe, we noticed a lack of green grass, except within the walls around the homes. Most all the families had Hispanic names, and so many of the surnames were the same, which made it hard for us to locate the homes of mothers and newborn children whom we visited.

In order to have some income, we had to get our R.N. license to practice in New Mexico, and then we were able to work in the local hospital several shifts a week.

On the weekends, we did some traveling to see places in New Mexico, and also in Arizona, such as the Grand Canyon, the Petrified Forest, and some of the pueblos of the Indian tribes. I had a chance to visit two of my schoolmates from the Lutheran Bible Institute who were doing mission work among one of the tribes. Some of the "main roads" we traveled to see them took us over rocks and very bumpy trails – but we did arrive at our destination.

It was most interesting to see the arts and crafts of the different Indian tribes, to listen to their native languages, and to see peppers strung up to dry.

In December, we drove back to Minnesota and attended our graduation service at the University of Minnesota. Carol Anderson, my Fairview nursing roommate's older sister, graduated with me, and we both graduated "With Distinction." My parents came to Minneapolis for the occasion, stayed at the Curtis Hotel, and held a festive party for Carol and me.

# CHAPTER 5

## Missionary Call to Taiwan

Since graduating from Fairview Hospital School of Nursing in Minneapolis, Minnesota, and the University of Minnesota with a B.S. and a Certificate in Public Health, I was awaiting a call from our Evangelical Lutheran Church (ELC) to serve as a missionary in Taiwan. I had flown out to Seattle, Washington, where my sister Bonnie lived and worked as a church secretary at Phinney Ridge Lutheran Church.

I found employment working first in Swedish Hospital at night in Delivery Room. Without a car, it was necessary for me to take the bus and transfer in downtown Seattle at night. One evening my second cousin came in to have her baby, and I had the joy of assisting in her delivery! Then I thought it would be nice to work in a day position since Bonnie and her roommate did. So later I worked for three months in a doctor's office.

While I felt that I had a call to the mission field, it wasn't in my plan to go as a single worker. So when a call came from Taiwan on August 13 to serve as a missionary, I had a problem. One night in bed I was struggling with this issue. Amid tears I opened my Bible to Psalm 34 and read the following words:

> "I sought the Lord and He answered me,
> and delivered me from all my fears. Look to Him
> and be radiant."

This was God's message to me. I had recently been talking with Christian friends who had said that if I felt confident of

God's call, then when difficulties arose, I would have the assurance that I was where I was meant to be.

That call from Dr. Marcy Ditmanson in Taiwan on August 13 was to ask if it would be possible for me to come to Taiwan to Morrison Academy, a boarding school for missionaries' children. Therefore I had to put a call through to Dr. Rolf Syrdal, Executive Secretary of the Board of Foreign Missions of the ELC, to receive permission to be assigned to Morrison Academy in Taichung. There I would serve as school nurse for the entire campus and dormitory mother for all the girls in grades 1 through 12. The school had about 120 students, including day students. With Dr. Syrdal's permission and blessing, I prepared to go to Taiwan.

Three generations for China

After a quick trip to Minnesota to have my wisdom teeth pulled by Dr. Brown, whom I had worked for one summer during my college days, and saying goodbye to all my relatives (while with swollen jaws!), and purchasing items I would need overseas, I flew back to Seattle.

My Commissioning Service was held on October 13, 1957 at Phinney Ridge Lutheran Church. My father, Rev. John Skepstad, missionary to China, was granted permission by our Mission Secretary, Dr. Rolf Syrdal, to commission me as a missionary of the Evangelical Lutheran Church to Taiwan. Also participating in the Commissioning Service were my brother, Rev. John N. Skepstad, and three other pastors. A lovely reception followed.

The night I flew out of Seattle airport was exciting! It was the first time I had been on a commercial flight. A group of friends as well as my family were there to see me off. Then we heard that the plane needed some repairs – mechanical reasons – and it was 2 a.m., with only my family remaining, when the plane took off. Since it was my first commercial flight, I was waiting for my stomach to "churn," but all I felt was excitement!

Enroute to Taiwan we had a layover in Japan, where a group of Lutheran missionaries, including Grace Anderson's sister, Alice Marie Sanoden, and her husband, were there to meet me, and I visited there for several days before continuing my flight. In Taipei, Lutheran missionaries again met my plane, welcomed me to the island, and helped me with all the necessary transitions to living in Taiwan, including registering with the American Consulate.

Next, I took a train trip down the west coast of the island. With me on the train was Mrs. Aarsheim, a Norwegian Lutheran missionary who had four children attending Morrison but who were not boarding students. Not only did I learn a lot about the school from her, but also she invited me to come to their home on my days off, and to make their home my home away from home! On arrival in Taichung, a group from Morrison Academy welcomed me and drove me out to the school. In the dormitory I found I had 17 girls in grades 1 to 12 to get acquainted with, as well as faculty. It was a challenge – but I loved it! I, too, had been to a boarding school in China and had some understanding of what the girls were going through. Yet I personally felt that first and second graders ought not to be away from their parents at such a young age. However, some missions required it.

There were many buildings on the campus. In addition to the girls' dormitory, there was a boys' dormitory that included high school classrooms on the second floor, an elementary school, a dining room, and some faculty homes. We also had day students from missionary or American military homes, for a total of 105 students and 23 faculty and staff. I came to realize that the school had excellent teachers, each outstanding in his or her field. In addition to academic classes, the school provided music classes and extramural athletics, and our teams would have competitions with other schools, including Taipei American School.

Since I was nurse for the entire campus, when a student became ill he or she would be moved to a room next to mine, and for me, it could be a 24-hour-a-day job for a few days. There were football injuries to be treated. One day our principal's wife had a dislocated shoulder, and I had to fly with her on an American military plane to Taipei for treatment.

The flat roof above our girls' dorm provided a great place to sleep at night in the warm weather, and to stargaze across the heavens. I loved my new challenge and enjoyed getting acquainted with each of my girls, among them a pair of twins!

Each evening we had devotions in the dorm lounge. Every month I measured the girls' height and weight and recorded it, to make sure they were doing well physically. During part of the year, we all had to use mosquito nets over our beds.

All of my girls with me at Morrison Academy

All the dorm students on campus had their meals together in the dining hall, so preparing for meals was not one of my responsibilities. I joined the students sitting at long tables, with a member of the staff at each end. I did have to supervise the laundry and hunt for items not returned to their owners!

At Christmastime we decorated my dormitory using the fronts of Christmas cards taped to one side of the windowpanes in the hall. The students went to the other side of the hall and with paint colors imitated the cards. Then the cards were removed and only the paintings they had created were visible. At Christmas school was recessed and students went home for vacation. They also had long weekends every six weeks to enable them to travel to their homes.

Me with some of the girls at Morrison Academy, Taichung

In addition to receiving a wonderful academic education at the school, the students also had music: a band, a choir and trios and quartets, piano lessons, and many kinds of sports: swimming, soccer, basketball, softball, and track along with cheerleading teams. The school's teams played teams from other schools around the island, and once one of our basketball teams was flown to the Philippine Islands to play a team at Faith Christian Academy. Our students also presented dramas, like the three-act play, "Our Hearts Were Young and Gay." The school's Junior-Senior Banquets were a work of art: the tables were beautifully set with flowers and candles, one of the juniors dressed as a seer and made predictions for the seniors, and a band played live music.

One of the older boys in the dormitory was a descendant of Hudson Taylor, founder of the well-known China Inland Mission, or "C.I.M." My grandfather, Sigvald Netland, in Norway in 1890, read a book that Hudson Taylor wrote about the great need for missionaries in China. So the day after he turned 21 years of age, Sigvald left Norway to head for China to share the Good News of Jesus Christ to the people there. How interesting to have a descendant of Hudson Taylor's at the school!

When the school year ended and the children had returned to their homes, I was free for the summer. I decided to visit Hualien where Dr. Marcy Ditmanson and his family lived. It was a three-hour train trip up the coast to Taipei and then a flight over the Cliff Road to Hualien ("Flower Garden"). Marcy was then serving as a physician at the Mennonite Hospital along with Canadian Mission personnel. While I was visiting, a typhoon struck the island with devastating force. Marcy was at the hospital while I was at his house staying with his wife Joyce, who was expecting to deliver their fourth child at any moment. I hoped and prayed that this would not happen during the storm. I was standing by a glass window, watching as the storm approached. The fierce wind, rain, and ocean came storming in and beat upon the glass. I saw the window bend and not break! And I heard myself singing:

> "My Heavenly Father watches over me;
> I trust in God, I know He cares for me;
> On mountain bleak, or on the stormy sea;
> Though billows roll, He keeps my soul;
> My Heavenly Father watches over me."

In the week following, I assisted the hospital staff in getting bedding, equipment and surgical instruments out in the sun to dry so the instruments could be re-sterilized. The hospital roof was damaged, and the mountain people for whom the hospital was built left their own thatched roof homes in their villages to come and help repair the hospital. That was gratitude in action.

Another school year went by. Because of the semi-tropical climate in Taiwan, our mission physician, Dr. Wilkerson, recommended that we get away from the island for two weeks every two years. So two summers after I went to Taiwan, I vacationed in Japan for several weeks. I had received an invitation from two Lutheran missionary friends in Japan (with whom I had attended the Lutheran Bible Institute in Minneapolis) to join them at their cottage at Nojiri-ko and to bring a friend. I invited Rachel Sarason, a teacher on staff at Morrison Academy, to accompany me. We flew to Japan and took a train up into the mountains of Nagano Ken to the picturesque village of Nojiri-ko. There in the midst of the mountains was a beautiful lake and a community of rustic missionary cottages built for summer use. Activities included swimming, boating, water-skiing, and sail boating. There were weekly Bible study courses and hymn sings on the lake – with some folks on shore, and some in boats on the water, singing antiphonally. It was inspiring.

During our stay, we learned that there was to be a hiking expedition in the Japan Alps, and we decided to join the adventure. It was to be led by a Japanese guide and an Austrian guide, with the hike beginning at midnight. By the light of a full moon, and our flashlights, we began from a starting point at 2,000 feet, with the goal of scaling Mt. Myoko, and reaching the top at 8,000 feet by sunrise. As we walked along, stones that rolled off the path and down the steep mountain took what seemed like forever to reach the bottom. We needed to be careful and sure-footed!

As day dawned, and we were hoping to reach the top by sunrise, we found that the morning sun was clouded over. It was a bit of a disappointment, but we had reached our goal! We ate our bag lunches and viewed the mountain ranges. Once back down the mountain, we all soaked in the Japanese hot baths to give our aching muscles much needed relief.

My life has never been the same since that day, for it was on this hike that I met a young ordained Presbyterian missionary, vacationing there from Taiwan. His name was Blake Bradley.

A few days later when I was participating in a tennis tournament, Blake waited to engage me in conversation:

"Do you have any plans for tomorrow afternoon?"

"Oh, I was planning to go on a Lutheran picnic."

"Well, a Presbyterian steak-fry is better any day!"

"Oh, how many are going on the Presbyterian steak-fry?"

"Well, if you think we need one, I could ask Miss Marion Wilcox (senior Presbyterian missionary from Taiwan) to be our chaperone!"

And so our first date was arranged.

Blake had bought some Kobe steaks and made all the preparations for our meal. We took a rowboat across the lake. Reversing the usual male/female roles, since I loved rowing (remembering times at Ottertail Lake in Minnesota when growing up), I rowed across the lake. In between our conversations, Blake sang songs he remembered from Boy Scouts and camping days. One I especially remembered was, "Dem Bones Gonna Rise Again!"

We found a neat cove across the lake and beached the boat on the shore. It was getting dusk, so Blake hung his flashlight on the tree branch overhead and built a fire over which to grill our steaks. The smell of steaks cooking over the charcoal fire whetted our appetites and we enjoyed a delicious meal together.

And as we ate, we had time to get better acquainted. The time passed all too quickly and we had to head homeward.

The next morning, Blake came over to where I was staying and said that we had somehow left the grill at our campsite. He invited me to go back with him to retrieve it. The Japanese cooks at his house were snickering and giving him a bad time about the oversight. We found the grill and returned it with a smile.

That very afternoon Rachel and I were leaving Nojiri-ko to return to Taiwan. Vacation was coming to an end and school was about to begin.

Blake didn't travel with us, but accompanying us on our train trip south was another young Presbyterian missionary bachelor. Blake wasn't too happy when he heard about this since this man could be a possible suitor. But Irving Mitchell was God's gift to us for that part of the journey. Rachel and I had disembarked in Kyoto to spend the night with a new friend, Shirley, who was a teacher of missionaries' children there, while Irvine went on to Osaka. He would meet our train in Osaka the next day.

In the morning Shirley saw us off at the train station in Kyoto. Rachel and I boarded the train and found our seats just inside the entrance. I set my beautifully hand-tooled leather purse, given me by my folks, down on the seat beside me while I lifted my suitcase to the overhead rack above. Just then the train began to pull out of the station, and I leaned out the window to wave goodbye to Shirley and then reached for my purse. It wasn't there. It was nowhere to be found! Just that morning I had put all my money in my purse, along with my passport, inoculation card, plane ticket, Okinawa permit, address book with addresses of friends around the world, and my keys. Passengers saw that we were upset and called for the policeman on the train. When he appeared, he said we would have to make out a police report at the train station in Osaka.

Irvine met us as promised. When he heard about my predicament, he was very helpful in filling out the police report and taking us to the American Consulate. The Consul had just left by boat for the United States. The staff lectured me at length for not holding onto my passport. It was a Friday afternoon and soon offices would close. They told me to return on Monday.

Rachel flew back to Taiwan that day. Before she left, she gave me three signed blank checks. Because Irvine was well known at the bank, I was able to cash one check and get a little money. Our next stop was at a locksmith who was able to get my suitcase opened. Then Irvine found me a place to stay.

That night, sitting in my room, I took out my Bible and read the book of Philippians. Verse after verse spoke to me and quieted my heart. "Our citizenship is in heaven" (3:20). I breathed a prayer, "Thank you, Lord, that no one can steal my passport to heaven." "Rejoice in the Lord always; again I say rejoice" (4:4). Then some of my favorite verses in Scripture were tested and proved. "In nothing be anxious, but in everything by prayer and supplication with thanksgiving, let your requests be made known to God. And the peace of God that passes all understanding shall keep your hearts and minds in Christ Jesus" (4:6-7). As I read those familiar words, a sense of peace filled my heart and I fell fast asleep.

On Monday, a trip to the American Consulate was heartening. A red plastic China Airlines travel folder containing my passport, inoculation card, and plane ticket had been found on the streets in Kyoto by a secretary on the way to work who sent it to the American Consulate. In looking at my passport, I saw that it was good for only two more weeks, not enough time for someone else to make use of it.

When I first arrived in Osaka, I had visited the airline office to let them know my purse had been stolen. But because I had already re-confirmed my flight out back to Taiwan, the agent had agreed that I could fly back without my ticket when I had a passport. Now I returned to the office to share my good news. I showed the agent my ticket. Then I heard the words, "Oh, I am so sorry, miss! Your ticket was a special excursion fare that expired the day you were scheduled to leave. Now you must pay an additional amount." Check #2 from Rachel was needed and used.

It was a full week before I could get another Okinawa permit from Tokyo (which specified the time of arrival and departure from the island), and then all was in order for my flight home. On Friday I was going to cash check #3 so I'd have a little money for my departure from the island, but … Rachel had forgotten to sign her last name on the check! Penniless, I boarded the plane in Osaka. It flew to Fukuoka. Then, after a short stop there we took off, and I dropped off to sleep. I was awakened by a voice over the loudspeaker, "In 20 minutes we will be landing in Fukuoka. Due to typhoon conditions, we are unable to proceed and are returning to our port of departure." That got my attention!

Another prayer winged its way heavenward: "Lord, I need you to look after me again. Please, Lord, I trust you." There was no one on the plane that I knew – but God did. There was a missionary couple from Japan headed to Okinawa to see about the possibility of opening up mission work there. When I learned this, I stayed close to them! The airlines paid for our accommodations over the weekend but said that if they couldn't fly us out on Monday, we would be on our own!

On Sunday we attended an American military church service. A misprint in their bulletin has stayed with me through the years. We were to sing the well-known hymn, "Love Divine, All *Lovers* Excelling"!

By Monday, the typhoon had passed and we flew to Okinawa – and back home to Taiwan! How grateful I was to be on Taiwanese soil! When I arrived back to Morrison, I learned that one of the mothers had been asked to help out during my absence. She warmly welcomed me back – along with all my girls and the staff at school!

I was glad when Blake visited me, a few days later, on his return to the island.

It was great being back at Morrison Academy with my girls in the dormitory! Classes had begun. The girls had to make up their beds and clean up the room before leaving for class, and I checked to make sure that this had been done.

I had been given a tiny black-and-white puppy to keep in the girls' dorm several years earlier when I first went to Morrison, so tiny at the time that she could sit in the palm of my hand. I named her Pepper. The girls enjoyed playing with her, especially one little first-grader who arrived late in the school year because her family had just come to Taiwan. She had had surgery in the United States for crossed eyes but needed additional surgery later. Finding it difficult to be a late arrival, and with this medical problem, she had a harder time relating to all the girls in the dorm and found that playing with Pepper helped with the adjustments she had to make.

One day one of my second-graders came to me and said, "Miss Skepstad, I have the prickly heat!" On examination, I realized that she had the measles! So she moved into my extra room were she was quarantined. She would look out the window at all the students having fun outside at recess time and sigh. Having one child ill increased my responsibilities. At times I might have children ill in both dormitories.

On Sundays each of my students was to write a letter to their parents telling about school and how they were getting along. In the afternoon we sometimes took Christian pamphlets out into the fields and shared them with folks who walked by.

On my days off I would bike over to the Aarsheims' home to relax and enjoy their company. They were so hospitable. It was also a time for me to write my mission letters home to be sent out to a list of my friends.

From time to time this year I kept my eye out for the postman on a bicycle bringing me a "kwai-syin," or fast delivery letter, from Blake. He was busy with trips into the mountains, visiting over 25 Bunun tribal churches or preaching places on the east coast of Taiwan, but he found time to write letters on the run. He came by to visit me on one of his trips. Plans were made for me to visit him in Yuli at Thanksgiving time, and to go on a trip with him, plus Miss Marion Wilcox, senior Presbyterian missionary stationed in Hualien, and Sister Kuni, a German Lutheran deaconess dentist.

To prepare for the four-day trip I made brownies, and I mixed cocoa, coffee, and powdered milk in a tight container to use with hot boiling water. Good hiking boots were rain proofed and clothes packed.

For our Thanksgiving dinner we would be munching on turkey sandwiches on a trek high up into Bunun tribal country, visiting churches on the way and giving medical and dental care to the isolated mountain folk between services. They say this area has the most beautiful scenery in all of Taiwan. We would be earning our views by climbing the heights and crossing those swinging bridges over deep chasms. Most rewarding of all would be the inspiration that comes from being able to share with these tribe's people the joy Christ has brought to us, and the medical care that they so desperately needed.

# CHAPTER 6

## Wedding Bells


In preparation for the mountain trip I had to apply for a mountain permit, which was good for three months. The Chinese government didn't allow foreigners to go to the tribal people without one. I needed a sleeping bag and an air mattress. Blake had written, "Come prepared to sing, prepared to walk, prepared for fleas and rats, and I don't know what all!" Some fudge and some cocoa powder and coffee powder would be good.

When Thanksgiving arrived and the children at Morrison Academy had left for their homes, I took a train up to Taipei, then flew over the Cliff Road to Hualien and boarded a train to Yuli (Jade Village), which was about two-thirds of the way south on the east coast. Blake met me at the train station, and we walked to the mission house where Miss Gussie Fraser, senior Presbyterian missionary, lived. Blake had moved here after a year of language study in Taipei. (His first year of study was while he was in the U.S. Army in Monterey, California.) Now he lived here, ready for work, and living in a servant's room!

It was good to be back together again! In the evening we talked of many things – that actually ended with our becoming engaged! However, we shared the news with no one then. This wasn't the time to share this good news!

In the morning all those going on the trip gathered together. The villages we were to visit had sent carriers down to help with the baggage. There were books in boxes to be given out at the Bible studies, medicines to be dispensed, and a slide projector for showing films in the evening after dark. At last we were ready. We took the train south to the village nearest to the mountain trail leading to these villages. Then began the upward trail, crossing streams, following the paths around the side of the mountains, and upward! Upward!

When we arrived at a village, I would set up for a medical clinic, outdoors if the weather permitted. I could speak Chinese to some extent, but not Bunun, so Blake had one of his workers interpret for me. Sometimes the whole village was there to be seen! Medicine for worms needed to be given to almost everyone. Many asked for aspirin for headaches (present or future!); many had coughs and abdominal problems. Some were very ill and needed to be transported down the mountain to the train station to take the train to the Mennonite Hospital in

Thanksgiving mountain trip in Bunun country with Blake

Hualien. It was under the auspices of the doctors there that I was doing my nursing here.

At the first village Sister Kuni, our dentist, and her assistant went to work pulling teeth – pulling a total of 100 that could not be saved. The Bunun people knew what it was like to have a bad toothache and not be able to do anything about it. Sister Kuni's assistant was running a foot-powered drill and filling the teeth that could be saved.

Marion Wilcox was holding meetings with some of the women who taught Sunday School or did women's work. She also talked with the children who gathered around her. Blake met with the elders of the church in Bible studies.

In the evening when darkness fell, Blake would show slides on a screen using a battery-powered projector. He had the attention of the whole village! What a wonderful opportunity to share the news that Jesus is the Light of the World. He loves everyone and gave His life that we might become the children of God!

The villagers prepared a meal for us using their primitive methods of cooking. I slipped my chopsticks under the table and wiped them with alcohol to make sure they were clean. These people shared the best that they had, and we appreciated their hospitality. At night we slept in their thatched roof huts on the tatami (straw-matted) floors. Mosquitoes were prevalent, and sometimes bedbugs too. It is all a part of the journey of missionary work.

The next day we traveled on to the next village and set up our work again. This one had a thatched-roof church. Seats were made of planks placed across sawhorses. There was a center aisle. Men sat on one side and women on the other. Up front there was a table with a cross on it. Most of the singing was done without any musical instrument accompaniment. Bunun singing resembled the wind and the waves, an up-and-down melody of sorts.

In one of the villages, as I was treating some of the people with the medicines laid on a table under a tree, someone called to me, "Come quickly!" The person pointed to a village shack. It was dark inside with no windows. When my eyes adjusted to the darkness, I saw a woman in the corner on the tatami floor who had just delivered a baby, and she couldn't get the baby to breathe. Applying some nursing skills, I was able save the baby. I was glad the umbilical cord had not yet been cut because the mountain people do this with a piece of bamboo, which is host to the tetanus organism! The Bununs lose many of their newborns. With "sterile" scissors, I cut the cord, tied it off, and the baby girl was placed back in her mother's arms.

The Bunun tribal men had been headhunters up until the time of World War II. Japan had been in control of Taiwan at that time, and the Japanese soldiers who were in the mountains then lost a lot of their heads! Some time had elapsed since that time, but we were mindful of the past. The Bununs had come a long ways since then.

In all we visited four villages, bringing the saving news of Jesus Christ and His love for them, along with medical and dental care, and friendship. We headed down the mountains, crossed streams, boarded the next train on the narrow gauge railroad, and once we were back at the house in Yuli we relaxed, with our feet in a pan of warm water! This was a Thanksgiving that I would never forget!

Back at Morrison I was able to attend a Women's Retreat off campus, and when I came back to the dormitory I had a sign on my door that read, "Miss Skepstad, I love you, we all love you. Guess who wrote this." Of course, I couldn't guess!

Blake wrote his folks about our engagement, and they were thrilled. They had asked for a photo of me, so he sent them his copy of my prayer letter that had my photo on it. Blake asked me what kind of a diamond I wanted and what size ring I needed. So I went to the PX in Taipei and found out it was 5 3/4. And I wanted a diamond with a plain gold round band. My preference was a small solitaire but with more cuts in the diamond. I had to be careful that no one I knew saw me as I looked over the rings! While I was at the PX, I bought us an electric frying pan, and I looked around at electric mixers and a small steam travel iron for later purchases. I also wrote my parents, and my brother John and sister Bonnie, about my engagement, and told them not to share the news yet.

When I had heard back from both John, a Lutheran pastor, and Bonnie, I had their blessings, although John wasn't expecting our engagement to happen this soon. My parents, however, were unhappy that I was leaving the Lutheran Church.

That night at the supper table, one of my first graders asked, "Is Blake your boyfriend?"

I responded, "He is a good friend." She seemed satisfied, and the others didn't seem to pick up on it.

Blake had heard from his dad, Dr. Hugh Bradley, who was the Area Secretary to the Board of World Missions for the Presbyterian Church, U.S., that there had been more trouble in the churches in Korea, and he might have to come out to the Orient earlier than he had planned.

When Christmas vacation began, all the Morrison Academy students went to their homes. Faculty members lived on the campus. Blake's dad was coming and would arrive in time to spend Christmas with us at the school in Taichung. One of the staff members said that Blake and his dad could stay in her apartment. As the time drew near, I must say I had butterflies in my stomach! I was about to meet my future father-in-law! When he arrived on the campus, I headed over to meet him. I took one look at his smiling face and outstretched arms, and was then enveloped in a big hug. No more butterflies.

Blake, his dad and I had some time together at my home in the dormitory, and we had much to share with one another. Although Blake's dad had heard of our engagement just before he left home on his trip to Asia, he still had time to purchase and bring along a beautiful necklace and earrings set for me. He had also shopped for my diamond in Japan on his trip over, but that was to arrive later. We ate Christmas dinner with Bob and Jane McKinnon, who were Conservative Baptist missionaries on the school faculty. The McKinnons had invited the faculty to a Christmas tea later in the day. As we walked in to the tea, I introduced Dr. Bradley as my future father-in-law! The principal, Mr. Means, was drinking a cup of tea, and his hands started to shake as he realized he was going to lose me as dormitory mother to the girls in the following year.

During the few days Blake, his dad and I had together, we met with the other Presbyterian missionaries in Taichung and those on the faculty at Tunghai University nearby. They were a wonderful group of mission folk, and I found myself very much at home with them.

I had to write a letter to Dr. Rolf Syrdal, the Evangelical Lutheran Church's Mission Secretary, to notify him that I would be getting married in the spring and would no longer be with the Lutheran Evangelical Church in Taiwan. Dr. Bradley had brought out a set of candidate papers that I filled in while he was there for the Southern Presbyterian Church, U.S. to become a bona fide member of their missionary community. He said I passed with flying colors!

Once Blake and I were engaged, we were busy making plans for our wedding day – and our life together! However, we were still busy in our work, I at Morrison Academy and Blake with the Bunun tribe on the other side of the island.

When I returned from a brief trip to Taipei after Christmas vacation, five or six of the staff at the school started singing "congratulations" to me as they saw my pedicab pull in. Just then Larry Brown, faculty member, breezed in and started whistling the wedding march in peppy style! When the girls all arrived back at school later in the evening, they had to hear all about it, so we all pulled our chairs together around the fire in the fireplace in my lounge, and I told them highlights of Blake's and my courtship. I couldn't have had a more receptive audience! They were very happy for me but couldn't figure out how we had been able to keep it all so secret!

The next morning I was able to see our principal, Mr. Means, and set May 20 as our wedding date. I didn't want to wait until school was out to get married because some of the faculty members from Morrison Academy who would want to attend the wedding were sailing back to the United States right away, and I wanted them to be able to come.

My father-in-law, Dr. Hugh Bradley, was the Area Secretary to the Far East for the Board of World Missions, PCUS. Therefore, our invitations to the wedding needed to be sent to all the Presbyterian U.S. missionaries, all the Canadian Presbyterian missionaries, all the English Presbyterian missionaries on the island, as well as all at Morrison Academy and our Chinese friends!

In planning for the wedding I made many lists, as well as a list of all the lists! I had to get some items from the United States, some from Japan, and some from Hong Kong. Where should we be married? We decided to be married in the beautiful oriental-style Chapel at the Presbyterian Seminary up the mountain from Taipei. My attendants would be Jane McKinnon, Morrison faculty member, as my matron of honor, and Marjorie Bly and Elaine Elness, both Lutheran missionaries on the island. Six-year-old Maia Lee would be my flower girl.

My parents were not able to come to the wedding, so I asked Dr. Marcy Ditmanson if he would walk me down the aisle. This was appropriate since he was the one who enabled me to come to Taiwan, and he had hoped that eventually I would be able to work with him in a hospital he planned to build on the west coast. This was not to be, so he would be "giving me away!"

I was able to leave Morrison Academy ten days before the wedding and went to stay with Dr. Ken and Kay Kepler, faculty members at the Presbyterian Seminary. They had a car and drove me to the many places I needed to go to prepare for the wedding: the dressmaker who made my dress; the printer who printed the service folders, thank-you notes, and our names on the napkins my folks had sent; the floral shop for flowers, candles for candelabra and on the aisles, and gifts for my attendants. A friend who had connections with the American military ordered my cake through one of their chefs.

As it turned out, Generalissimo Chiang Kai Shek, who lived on the same mountain above Taipei, announced that May 20 would be the date of his re-inauguration, with parades taking place throughout the city. I called to find out when and where the parades would take place and received several different answers. This meant that I would have to have everything for our wedding delivered before the parades began!

Blake flew in from the east coast three days before the wedding. He went to the British Consulate to get visas for us to fly to Hong Kong for our honeymoon.

Blake's father had to make a mission trip from the U.S. out to Korea near the time of the wedding, and he was able to bring his wife Agnes along, so they came to Taiwan from there, arriving two days before the wedding. They brought me many gifts from my folks, including the small white book, *Consecration*, and some artificial lilies-of-the-valley that I carried in my small bouquet, plus several dresses, a silver bracelet and cufflinks.

On May 19 we had a wedding rehearsal at the chapel. Beth

Farlow, who had been in Japan the same summer Blake and I had met, and who had met Joe Farlow there and married him in March, took the place of the bride. All went well. Would the wedding go as smoothly? After the rehearsal, we had a dinner for all involved plus their mates, hosted by Dr. and Mrs. Bradley.

The weather did not co-operate. The day before, the day of, and the day after the wedding, the rain poured down. I had hoped that we would be able to see all the sparkling lights of the city of Taipei below

Oriental Chapel at the Presbyterian Seminary where Blake and I got married

from the mountain in the evening, but clouds and rain prevented this view.

The day of the wedding, I made sure that the flowers, the white carnations for the men attendants, the wedding cake, and the wedding folders were delivered before the parades took place. I had hired a bus to bring students and faculty from Morrison Academy up to the Seminary chapel. Since my parents could not attend the wedding, I asked Jerry Elness, Lutheran missionary, to take movies of the service that I could send to them.

He bought film on the black market on the streets of Taipei, which turned out to be no good. The individual photos turned out very well, however. Jessie Junkin played the organ that had been loaned to us for the evening by friends. There was some difficulty in getting the organ to play before the wedding started, but that issue had been resolved.

My attendants were lovely in long blue dresses and pearl necklaces, and little Maia was precious in her blue dress made from material that my sister had sent. She wore a silver chain with one pearl on it, and a big smile!

At the last minute we could not find the white boutonnieres for the groomsmen. Ken Kepler walked up to the organ that was on the side isle and began breaking off pink carnations from the bouquet sitting on the organ – while Jessie was worried something might happen to the organ and there would be no music! She said to Ken, "Ken Kepler, you stop that. Ken Kepler, you stop that!" Ken *carefully* picked three.

Finally all was ready. Rev. Herman Bly from the Lutheran Mission (who had been in China with my parents and me) and Dr. Hugh Bradley were up front, and the wedding music began to play. Mary Ellen Boehr sang the "Wedding Prayer." Blake and his three groomsmen, Joe Farlow, Bob Montgomery, and Gene Craven, were in place. Then my attendants walked in one-by-one, followed by Maia, throwing flower petals on the aisle. Dr. Marcy Ditmanson walked me down the aisle to Blake as Jessie played "Wedding March."

Dr. Bradley gave the sermonette based on Scripture passages from Ephesians: 4:1 "Lead a life worthy of the calling to which you have been called;" 5:2 "Walk in love, as Christ loved us;" 5:7 "Walk as children of light;" and 5:15-16 "Walk as wise men, making the most of the time, because the days are evil." Rev. Herman Bly then united us in marriage.

Coming down the aisle after the wedding

Mary Ellen Boehr sang "The Lord's Prayer," then the congregation rose and sang "Savior, Like a Shepherd Lead Us." Rev. Bly pronounced the benediction, and we all joyfully recessed to "Wedding March."

Our reception was in a nearby building and we hurried over there in the rain. Blake and I sampled a piece of the wedding cake before standing in the reception line, with Maia Lee beside us beaming at everyone who came through. It took an hour for everyone to come through the line! Then we had to dash back into the sanctuary for pictures to be taken. That took an hour too, for Jerry used three cameras! By this time most of the guests had left, and the food had been taken away, so we never had a chance to sample the sunbakkles, Russian teacakes, brownies, nuts, and punch!

Those helping at the reception were my 7th ands 8th grade girls from Morrison who served at the tables, Marit Hanson who served at the punch bowl, and Beth Farlow and Rachel Sarason were at the gifts table.

Our wedding cake was something else! I had asked for a traditional white layer cake. What I got was a five-layer cake, with the bottom layer made of wood and covered with white frosting. On that bottom layer were four miniature mountain chapels with battery lights inside! The edible part was fruitcake! Crowning the top layer were a bride and groom and lilies-of-the-valley.

We had invited Jane Young, the American Consulate General in Taiwan, to be with us, and she was happy to be there.

Well, it was still pouring rain! Many guests had difficulty getting taxis when they were ready to leave, and some guests didn't get away from the Kepler's (where the stragglers had gathered) till 1:30 a.m., including the Ditmansons and Joyce – who was expecting a baby the next week!

Groomsman Joe drove the "get-away" car. (We had heard that some of the guests planned to kidnap me, so Blake and I stayed hand-in-hand most of the time.) He drove us to a Taiwanese inn for the night. The next day we were on a plane to Hong Kong where we spent our honeymoon.

In making preparation for our honeymoon in Hong Kong, I had contacted Mrs. Charlotte Martinson in the Lutheran Mission in that area, and she had reserved a nice room for us in The Four Seasons Hotel. When we arrived and registered at the desk, I had to sign in as Faith Skepstad because there had been no time after the wedding to have the name on my passport changed to my married name. In our room, there was a beautiful bouquet of flowers to welcome us, which Mrs. Martinson had arranged for.

It was wonderful to have time to relax after our extremely busy schedule before the wedding. The weather was lovely, and we spent many happy hours on the beach. During the time in Hong Kong, Charlotte invited us out to their mission community for a lovely tea. Her daughter Char and I had gone to boarding school together in China during wartime, and all these missionaries were good friends of my family.

Blake's parents spent some days in Hong Kong after the wedding, and we often ate dinner together. During their stay, my mother-in-law fell and injured her arm and, as I remember, had to use a sling for her arm.

Hong Kong was a shoppers' paradise! The colony was a member of the British Empire and had merchandise from all over the world, at very good prices, if one knows how to shop. I had graduated from high school in Hong Kong 11 years earlier, and one of my graduation gifts had been a carved cedar chest. I had chosen the designs that I wanted to be carved in the chest, and I had treasured it ever since. This visit I bought a beautiful aqua brocaded silk jacket with floral designs in it. It was reversible with beige, creamy color with floral designs on the interior.

All good things come to an end, and we flew back to Taiwan. The mission allowed me to have one quarter of language study in Taipei, which was very helpful; when I had lived in China growing up, it was wartime and we had to evacuate and move many times, and the dialect had been different in different locations. While I was studying, Blake had a knee operation at the Seventh Day Adventist Hospital. Years ago, he had injured his knee when jumping over the net to shake his opponent's hand after a game of tennis. He didn't entirely clear the net. The knee had bothered him increasingly, with all the mountain travel needed in his work with a mountain tribe. So while studying the language, visiting Blake in the hospital, and taking him food that appealed to him, I began to realize that I was pregnant! At the end of the term, we flew back to the east coast and took the fast express from Hualien to Yuli. It was a narrow gauge railroad, and it took two hours to travel 50 miles!

It was getting closer to Christmas when we arrived. Aunt Gussie Fraser, senior Presbyterian missionary, had told Blake that when we were married, she would give us half her house. We would have a second entrance to the back of the house, with a small living room, one bedroom and a bathroom. A new wall in the long hall separated her half from ours. We had asked that the outside door be painted green. When we arrived, it was blue. The painter said he didn't have green paint then. We walked up the few steps to our entrance and walked into the living room. For a kitchen, we had to convert a closet and have a sink installed in it. When checking out the sink, we turned on the water – and our feet got wet! No plumbing below! We joked that Yuli was "malfunction junction!" We had no refrigerator, but Aunt Gussie gave us some shelves in her refrigerator. So, to prepare a meal I would go outside to her door, go in to get what we needed for the meal, and return to prepare it. Our stove was a one-burner electric unit, and I had an electric frying pan. We set up a card table by a window in the living room and ate our meals there. I remember that there was a papaya tree outside the window.

Bunun was a very difficult language to learn because the Bunun people had no written language. Blake had a Bunun co-worker, Ki-shing, and Blake was learning the language from him. To help Blake acquire the tools to learn the basics of this Malayo-Polynesian language more easily, The Presbyterian Mission (PCUS) was making it possible for us to travel to Australia to attend the Wycliffe School of Linguistics for three months; the school was focused on the Malayo-Polynesian languages.

We had just moved back to Yuli when we needed to leave, and I was feeling the nausea that comes in the first three months of pregnancy; I wondered if I was going to be able to go. The morning we were to leave, I said positively, "I think I'm feeling a little better…" So I got dressed and packed a suitcase, and we walked to the train station to go to Hualien. Our missionaries there were having a Christmas dinner. We joined them at the table and afterwards I felt "a little better"! The next day we flew to Taipei. Again, the missionaries there were having their Christmas dinner. It went well! Then I knew that I would be going to Australia with Blake!

# CHAPTER 7

## Wycliffe Training

We flew from Taipei airport to Melbourne, Australia, via the Philippine Islands. We were traveling to a country where the people spoke English, yet we wondered if we were going to be able to understand them because of their accent.

The first night there, we stayed in The People's Palace, run by the Salvation Army. In the morning we ate breakfast at a small table where an Australian woman was sitting. She was congenial and asked us, "I say, did you have a 'baisin' in your room last night?"

I was pondering her question, but Blake responded, "Yes, we did have a wash basin in our room." Yes, language was going to be problematic! We needed to listen to the Australians' accent!

That morning we stood in line to buy tickets to the train that would take us out to where the Wycliffe School was located. I asked the lady behind me if we were standing in the right line. She answered arrogantly, "Well, where else do you suppose this train would be going?!"

At the school we had quarters in a house along with another family. The school had three classes a day: Phonetics (every sound, and know how to write it down), Phonemics (those sounds used in a particular language), and Grammar. They had both American and Australian tutors. Every Friday we students would be given a test. If an American tutor read the words we had to write down, we did well. If an Australian tutor called out the words, we didn't fare so well! The tutors helped us to understand something about the Malayo-Polynesian people and their customs.

The school required that everyone who attended its classes had to help out in some way. Those who gave haircuts gave them freely to others. Some people set the table for meals, others helped with the dishes afterwards. We had devotional services as well as worship on Sundays. We learned some new hymns from their hymnbook, which increased the number of hymns we enjoyed singing as we sang praises to God.

Blake had a birthday while we were there. I wanted to invite a few friends over for the occasion, so I needed to bake a cake. The Australians use weights and measures that I wasn't familiar with, so I went to one of the American tutors and asked if she had an American cookbook. She did, and she loaned it to me. So I skipped one of the classes and prepared a cake to be put in the oven. One of the ladies in charge offered to put it in the oven for me, so I thanked her and returned to the class. Blake was wondering where I had gone; was it morning sickness? Later I returned to check on the cake. Alas, while my cake was in a smaller oven in the kitchen, the chief chef had fired up the big oven right next to it, and my cake was charred on all sides. The lady in charge felt so bad about it. We had to cut off the burnt top, sides, and bottom, so the cake was much smaller. We needed a *lot* of frosting to cover it. The lady offered to make the frosting, but I was near tears (as happens during pregnancy!), and I answered her, "No, I want to make the frosting!"

At the afternoon tea following class, I saw the tutor who had lent me her cookbook. She was standing near Blake and me and asked, "How did the cake turn out?" Knowing, as I did, that this was supposed to be a surprise for Blake, the tears started to come, and I ran to the bathroom and let them flow! We did have a few guests to the house in the evening to celebrate Blake's birthday, despite the fact he never wanted folks to know when his birthday was. However, he finally agreed to build a fire in the fireplace, and that warmed things up, both literally and figuratively!

We made some good friends who were also studying at the school. One such couple there was connected to Wycliffe in the Philippine Islands. Their house in the Philippines was built on stilts over the water. I wondered how they kept their little children from falling into the water. Another young Australian couple at the school was expecting their first child also, and after we left Australia to return home, we kept in touch with them. Each Christmas since then we have received a Christmas letter from them. The husband was working for the Bible Society in different parts of Australia.

Occasionally during our time in Australia we took trips to see other parts of the country, including the Blue Hills and kangaroos in a park. These adventures helped us get the feel of the country "down under."

The school was intense, and Blake felt that it was the most difficult school he had attended, including seminary. A couple attending the school offered us the use of a cabin they had on the shores of the bay in Sydney for two weeks. There we were able to unwind, get in some swimming, and relax.

Armed with new tools for learning the Bunun language, learned in Australia, we flew back to Taiwan. While we had been away in Australia, the mission had begun building a house in Yuli for us to live in. Our friend and fellow missionary, Rev. Joe Farlow, was in charge of plans and supervising the construction. The house was built across the street from Aunt Gussie's house and our new address was 6-1 Ta Tung Lu, Yuli, Taiwan!

When we saw the size of the house, we questioned Joe, "Why so large?" Joe's reply was that one day there might be another missionary family assigned to Yuli, and the house could be divided into two parts. When the house was completed, we moved our furniture and belongings from Aunt Gussie's house to our new home. Besides our one-story three-bedroom house, another two-story building with an outside staircase was built in our compound, with rooms upstairs for our Bunun co-workers to stay in when visiting. Downstairs was an office where Blake and his co-workers could plan their work and trips into the mountains. There was also a room for our washing machine and dryer, and a pump, to pump water up to the holding tank on top of the second floor. This provided running water in our house.

Our baby was due in three months. Our families in the States had sent some baby clothes, and our fellow missionaries had hosted a shower as well. We readied a bedroom for our anticipated child, sex unknown. Our nearest western hospital was the Mennonite Hospital in Hualien, two hours away by train. I knew the Canadian nurses and doctors there, and they had assured me that they would go by my desires to have natural childbirth. So a few days before my due date, we traveled to Hualien and stayed with Aunt Marian Wilcox until it was time to move over to the hospital. I asked one of the nurses if there was anything I would need at this hospital, which was primarily for the mountain people, and she said I might want to bring an air mattress to lay on top of the tatami bed. All went well, and on a Sunday afternoon at 5 p.m., Karen Elizabeth was born, a healthy baby girl weighing six pounds 13 ounces! I felt like I had been to a vesper service! That night I felt so stiff and sore, and thought, I guess this is how one feels after having a delivery. Well, it didn't have much to do with the delivery; the air mattress had a leak in it and had gone absolutely flat!

While I was in the hospital other women came in for deliveries, and in the nursery there were a Bunun baby, a Toroko baby, a Toroko-Chinese baby, and a Taiwanese baby, giving it an international flavor!

The mountain food was not appealing to me at that time, so Aunt Marian prepared western-style food for me, and Blake brought meals over to me on his bicycle. Then as soon as I could travel, we had to fly to Taipei to the American Consulate to get Karen's birth registered.

Back home in Yuli I had two Chinese helpers in the home, one a cook and one to keep the house clean and launder the clothes. The cook had to go to the market each day to purchase fresh food in order to prepare it. No canned or frozen food was available in Yuli, so meals had to be prepared from scratch. I had to show our cook how to prepare meals western style, and she would write it down in Chinese characters in a little book. We would eat Chinese food once a day most of the time. Pork was available in the local market, but not beef. Each time we traveled to Taipei, we would purchase three pounds of frozen beef, packaged in one-pound units. These were saved for special occasions. Sometimes my parents would ship us groceries from the States, canned goods, with packages of Jell-O and puddings. A taste of home!

When it came time to have Karen baptized, we invited senior missionary E. H. "Ham" Hamilton from Taipei to officiate at the service, to be held in the Taiwanese Presbyterian Church in Yuli. On that Sunday, there were also six Taiwanese babies to be baptized, including the daughter of the local Taiwanese Presbyterian pastor, and Rev. Hamilton baptized them all.

We were fortunate to have electricity and running water in our home. We had an electric stove and a small electric oven, so were well supplied. However, the only heat we had in the house was a fireplace in the living room, and the temperature in the winter would be in the low 40's. We had an electric heater that we would plug in, in the bathroom at bath time.

Blake was eager to begin to apply his new knowledge gained at Wycliffe in Australia. He had a Bunun co-worker, Kishing, who helped him full time, and another helper Ebi, who had had two years of Bible School training. Ebi's main responsibilities were to translate Bible study material into Bunun, and to teach us Bunun. Blake spoke Chinese well, but Bunun was an entirely different language and that is where his co-workers were very helpful. There were about 20 Bunun villages on the east coast, and the three men tried to visit them as often as they could. There were only two ordained pastors in the tribe. On Sundays the village churches could only celebrate the Lord's Supper when an ordained minister was there.

Blake and Kishing would be out every Sunday to lead worship in one of the villages. Often they held conferences for several days for untrained mountain preachers. The two held Bible studies in order to help the preachers develop messages to give on Sunday mornings as they led their chapel services. At other times Blake and Kishing held Sunday School teachers' workshops with material for the coming six weeks. Then in the evenings they would show slides of Bible stories. One evening before Karen was born, I went with them to one of the villages. I played my autoharp to lead singing because many of the chapels had no musical instruments. Subsequently a Bible woman learned to play the pump organ.

Blake had previously asked Christians back in the United States to pray for various villages by name. The churches undertook the responsibility to pray for a specific church. We tried to write a description of the church for them, with their specific needs. As time went on, we were encouraged to see spiritual growth that couldn't be accounted for any other way! Prayer changes things!

In 1962 it was furlough time. About a month before we left Yuli, we had a three-day preachers conference in our home. We moved all the furniture from the living room and dining room into the back of the house. Blake had stressed to the attendees that they must bring their own bedding to put on the floor, but only seven of the 28 of them did! So we had to scout for extra bedding, curtains, bedrolls, air mattresses and winter housecoats – anything to cover the cement floor!

To cook meals for them all, we had to prepare food in the backyard over an open fire, using a very large cauldron borrowed from the local Taiwanese church. We cooked rice first, and then the cauldron was cleansed, and a variety of vegetables – cabbage, celery, green onions, and green beans – along with chunks of meat, went into the pot. Half of the vegetables were used in a soup and half were served with the rice and meat as a main course. Kishing's wife, Wuli, was our chief cook, and our house girl and gate boy and I helped as well. One of the preachers was to bring all the bowls and chopsticks but came with only six, so our gate boy had to bike to a nearby village to see if we could borrow some from the people there. We had a long screened-in porch on one side of the house, and we set up long tables and benches there for the preachers' meals. Breakfast meant getting up at four or four-thirty a.m. to serve this meal on time.

This kind of conference with Bible studies and aids for the preachers was so helpful. These villagers were men who had to work in their fields, as well as prepare for services, and they never had any time for recreation. At our home they learned about badminton, croquet, and horseshoes. After a very busy time of concentrated study, the conference closed with one of the two pastors leading a communion service.

After everyone had left, we did some cleaning and resting. Then Blake came down with a potent strain of the flu. The hospital in Hualien sent enough penicillin for three days, three injections a day, plus some other medications. It helped that I was a registered nurse!

The following Sunday the Watermann family arrived, eight of them, having caught an earlier train than expected. Their children, ages three, six, eight, ten, and twelve, were quite a handful, and we had some interesting episodes! The Watermanns came to check Bible translation work in the Bunun language. It was very helpful to have experienced translation workers oversee what Blake and his co-workers had done.

We then had to begin packing and preparing for the time we were to be on furlough in the U.S., when we would be continuing language study, and for Blake, would be itinerating to the Presbyterian churches, sharing what God was doing among the Bunun tribe in Taiwan.

Towards the end of May 1962, after five years of mission work in Taiwan, it was time to pack our luggage, say goodbye to our co-workers and fellow missionaries, take the train to Hualien, and fly to Taipei. Our overseas flight was routed to Japan, on to Anchorage, Alaska, and finally to Seattle, Washington.

All this travel was difficult for Karen, even though we had stopped over in Japan for several days. On the flight from Japan she could not settle down, and cried and cried. There were about four other infants on the plane, all of whom went off to sleep, but not ours! I fed her, burped her, changed her, the attendant walked her up and down the aisle. Not until we approached the Anchorage airport did she go to sleep. And here we had to change planes and head to Seattle!

My sister Bonnie and husband lived in the Seattle area. My parents had driven out from Minnesota, and my brother John had driven from California. They were all at the airport to meet me – and my husband and my ten-month-old daughter for the first time! We had to go through customs before we were free to get together. Finally we were able to go to Bonnie's home and rest up. Both Bonnie and I were five-months pregnant, she with her first child. It was wonderful to spend a few days together!

Our final destination was Richmond, Virginia, where we had an upstairs apartment at Mission Court. Blake studied at Union Theological Seminary (where he had studied for the ministry before going to Taiwan), as well as itinerating for missions when needed.

With my delivery imminent, I needed to make an appointment with a doctor; I saw him one time before delivery. I explained that I wanted to have natural childbirth. He said he could do this – if I came in before this Friday at 5 p.m. He would be off after that and his assistant would need to take over. Well, we came to Richmond Memorial Hospital on that Friday evening about 7:00 p.m., and as the doctor had said, his assistant took over with his "routine orders." Before I knew it, a nurse had inserted an I.V. and was giving me a medication to speed up my delivery. I tried to explain what I wanted, but I lost the argument. Then the nurse gave me an epidural so I wouldn't feel the pain. I was aware of all that was happening when our son was born, but I felt like I didn't have a part in this delivery. However, we had a healthy new baby boy, weighing 7 lbs. 13 oz.!

My sister Bonnie had a new baby girl two weeks later, and she and her husband named her Laura Dawn.

In choosing a name for our new son, my preference was to name him "David." However, three other missionary families that we worked with in Taiwan had all had baby boys named David. So we named our son "John Hugh Bradley," John for my dad and brother and Hugh for Blake's father.

Blake's father, Dr. Hugh Bradley, was born in China where his father was a medical doctor and built a hospital to care for ill and wounded folk.

Dr. Bradley was the pastor of Decatur Presbyterian Church, Decatur, Georgia for ten years, and then responded to a call – issued for the third time – to become the East Asia Area Secretary to the Board of World Missions for the Presbyterian Church U.S. In 1957, when Blake went to Taiwan, he stopped in Korea to visit his father who had had a heart attack and was being treated by one of our mission physicians. And now he was beginning to have some further heart problem. His physician said he needed to give up his mission work traveling abroad, so he became an instructor teaching Bible classes to students at King College in Bristol, Tennessee.

Dr. and Mrs. Hugh Bradley (Blake's parents)
with our daughter Karen

Blake, the two children and I were living in a building called Mission Court apartments. Blake's parents, who were in Richmond, Virginia, made it possible for me to have some help in the home with the two little ones who were thirteen-and-a-half months apart in age. Other missionaries staying in other apartments at Mission Court would invite our daughter Karen to come to their place for a few hours so I could have time alone with my new little one. Outside the apartment was a tennis court, and sometimes the two children and I would go outside to watch Blake play tennis.

Often Blake itinerated to various churches sharing the news of how the Bunun tribe high up in the mountainous regions of Taiwan was responding to the Gospel of Jesus Christ. Usually he would carry several items into the pulpit to help the congregations visualize the work, like a pair of mountain boots and a bottle of medicine. Some of the churches were ones that had promised to pray for an individual village church, and they were eager to find out what was happening in "their" village. It was really amazing how the Spirit of God was sweeping across the mountains of Taiwan among these animistic peoples who wanted to know more about this God who loves them.

Often Blake was asked to speak to youth groups. Some of the young people were interested. However, one group he spoke to talked to each other throughout the presentation, which was most discouraging.

My parents planned to come for a visit from Minnesota. Mother would never fly on a plane, so they had to come by train and transfer at several locations, sometimes in the middle of the night. But they arrived in Richmond and were welcomed by us all. While they were here, we went to see The Civil War Centennial Center. Later Blake took them to Washington,

D.C. to do some sight seeing. They were also able to visit Williamsburg, so had a chance to see more of that part of the country while still enjoying a visit with us and getting acquainted with their first grandchildren.

We attended Ginter Park Presbyterian Church, which was close by. I enjoyed attending a seminary wives' Bible study. Mostly, however, I enjoyed being wife and mother to my family. The year passed quickly, and it was time to return to our work in Taiwan.

We said goodbye to Mom and Dad Bradley in Bristol, Tennessee and drove to Minnesota to see my parents, continued out to Seattle to see Bonnie and family, then headed south to San Francisco. Our baggage was already on board the ship there, and we were due to sail the next day. That evening we had a phone call from Blake's parents. His dad said, "We just wanted to say goodbye to you one more time before you go." Something his mom said clued us that we might want to call his cardiologist, and we did so. His report was that Dad had anywhere from two weeks to six months to live. Blake was an only child. This was no time to be going overseas! So we had our luggage removed from the ship and immediately flew back to Bristol with our two children.

Ten days later, as I was sitting by Dad's bedside, he looked at me, held my hand, and said, "I love you, Faith." A few minutes later he had another heart attack, and he was gone, called into God's presence, to his Eternal Home.

Dad's funeral service was held in the chapel at King College in Bristol, Tennessee. His interment was in Anderson, South Carolina in the family burial grounds. We moved into the basement of Mom's house to stay and help her with all the emotional and financial needs at this time of loss. The days went by slowly, but bit-by-bit she was able to gain her physical and emotional strength, realizing that there was still a future for her. She had many friends and many talents, and financially she was going to be all right. Blake found the son of a professor at King College who was a high school student and was willing to come and live with her in her home while he attended school in the daytime. Peter was an answer to prayer!

In November we made plans to return to Taiwan; we flew back rather than going by ship, as we had previously planned.

# CHAPTER 8

## Our Second Term in Taiwan

Our flight back to Taiwan in November 1963 was fairly uneventful. However, while we were in Taipei registering with the government and the American Consulate, we heard the shocking news that President Kennedy had been shot and killed! How could that have happened in the United States of America! We felt a pervading sense of grief and loss, as well as a sense of uncertainty as Americans being in a foreign land at this time.

However, for Blake and me, we were returning to our home and work in Yuli on the east coast. For our two very young children, it was very different. There were mystified looks on their faces as they saw people who looked different from them.

Me with Karen and John getting places in Yuli

Blake was planning to put out five booklets in the Bunun language. The first one was about a Christian talking to an unbeliever, telling him about Jesus and His love for him, and inviting him to come to the church. The second one was about our Lord Jesus Christ, who came to earth, died for our sins, and rose again. The third one begins at creation, tells of Moses and the Ten Commandments, of Christ's life and crucifixion, and of our need to repent of our sins, be baptized, and share in communion. The fourth one we planned on putting out was to be about the Lord's Prayer. Each booklet had pictures on one side of the page illustrating the truths, and on the opposite page the words were all set to music. The Bununs love to sing, so it was easier for them to learn songs rather than to just read the words.

Since the Bununs had no books in their own language (though a Taiwanese pastor was working on translating a Bunun New Testament), they had to be taught to read. Once they had learned the basics they could study the first booklet. Then they were given a test. If they passed it, they were allowed to go on to the next booklet. In the third booklet there was a page in the back of the booklet that had a place for them to sign their name (or put a marker) saying they had received Christ into their heart, "and would to the death follow Him." Blake said to the committee that was overseeing the booklets that, that was pretty strong language to use, but they answered, "We have been through the killing times (during the Japanese occupation), and the killing times may come again."

Sometimes when we were walking or biking to the villages we could hear one or two of the villagers singing these songs as they worked their fields. How good it was to know that God's truths were becoming a part of their lives.

In April 1964, we were able to hold a second preachers' conference in our home for four days; it was four days of concentrated Bible study for leaders who came from villages far and near. With the mission house across the street being vacant at this time, we used their living room and dining room for sleeping accommodations for most of the preachers. In our home we had the two guest preachers, five Bunun leaders, and the women delegates. Our living room became the conference center. Some of the preachers forgot to bring a mat or anything to sleep on, and so we tried to find a blanket or something for them to use on the floor.

Each morning opening worship began at 6 a.m. Those who came earlier than that sat and sang while they waited for the prayer meeting to begin. Our two guest speakers, Rev. Kenneth Kepler and Rev. James Li, from the Presbyterian Seminary in Taipei, presented a series of fine, inspirational messages from God's Word. In addition to these messages, Blake led the group in a simple method of Bible study in which all could participate, using three questions concerning individuals in a passage studied:

- What are the person's good points?
- What are the person's bad points?
- What lesson does this have for me?

After they caught on to this method, and saw that it was a tool with which they could dig out gems of Bible truth for themselves, faces came alive with a glow of wonder and amazement! Forty-five minute periods lengthened into one-and-a-half hours, even cutting into recreation periods, as the participants were unwilling to call a halt before they had finished their discussion. Since they had caught the vision, we were hopeful that they would use this method at home in their churches so that each Christian would be actively involved in a Bible study program.

Recreation periods provided the needed breaks between sessions. What enthusiastic participants they were … in badminton, horseshoes, and croquet … all new to them, but available in our yard. Croquet was a favorite, and a number of churches ordered sets fashioned after ours for their use in "their" village.

Out in the backyard another activity was taking place, one even more important than recreation. As at past preachers conferences, Kishing's wife Wuli headed up the cooking crew, who were busily preparing food for the hungry crowd. We sometimes served up to 40 people at one meal. Over our three fire pits, we had thrown a canvas overhead on bamboo supports to protect us from the rain or sun. Seven pairs of hands were busily occupied in various activity, from riding bikes to the market to purchase big box loads of vegetables and pillowcase loads of rice, to washing and chopping all the ingredients and cooking the dishes of food. We cooked plenty of food, enough for seconds and thirds. From 4:30 a.m. – when my alarm went off and it was time to rouse and build the fires (yawn!) and wash the rice for breakfast – it was one steady push to have meals on schedule. Once one meal's dishes were done, it was time to start the next meal! But good food contributes to a successful conference, and it was worth every bit of effort involved.

Out of this conference came several fine results:

- A deepening of the spiritual life in those who attended.
- Better fellowship among the preachers, whereas there had previously been divisions and mistrust among certain ones.
- The spreading of the Bible study programs which "caught fire" in the mountain churches.

"For as the rain and the snow come down from heaven,
    And return not thither but water the earth,
  Making it spring forth and sprout,
        Giving seed to the sower and bread to the eater,
So shall my word be that goes forth from my mouth;
            It shall not return to me empty, but it shall
            accomplish that which I purpose, And prosper in
            the thing for which I sent it."

Isaiah 55:10-11

As you may have surmised, the need for additional missionaries to work among the mountain tribes was crucial. So it was very good news when we heard that Rev. Bert and Ann Downs and family were living in Taipei, had studied Mandarin Chinese for two years and Taiwanese for one year, and had been assigned to the mountain work. Bert had

Blake and Bert Downs in another Bunun church

105

accompanied Blake on a two-week trip to experience the mission work being done among the Bunun mountain tribes. Bert was so healthy and physically suited for work among the mountain churches. He had been assigned to work with the tribal folk west of the high central mountain range.

Then on June 20, 1964, before he had actually started the work, we heard the news that Bert had been in a fatal plane crash on the west coast of central Taiwan! No survivors! The lives of 57 people snuffed out in moments. We found this so difficult to comprehend.

Concerning this tragedy, here I'd like to quote the words of Margaret Sells, senior Presbyterian missionary in Taipei: "Last Sunday morning, after having received the tragic radio announcement, Ann and I prepared for bed. It was 3 a.m. Baby Bryan (15 months old) had awakened and was standing in his crib. He gave me some very searching looks as if to say, 'What are you doing here?' He looked and looked around the room. We knew for whom he was looking.

We had two-and-a-half hours' sleep that dark, dark morning. Then Punt (Bert, Jr.), not quite eight years old, came into the room, got into the bed and asked for his daddy. Ann told him, 'Daddy won't be coming back, Punt.'

'Is Daddy dead?' He asked in stricken tones. Ann then took him out into the living room and told him that his Daddy was with Jesus. Dear friends, please note what this little boy said. It has wrung our hearts – and many hearts...

'Then who will go to the mountains?' he asked, and the tears began to flow. Can't you picture that home where the zeal of the parents was reflected in this question of their little boy? Unconsciously, he was saying with Isaiah, 'How beautiful upon the mountains are the feet of them that preach good news... Whom shall I send and who will go for us?' And, in essence, that question echoed the voice of Paul ... 'Whosoever shall call upon the name of the Lord shall be saved... How then shall they call on him in whom they have not believed? And how shall they believe in him of whom they have not heard? And how shall they hear without a preacher?'

'Why this waste, Lord? Why did it have to be Bert, ... a man so gifted, so dedicated, so needed?' God's answer comes quickly: 'My children. I make no mistakes. Bert's work was finished.'

'But Lord, how could it be finished? He was only 32.'

'Have you forgotten? My Son died at the age of 33, on the cruel cross.

Do you remember how He cried out, "It is *finished*?"'

### BERTIS E. DOWNS III
#### Has Been
#### Promoted to Higher Service
## BUT WHO WILL GO TO THE MOUNTAINS?"

When we heard the tragic news, we made plans to travel to Taipei for the Memorial Service. All planes in Taiwan had been grounded since the plane crash, so this meant that we would have to travel in a vehicle by very rough roads, including riverbeds in places. From beyond Hualien we would have to go on the Cliff Road, which had one-way traffic only, going opposite ways according to the times scheduled. I was over four months pregnant with our third child but was not willing to miss the service, so our whole family was there. In Taipei we stayed with one of our mission families.

I remember the Memorial Service. Bert's wife Ann was sitting up in the front row with her three little boys. One of the hymns Ann had chosen for the service was "Lead On, O King Eternal."

Shortly after the service, Ann and the three boys flew back to the United States. Ann Broom, another of our missionaries, accompanied them on their trip home.

Our third baby was due in November 1964. One day when I was eight months along and Blake was out on a conference with the Bunun preachers, I began having contractions that were becoming more regular, and I kept looking for him to arrive back home. The time went by and he didn't come. Blake knew that these preachers have so little time for leisure, so he treated them to some hot baths to help them relax after their study sessions. When he did arrive, and learned that I was having some regular contractions, he immediately hopped on his bicycle and hurried to the telephone office in town. Quickly he put through a call to the Mennonite Hospital in Hualien that we would be taking the last fast express train that night because I was in labor. I packed clothes in a suitcase and we walked to the station. When we arrived in Hualien two hours later, folks from the hospital were there to meet us. By then my contractions had stopped. Wouldn't you know it! We ended up at the home of Miss Marian Wilcox, who welcomed our whole family into her home.

That night there was an especially bad storm, and the rail line was disrupted in 18 places! We certainly were grateful to be near the hospital. As it turned out, Anne Sharon was born fairly close to her due date, a month after we had arrived in Hualien.

Here are a few glimpses into our family life as our children grew. Hugh, a young man of two, had become a ready diplomat. Whenever he got into difficulty with mommy or daddy he said, "Okay, I'm not going to do dat anymore!" One day in Hualien, we were late in coming to dinner, and I suggested he tell Aunt Marion he was sorry to be late. To my surprise I heard his truthful apology come out like this, "I'm sorry I had to run so fast!"

In June 1965, one of our fine mountain elders from Cho Le village, while hunting alone in the mountains, was bitten by one of the most deadly snakes on Taiwan. This kind of snake is so deadly poisonous that it is called the hundred-pace snake. People bitten supposedly die before they walk 100 paces.

Immediately after being bitten, Elder Sungyi cut a hunk of his flesh out of his leg around the bite, applied a makeshift tourniquet, and started walking. He walked for *three hours* before collapsing on the mountain trail, still far from the nearest village. Just then two men from his village came up the trail on another errand. As this is not a commonly traveled trail, we felt that their arriving at this particular moment was surely of God's doing.

One of the men started carrying Sungyi on his back while the other man ran ahead toward the village for help. At that time there happened to be a number of men on the path along the way, and they immediately ran back to carry Sungyi in by fast relays while others prepared a cart to bring him down to Yuli where we lived.

The first two doctors in town told him there was nothing they could do … it was too late. Finally he was admitted to the new government hospital in town. It was 6:00 p.m. by that time, five hours after he had been bitten. The doctor there told Blake in English, "Pastor Bradley, it is most critical – very, very bad – I fear it is too late."

The news traveled fast by "mountain grapevine," and Christian tribesmen began to arrive from the nearby villages. They began a continuous round of intercession, with one Christian after another sharing in the responsibility for prayer to God.

Prayer continued all night, but in the morning the outlook was even more critical. There was no anti-venom serum of the right type available, and the poison was destroying the nerves as well as the blood vessels, causing internal bleeding in addition to bleeding from the wound. The bleeding could not be stopped. All that could be done was to replace the blood at the same rate at which he was losing it.

There was no such thing as a blood bank in Yuli, and local donors would have expected pay that was beyond the villagers' means, even if someone could have been found who was willing to give. Several of the mountain Christians began rolling up their sleeves and said, "We have no money to give, but here is our blood." And so the transfusions began with the blood of Christian brothers going in as the poisoned blood flowed out. By the next evening all available donors had given their blood, but Sungyi was still bleeding his life away. The doctor said, "I'm afraid it's hopeless. He won't stop bleeding and there are no others here who can give blood."

A mountain preacher replied, "Wait! We have more blood in the mountains and we will bring it here tonight." He left in a motorized cart and returned at midnight bringing a cartful of mountaineers with the life giving blood. A verse from Scripture came to us that was full of meaning. "The life of the flesh is in the blood." Another verse about Christ came to us, "Thou wast slain and by thy blood didst ransom men for God from every tribe and tongue, people and nation." (Revelation 5:9)

In the morning we were to have a station meeting in our home in Yuli, and the Montgomeries and Miss Wilcox had just arrived when the bad news came from the hospital that all the blood had been used up. There was no time to wait for donors from the mountains to arrive. We called off our meeting and hurried to the hospital where we found, fortunately, that three of us had the right type to give.

As our blood was being tested in the laboratory, the Chinese chief surgeon, himself a Christian, asked why so many mountain people had been willing to come and donate blood for Sungyi. Blake replied, "Doctor, Sungyi is well liked, a Christian elder in the church. These people have come because Sungyi was in need, and they as Christian brothers and sisters are helping out as they feel Christians should."

Despite the repeated transfusions, Sungyi's condition remained critical. He was in such poor condition that the doctors wheeled him in to the operating room for possible amputation, believing that they might save his life in that way. Sungyi and his family were most upset and declared it was better to die than to lose a leg. A one-legged man in a tribal society is considered a great stigma, and, of course, in a mountain agricultural economy is useless – just a mouth to feed. The doctors were about to operate.

On this day Dr. Frank Dennis and family of the TEAM mission were driving up the east coast. Arriving in Yuli, Dr. Dennis remembered that Blake and I lived here. He had met us at a missionary conference the year before and decided to stop and say hello. He asked the villagers where the foreigners lived, found our home, and knocked on the door.

We were there, ready to begin our Mission Meeting, when we heard his knock on the door. Blake opened the door and said, "Frank! You're an answer to prayer!"

Blake told him about Sungyi's critical condition. Dr. Dennis thought, "Whoa, the University of Minnesota was real weak on tropical snake bites, and even if I were an expert, I have never been to Yuli before, know no one, and why would they listen to me?" But he said, "Let's go see what God has in mind."

When Blake and Dr. Dennis got to the hospital, there was not a person to be seen. The two men looked around and found a "No Admittance" sign, and on past it, closed doors. They went through two pairs of doors and were looking into the Operating Room where there were four people in gowns and masks standing around a patient on the table. Out of the room a voice said, "Tan Yisheng! Ching jinlai bangmang!" "Dr. Dennis! Please come in and help!" Amazing!

"Who are you?" Dr. Dennis asked.

"Dr. Lin. I was at Chiayi Air Force Hospital and came down to Pingdung Christian Hospital last summer to learn polio operations from you. You are my teacher!" God had really opened the door!

As Dr. Dennis examined the patient, he saw a strong man bleeding from everywhere, his nose, mouth, eyes, bladder catheter, and especially from an ugly wound on his leg where he had taken a knife and cut it to let the venom out (and dirt in). He asked the doctors why they were planning to amputate his leg. "To stop the bleeding and to prevent infection, because if we sew up this dirty wound to stop the bleeding, it will get gangrene." Dr. Dennis asked if they had any catgut suture that was absorbable. The scrub nurse found some in the storeroom. They tied off the visible bleeders, put a saline pack on the open wound, which would be closed later when clean, and Dr. Dennis told them they would need fresh blood to stop the bleeding. He returned to our home and said, "No amputation, but he will need lots of blood." More villagers arrived in Yuli to give blood.

Two weeks later Sungyi was discharged from the hospital. When he was well, he traveled among the tribe with this testimony. "My life was saved from the sting of the snake by the blood of friends who loved me enough to donate their blood to me. And in the same way, my soul was saved from the sting of death of that old Serpent Satan by the blood of Christ who even gave his life for me on the cross." Many people who never understood the simple Gospel were able to understand and believe because of this faithful elder's testimony!

☙❧

In the summer of 1965, our family spent two weeks vacationing in the mountains in Nojiri, Japan, and had a time of physical and spiritual refreshment. You may remember that this is where Blake and I met!

Back in Yuli, Taiwan, it was time to resume the work with the Bunun tribe, which was our field of mission. Blake was off teaching and preaching in various villages with his co-workers. On arriving home after one trip, he was feeling ill. I thought that he was just getting acclimatized to being back in Taiwan and gave him some sulfa medication. This didn't help, and he went up to the Mennonite Hospital to see one of the physicians. They were unable to diagnose him accurately because of the sulfa medicine that disguised his symptoms. Karen was also ill, and the physicians at the hospital *did* diagnose her illness as typhoid fever and treated her with medication. Blake had had his injections for typhoid fever on schedule, and had just had his booster shot.

He continued to become increasingly ill with symptoms of abdominal pain, colitis, diarrhea, fever, and weakness, and was confined to his bed. I attempted to communicate with the Bunun workers who came down from the mountains to see Blake through our Bunun gate boy, Suna, as well as caring for our three children. The weeks went by. Sometimes the night hours would be so long, and I would get a mystery thriller book to read to him a chapter or two at a time. Finally Blake felt able to make a trip to see our Presbyterian physician who was located at a hospital on the other side of the island. In order to see him, Blake had to travel alone two hours on the "fast express" train from our town to Hualien

113

A mountain Bunun village church

(50 miles away!) From there he had to fly to Taipei. Then he took the train south for three hours, where he boarded a bus that traveled over rough roads out to the mission hospital. Finally he was able to see Dr. Wilkerson, who was an excellent diagnostician. Blake was diagnosed with typhoid fever and was treated for it. However, the illness had taken its toll on Blake, and he didn't regain his energy and strength. We continued to stay in Yuli and do as much as he was able to accomplish at that time. As summer approached, we felt that we needed to return to the United States to seek further medical help, to enable us to return after a medical furlough.

We were grateful that three of the booklets of the Good News Bunun Language Gospel Course had been printed and taught to our co-workers, who could teach them to the others, as they passed a test on each one.

Book #1 "From Sadness to Joy": 375 of those enrolled had already completed Book #1.

Book #2 "Life of Christ in Song": 187 of them had gone on to finish Book #2.

Book #3 "Singing Picture Catechism": Book #3 was completed and had arrived in December, in time for Blake to teach it at a conference for 26 churches.

Miss Nettie Junkin, one of our Presbyterian missionaries at our Bible School, had offered to come to Yuli to continue the work with the Bible course while we were away. And she was able to introduce Book #4, on "The Apostles Creed."

Another blessing was the arrival of Rev. and Mrs. Eugene Ayton of the China Inland Mission, who moved into "Aunt Gussie's" empty house across the street and came to assist in our work, visiting the tribal village churches on Sundays.

One of the Taiwanese pastors had put out a hymnbook in the Bunun language, which also needed to be introduced.

We packed only what we needed to have while in America, and when we left Yuli on the train, we waved goodbye to our friends, fully expecting to return.

# CHAPTER 9

## Pastorates in America

We flew home from Taiwan on July 6, 1966, taking it in easy stages, and landed in Seattle. My sister Bonnie was still living in the area, and she met us and welcomed us to her home. She had two small daughters, Laura and Mary, and her husband Milt was an acoustical engineer at Boeing Aircraft Company. My parents were also visiting them at that time.

The day after we arrived in Seattle, there was a plane strike. Since Blake was ill and had a medical priority, he was allowed to fly on to Nashville, Tennessee, for his medical appointment. The children and I had four days with Bonnie, and then feeling that I needed to know what was happening to Blake, we flew "standby" to San Francisco. Period! I wandered around the airport with our three little children, ended up at Traveler's Aid and asked the lady on duty there for help. She looked at me and the three children, the oldest nearly five, a three-year-old, and a twenty-month-old, and said, "Lady, I recommend that you get a hotel room and stay there until the strike is over!"

Then it occurred to me that there was a place near Oakland called the Home of Peace, which was a missionary home that housed missionaries coming and going overseas. Our family had stayed there once before on our way back to Taiwan in 1963. I looked up their phone number in the phone book and called them. I asked if they had a room that we might stay in until the plane strike was over. The receptionist's response was, "Due to the plane strike, we *do* have a room available," so they sent a car to the airport to bring us to the home. The plane strike was affecting them too. What a blessing this was for us! They served meals in their dining room. One positive result of our necessary stay was that my older brother John, who was living in Los Angeles, was able to drive up to see us one day.

I was in touch with our mission board, and they were able to get plane tickets for us to leave before the strike was over. Traveling with the three little children was no simple matter! After being cooped up in one room for several days, they were not in the best of moods. Our plane left San Francisco around 5 p.m. Five minutes later the children were unhappy, having to sit still once again. Across the aisle from us was a young woman busily preparing a talk she was to give at her destination; it was to be about people who are so busy that they can't look around and see the needs of others. She looked across the aisle, saw my children, and put her talk away! She was a wonderful help, reading to them and telling them stories. She was God's answer to my prayers! When we landed in Texas, she disembarked while we continued on to Nashville, arriving at 2 a.m.!

There to meet us were the Walt Shepherds from our Mission Board! Since we didn't know how long Blake would be in the hospital, they took us to a hotel where we stayed for ten days, eating our meals in the hotel. At that time, a Presbyterian family in Nashville, the Overton Thompsons, was going on vacation, and they opened their house to us! We moved from the hotel to their home. What generosity! They even had tricycles and toys for our children to play with. It is while we were there that Karen celebrated her fifth birthday with children in the neighborhood!

Meanwhile, Blake was having tests run in the hospital. When he was cleared to leave, we all headed for Montreat,

North Carolina and a reunion with Blake's mother who had a summer cottage there.

After our visit there, we went to Mission Haven in Decatur, Georgia, but since we had come home on a health furlough, we didn't have reservations for a home there. However, Decatur Presbyterian Church, one of our supporting churches, rented a house for us a block away from the church. Church members had thoroughly cleaned it, moved in furniture, curtains and pictures, and had filled the pantry and refrigerator with food! All we had to do was move in with our suitcases! What a blessing!

Blake began a light study schedule, working on a course in Missionary Anthropology, and getting a good rest. I began taking typing lessons, as I never had them in high school – in China!

Karen and Hugh attended the church kindergarten classes, so they had entered the "halls of learning." Karen was studying about the Pilgrims and the early days in America. At home one day she asked, "Who was it that disgusted America? Oh, yes, Columbus!" Both of the children enjoyed the daily rhythm and music class. One morning at family devotions, we were surprised to hear Hugh repeat a Bible verse he had known a long time in the following way, "And Jesus increased in 'rhythm' and in stature, and in favor with God and man." Anne, while not in school, was also in the process of learning and interpreting things according to her level of knowledge that was then hers. One day we were at Stone Mountain and heard the chiming of the magnificent carillon bells that had been installed in a tower there. Our two-year-old tugged on my skirt and said, "Listen, Mommy, music box! Hear it?"

On August 1, 1967 our fourth child David was born, and we welcomed a chubby, lovable baby with chuckles and smiles for everyone. Anne, our nearly three-year-old, was allowed to attend nursery school two days a week at Decatur Presbyterian Church; she was one of their most enthusiastic pupils! Her frequent – and hopeful – question at the breakfast table each morning was, "Is *today* I go to school?"

One day two ladies from Decatur Church came to visit. I told them that Blake was putting out the Good News Bible Course in Taiwan and needed illustrations to include

The family in front of our home in Decatur, Georgia

depicting the teaching. *I* wasn't capable of helping. Then one of the ladies, Doris Hancock, invited me to her home for art lessons once a week, since she was an art teacher. The other lady said, "I will supply your oil paints for you." And thus began my interest in oil painting, which continued on for many a year. While David was still small enough to sleep in the mornings, I took him along and lay him on a bed in another bedroom. Later on, with my teacher's assistance, I had progressed far enough to paint portraits of my four children, but I was relieved when I had completed all four of them. It was not my favorite thing to paint! However, oil painting opened up an art that I have much enjoyed through the years.

For two years we lived in this home in Decatur, Georgia. The first year was a health furlough. When it became evident that Blake's health was not adequate enough to return to the mountain work in Taiwan, he was granted a second year of furlough. During that time he began serving as a pastoral visitor for Decatur Presbyterian Church. The second year in Decatur, Karen went to first grade at Winnona Park Elementary. At the end of the second year of furlough, Blake was still not well enough to return to the mountain work, and it became clear that our work on the mission field in Taiwan was over. With deep regret, we had to resign from the Mission Board. It was the hardest thing we had ever had to do.

The next step was to seek a pastorate in Georgia or one of the other southern states. Blake was able to visit a number of open parishes, and on July 7, 1968 he preached at Salem Presbyterian Church, a short distance southeast of Atlanta. He was issued a call, and accepted. And so began our experience of serving a church in the United States.

Our family moved from Decatur, Georgia, into the manse at Salem Presbyterian Church in Lithonia, southeast of Atlanta outside the newly built beltline. It was a small white wooden church, with mainly two families keeping the church going through the years. Blake and I learned that they still liked to maintain control in a number of ways.

We had only one car at that time, so I used to drive Blake to the church office early on Sunday mornings, then return home to get the rest of the family ready to go. The church had a good organist and a small choir that sang every Sunday, enhancing the service. Preceding the service, we also had a Sunday School, with combined ages in some classes. On Wednesday nights there was a Bible study and a song service.

Slowly the church began to grow as new members joined the congregation. Every summer the church held a Vacation Bible School, inviting neighborhood children to come and take part. After a number of years, the church made plans to build a new sanctuary on the land right next door. It took some time for the Session to plan with an architect what all would be included in the plans for the church, and it took time to raise money to have it built. The exterior was made of brick and wood, and there were steps in the front leading up into the sanctuary. When

Our family outside the manse for Salem Presbyterian Church

finished, it was beautiful and worshipful. The organ and choir loft were on the right side at the front of the church. In the basement were the Sunday School rooms and the nursery. Two of us painted the scene of Noah and the Ark on the wall of the nursery.

Our children attended a different school here, Murphy Candler Elementary, with Karen in second grade and Hugh in first grade. At this point Hugh said, "Now when I'm going to school, I want to be called John. That's my first name," and we agreed with him. There was a school bus that went by our home to the school, and the children rode the bus together.

At Halloween time, we helped to make costumes for them. Karen was a fairy, John was a Viking, and Anne was dressed in a Japanese gown given to her when we were in Japan.

In 1970 we drove to Florida for our vacation. We had just purchased a new camping trailer that we were pulling. Blake needed a rest from driving and asked me to take over. On highway 1A1 along the coast of Florida, the winds were blowing in from the ocean, and I adapted to that. Then a huge semi passed us and pulled in right ahead of us. The trailer began to weave back and forth and finally broke loose and turned over on its side. In the process, our car swung around and was headed in the wrong direction on the interstate. Fortunately, there was no traffic immediately behind us. A trucker coming north in the other lane swung over and stopped. He had the equipment to set the trailer upright. Having done so, we were able to pull it off at the next exit. The trailer was demolished. After a lot of effort, we were finally able to open the door to get a few things out to continue our trip. Inside we saw the refrigerator door open, food everywhere, blankets, pillows, clothes soiled. We were able to leave the trailer at that exit, and having notified the insurance company, continued on our way to Miami. We learned later that the trailer was under warranty, and the company would supply us with a similar trailer back home. Our lives had been spared by the Lord on the Florida freeway!

In 1972 Blake's mother Agnes Bradley became seriously ill and spent three months in the hospital. From there it was necessary for her to move to a nursing home in Atlanta and to sell her home in Bristol, Tennessee. Blake was her only child, and it was up to us to accomplish the sale of the house for her. She lived for another year or so, and when the time came, I was by her bedside in the hospital as she entered Life Eternal.

The family liked to go camping at Stone Mountain Park at Easter and on weekends, but we were back at our church on Sunday mornings. One day while we were camping, Karen went to the restroom, and as she was washing her hands, a lady came in, took one look at her and asked, "Is your mother's name Faith?"

"Yes," Karen responded. Karen looked so much like me that the lady had guessed correctly. It turned out she was a classmate of mine from Fairview Hospital in Minneapolis in 1955! And we were parked right next to each other here in the park in Georgia!

In 1972 I was able to fly to Seattle where my sister lived, to help celebrate my parents' fiftieth wedding anniversary! My parents, siblings and I enjoyed a teriyaki meal at the Cliff House overlooking the water and the sparkling lights of Seattle!

During our time at Salem Presbyterian, soccer was a big sport for children. At one time we had three of our children playing on different teams. On Saturdays, it was difficult to get to all their games held in different places! And sometimes the two girls were cheerleaders for boys' teams. I can remember one Friday night, sewing on outfits for both girls. That same night, Karen had a friend over to spend the night in the camping trailer. Meanwhile, I sewed all night. In the morning I still didn't have the zippers in; I had to pin the two girls in for the first games. John's team, the Green Panthers, won the Atlanta city championship two years in a row.

At Christmastime, we initiated a re-enactment of the Nativity Scene outside the church. The young people played the parts and were in costumes. Night spotlights lit the scene. We had a throne for King Herod. Later, we even used live animals and had shepherds warming themselves by a fire. We wanted the community to know the real reason for Christmas, Christ's birth in Bethlehem, that he might later redeem us from sin, that we might become children of God.

John and Anne tried out for the Young Singers of Callanwolde, a group that included young people from all over Atlanta and neighboring towns; they were accepted. They practiced twice a week in Atlanta, so I drove them back and forth. Later the choir went on tour and sang in many places all over the south. In Houston, Texas they sang "The Star Spangled Banner" at the start of a major league baseball game in the Astrodome!

One of the members of the church contributed money for an octave of Schulmerich handbells to be used occasionally during services. Eventually the church had two octaves. Our bell choir was composed of both children and adults, and I was the director.

In 1975 the Salem Presbyterian Church celebrated its Centennial as a church. We dressed up in old time clothes and had a number of events at the church, such as singing by a barbershop quartet and a feast at the church. The celebration went on for several days. People in town commented, "Those Presbyterians are still celebrating!"

In 1976 we received a call from the Monticello Presbyterian Church in Monticello, Georgia. It was the end of the summer and time for school to begin, so we accepted the call and made the move as quickly as possible.

Monticello was a small town with a population of about 4,000 people, located an hour's drive southeast of Atlanta. The town had a number of large antebellum houses, and there was much of historical interest there.

Blake's call was to a two-church field, the Monticello Presbyterian Church in town, and to a smaller church 18 miles away in Jones County, Wayside Presbyterian Church. On Sunday, services at Wayside were at 9:30 a.m. and at 11:15 a.m. in Monticello. The manse was in Monticello, several blocks from the church.

This was the time of integration in this town, and some parents did not want their children in integrated schools. There was a larger elementary school, a junior high and a senior high school. There was also a private academy. Children in our church attended all these different schools. One of our elders at church was the superintendent of the public schools, and it was our preference for our children to attend the public schools.

The school year began immediately after we arrived, and we brought our four children to the public schools to be registered. Karen was a sophomore in high school, John a freshman, Anne in seventh grade, and David in fourth grade. There were no soccer teams here, no Young Singers of Callanwolde, and no girls track team for Karen, but the children easily made new friends and found other interests. Karen made the varsity cheerleading squad, Anne was a cheerleader for the junior high teams, and John started guitar lessons. He and David looked forward to tennis in the spring. Karen and John sang with the high school glee club. Even the football players tried out for this event, as *this* was the organization to belong to!

After planning for services at both churches for several years, Blake terminated his call to Wayside because the Monticello Church had grown and was now able to pay the full salary. In addition to his regular work, for a week in the summer of 1978 Blake was the director at Pioneer Camp for the Presbytery. I was camp nurse and was in charge of the music. Karen and John were junior counselors, Anne a camper, and David a babysitter for two children of one of the counselors, so the whole family was involved! Later, Blake also led three mission workshops in the Presbytery during the year.

The year that we moved to Monticello, we borrowed the two octaves of handbells I had used in the choir at Salem Presbyterian Church. Monticello and Wayside churches tried them out and were immediately interested. Each church then bought one octave of Schulmerich handbells. During the two years that Wayside was a part of the call, I carried them from church to church for practices and to the services at which they were going to be played. Then the Monticello church bought the second octave of bells from Wayside. Our four children were all ringers. (And so was the football coach at the high school in Monticello!) One week we took part in an area festival in Atlanta in which 400 handbell ringers took part. It was a thrill! The final concert took place at Six Flags over Georgia.

Monticello was a town that appreciated music. The high school music director formed vocal trios and quartets, and they attended regional and state tournaments. As I remember, Karen's trio received second place in state and John's quartet also came in second in state. The band director formed small instrumental groups as well. David sang with one of the groups. He also was drum major of the band.

Our first summer there we flew out to Washington State to visit my sister Bonnie, her husband Milton Jeter, and their daughters, Laura and Mary. While there we did some hiking in the mountains and saw magnificent views of Mt. Rainier.

The second summer we had purchased a 17-foot travel trailer, and we drove all the way from Monticello up to

Minnesota to visit with my parents. We also took this opportunity to go up along the north shore of Lake Superior to the boundary waters with Canada. Having made previous arrangements, we were able to rent three canoes plus tents and food supplies for a four- or five-day trip. It was the best family vacation we had ever had together!

During our days in Monticello, three of our children graduated from high school. Following graduation Karen attended Presbyterian College in Clinton, South Carolina. The next year John attended Furman University in Greenville, South Carolina. Anne, too, graduated from Monticello High School and attended Furman University for two years, then transferred to Presbyterian College. They all received scholarships. Only David was at home with us.

Blake's health was becoming more and more problematic. Ever since we had returned from Taiwan in 1966, Blake had required and had psychological counseling from many different counselors. He was put on antidepressant medications. He also had physical problems requiring a number of surgeries; one was for sinus problems in 1979, and in January 1981 he had emergency surgery in Atlanta for a bleeding ulcer. Recovery was slow.

The Monticello Presbyterian Church was so helpful and understanding and prayed for his return to health. The congregation gave him a six-months leave of absence. When he still was not able to return, they gave him another three months off. During this time I worked at the small local hospital part-time and also in the county health department for some months. With three children in Christian colleges out of state, we needed all the income we could manage, even though the children were all working at college part-time along with a full load of classes.

To be able to work as a nurse I needed to re-activate my nursing license. This meant either taking a refresher course in Atlanta or working under the supervision of the director of nurses at the Monticello Hospital for 30 days. I chose the second option. To activate my license I also had to get recommendations from three doctors or nurses. I wrote to my nursing school, Fairview Hospital in Minneapolis. The director of nurses had changed, but the current one knew my parents and was glad to write a letter of recommendation. I sent another request to a doctor whom I had worked for at his clinic in Seattle for three months before leaving for Taiwan. He wrote the nicest letter, and sent me a copy. He also said that my request was very timely, as that day he was retiring and selling his clinic to the city of Seattle! The Lord had his hand in all of this!

When the summer leave of absence ended, Blake and I went and sat in the Monticello Presbyterian Church and prayed. The stained glass window in the front of the church was of Jesus praying on a rock in Gethsemane. We stayed there silently in prayer until we had our answer. We needed to resign from the church because of Blake's ill health. Where were we to go… to our two-bedroom cottage in Montreat, North Carolina?

When we got home the telephone rang. It was our friends, the Gautiers, who had been our next-door neighbors in Lithonia. They had to move out to Denver for health reasons. Did we know anyone who would want to rent their home at Lake Capri? We assured them we did. *We* did!

When the Gautiers gave us permission to move into their home at Lake Capri, they said it was fine with them for us to use whatever furniture of theirs we wanted to use. Whatever we wanted to use of ours was fine, also. Unused items, theirs or ours, could be stored in the large basement with a screened-in porch. We had U-Haul trucks coming and going, and finally we began the process of settling into their home and enjoying the scenic view of the lake.

For a month things were hectic, with Karen heading off to Presbyterian College for her senior year and John and Anne both attending Furman University. During her last two years of college, Karen was the accompanist for the Presbyterian College Choir. Both Karen and Anne had Georgia Pacific Scholarships, and John had a scholarship from Furman University. With none of them owning cars, we spent time on the road getting them to and from colleges!

Our move meant that David, as a freshman, had to enroll in Rockdale High School, a countywide high school in Conyers, Georgia. He didn't know any students there and for some time he ate in the cafeteria by himself. He wanted to choose his friends carefully. One day David was sitting on a chair outside an office, wearing tennis shoes, with one foot resting on his other knee. The tennis coach came by, noticed his shoes, and asked him if he played tennis. David said "yes."

"Want to try out for the team?" asked the coach.

Again, David said "yes." He had begun to find his place at this large high school. His other main extra curricular interest was in the band, and he had just returned from Orlando, Florida, where the Rockdale Marching Band had participated in a band festival.

In Monticello I had been working in the small hospital part-time. In Conyers, Rockdale Hospital was a 100-bed facility five miles from home and had 77 physicians on staff! I went to apply for a part-time position. I told them that we had recently moved to town, that my husband, a minister, was unable to work and we had three children in college. The nurse in charge worked out a way that I could work on the night shift several times a week, and she would enroll me in an orientation program for Rockdale Hospital. I must admit that in those days, I thought "nursing," every waking hour of the day – and of the night! Even after working at the small hospital in Monticello, this was a huge change!!

I preferred not to leave Blake alone in the house, so by my working the night shift, David could be with him at night and I would be there in the day, although I would be asleep part of the time. Gradually I picked up the nursing skills required to work in this hospital, and later was able to work as nurse in charge as needed on the night shift.

Blake was now receiving a disability pension from the Board of Annuities and Relief of the Presbyterian Fund, which certainly was a financial help.

We enjoyed getting in walks around Lake Capri, and across it over a bridge. From the house we could see the lake, so we enjoyed it both inside and outside. Blake mowed the lawn and took care of the yard.

In the spring we had a phone call from the Gautiers saying that they needed to move back into their home on Lake Capri. So once again we began to hunt for another location in which to live.

A Presbyterian minister's wife whom we knew well was a real estate agent, so we sought her assistance. And in the end we moved into a house that belonged to them, that they had available to rent out. In June 1983, we moved to this new place, 4068 Sweetwater Court in Conyers. Fortunately, this meant that David didn't have to change schools again.

At our new location, we barely had room to get all our belongings into the house. The garage was full of unopened boxes, with no room for the car. But with three off at college, we only had three of us in the house much of the time and we got by with what space we had.

Each year Presbyterian College sent two graduating seniors to Zaire to teach English to Zairian high school students. This year it happened to be two pre-med students who were chosen. One of them was accepted into a medical school and decided he needed to forego the travel opportunity. Karen, now a cum laude graduating senior with an elementary education major, heard of this opportunity at church while still at college and immediately signed up to go. We heard the news when at Sunday dinner the phone rang in our home, and Karen told us she had signed up to go to Zaire as a mission volunteer!! She needed to raise funds to enable her to go and so wrote letters to many of our friends asking for financial help. Because she had no knowledge of the French language spoken there, she had to attend the Peace Corps language school for ten weeks. As it turned out, her assignment was changed, for the missionaries in Zaire needed her to teach elementary school for their children. Right down her alley!!

While at Furman University, John had an opportunity to travel with fellow students and two professors overseas to Lebanon, Syria, Israel, Egypt, Kenya, and London. John and several of the other students stayed on and visited Switzerland, Austria, and Italy before coming home.

The following year John graduated from Furman University cum laude, with a major in religion. He became a counselor at Outdoor Therapeutic Program, a state-run facility in the north Georgia mountains, working with teen-aged boys with emotional problems, some of whom were one step away from going to prison. In this setting, they lived and worked outside. There were ten boys in a "tribe" with two counselors. Each counselor had two days a week free, which meant that often there was only one counselor with the boys. The boys learned to build their own lodges and do much of their own cooking, while learning qualities of trust and interdependency.

Anne was a junior transfer to Presbyterian College from Furman University, a psychology major. She sang with the Presbyterian College Choir during the time they traveled to Europe, including England, Scotland, East and West Germany, Austria, and Italy. In Edinburgh they sang at St. Giles Cathedral, in Germany at the Cologne Cathedral, and in Rome at the Vatican!! What great opportunities for overseas travel our children have had during their college days!

However, since we had returned from Taiwan in 1966, Blake had been seeing counselors to assist him in uncovering the mental and emotional difficulties he had had in recent years, which complicated his recovery from typhoid fever. He had monthly visits with Dr. Ben at Brawner Institute in Smyrna, Georgia. I accompanied him and sat in on the visits, often not saying anything, unless a correction needed to be made. Blake wrote, "At present I am seeing a psychiatrist about once a month. Have tried a lot of antidepressants over a period of seven years, with little or no results except for the present drug Ascendin, which seems to be helping although can only take small doses without producing skin rash and makes me irritable. Also on Valium."

Missionaries working overseas build up little credit, but in 1987, our monetary funds came together and enabled us to look for a home of our own. Blake was the one who chose it, our two-story brick-and-frame house located on a beautiful half-acre lot, graced with maples, pines, and azalea bushes. I took on a full-time position working in Clinical Arts Home Care with home office in Covington, Georgia. There were six of us registered nurses who visited patients in their own homes.

In 1987 David was in his junior year and attending King College in Bristol, Tennessee on a tennis scholarship. (Bristol was the city where Dr. and Mrs. Hugh Bradley had a lovely home, in their lifetime, close to the school campus.) We had happy memories from spending some days at Christmastime and in the summer with them.

# CHAPTER 10

## Thru the Valley of the Shadow

Blake's depression grew more severe, and several times he had to be admitted to the Psychiatric Institute for a brief time. Electric shock treatments were of no help. He was treated by Dr. Ben, a very experienced psychiatrist, who at first thought that he would have Blake back in the ministry in a year's time. However, the years went by, and after using many medications and combinations of medications, and being treated several times as an in-patient, Blake was still in very poor mental and physical health. While at the Institute he was diagnosed with obsessive-compulsive disorder. In his mind, he thought over and over again, "I am no good. I am no good."

After Blake's ten years of medications at the Psychiatric Institute, Dr. Ben called another very experienced psychiatrist to go over all of Blake's records to see if he could suggest anything. After reviewing them all, the consultant said he had nothing additional to suggest. Because the psychologists could not offer any other treatment for Blake, even as an in-patient, he was discharged to come home. He had tried all treatments and medications available to him at that time. Knowing this, and depressed beyond measure, he attempted to end his life; he was in his car in a public parking lot, got out of the car and lay down on the pavement, and then shot himself. He did not succeed. The police were notified; the officer who responded to the call asked Blake who had shot him. He replied, "I shot myself because I am tired of living." Blake was hospitalized and underwent surgery.

The night before, Anne was driving her car in Savannah, Georgia, when two Georgia Southern students ran a red light and totaled her car. Her life could well have been snuffed out! When she received Karen's phone call, she made arrangements for a rented car and immediately drove up to Atlanta with her husband Reed to be with us.

David was attending Union Theological Seminary in Richmond, Virginia, when he heard the news. He immediately took a flight to Atlanta. John, who was attending Emory Law School, was nearby and met David at the airport.

After David had been with us more than a week visiting his dad in intensive care, and with the surgeon feeling that Blake would recover, I felt that David should return to seminary classes. His professor had told him that before he returned to seminary, he needed to tell his dad everything he wanted to tell him. David followed his advice and then flew back to school. That afternoon Blake took a turn for the worse. His nurse in intensive care was a Christian and suggested we bring a recording of some Christian hymns to play for him. I found a favorite one of Blake's and took it to him to listen to as he was on the respirator. One day when we had been with him at the hospital all day, the nurse suggested we go home to get some sleep. She would call us if we needed to return.

At 2:30 a.m. the phone rang and the nurse requested that we return. Karen, John, and I quickly drove to the hospital. Since Anne had needed to return to Savannah to appear in court concerning the car accident, she was unable to be with us. The three of us stood around Blake's bed and watched the monitor showing the declining heart rate during Blake's last moments with us. Then his struggle was over, and on March 29, 1992, he passed on to Eternal Life with our Lord Jesus Christ.

In the hospital, when Blake had breathed his last breath, it was a comfort to me to pick up the telephone and put through a call to Mr. Phil Jordan in Monticello, who was in charge of

Jordan Funeral Home. Phil was a member of the Presbyterian Church where Blake had lovingly served as pastor, and a good friend, and I asked him if he could come to the hospital for Blake. At that time I had wondered about cremation, but Phil had said, "All the folks in the church and many others would want to see him and have him buried here in the cemetery." Though I lived in Conyers at that time, much of my work as home health nurse was still in Monticello, so I had kept in touch with many of our friends there.

Blake's service was held on March 31, 1992, in the Monticello Presbyterian Church. Rev. Malcolm Davis was the pastor there at this time, and he led in the service for the overflow crowd.

The opening hymn was "Come Thou Fount of Every Blessing." The choir sang a favorite song, "Father God," and a friend of ours from another church sang my request, "Under His Wings I Am Safely Abiding."

Two other pastors with whom we had served in different parts of the world shared their memories of Blake's service. Rev. Harry Phillips, a fellow missionary from Taiwan, spoke of Blake's work with the Bunun aboriginal tribe, how he worked with 27 or more villages in the mountain area on the east coast of Taiwan. It had been such a strenuous task! For health reasons we had returned to the United States and were not able to return. In Georgia Blake had served three different churches. Rev. Charlie Cook, our Presbytery Executive, told about Blake's ministry here in America.

The closing hymn was a favorite of Blake's, "Be Thou My Vision."

"Be Thou my vision, O Lord of my heart,
　　Naught be all else to me, save that Thou art-
　　　　Thou my best thought, by day or by night,
　　　　　　Waking or sleeping, Thy presence my light. "

Westview Cemetery was close to where we had lived for six years in Monticello. Good years, happy years. And it was here that Blake was buried.

Rev. Davis, and Rev. Todd Hobbie who was my pastor at that time in Conyers, Georgia, officiated in the service at the cemetery.

The women of the Church had prepared a wonderful meal for all our guests, who had come from many different locations and included out-of-state friends. It was good to be able to visit with them, and my family appreciated their presence with us at this time of sadness.

# CHAPTER 11

## Continuing the Journey Alone

In 1987, after Blake and I had purchased a home in Conyers, Georgia, I began to work with a Home Health Care Service. At that time there were six of us R.N. nurses who were employed there. In the morning we would gather informally, chat about our assignments, and wish each other well. We had no cell phones at that time, and were on our own as we traveled to make our visits for the day. Later the organization grew to include many more visiting nurses, aides, and other employees who meticulously read through our notes for completeness and accuracy before they were accepted. I had

Our home in Conyers, Georgia with trailer on the side

the names of 36 patients on my team in 1991, and I would usually visit about six a day. Physicians had referred these patients to us to be visited. Depending on the care needed, the visits might be one time a week, once every other week, or once a month. The aides generally bathed the patients two or three times weekly.

During our visits we would take their blood pressure and

temperature, assess their health needs, and find out what particular problems they were having. We explained the symptoms of their particular disease to them; for example, a diabetic would be taught the symptoms of hyperglycemia (too little insulin) or hypoglycemia (too much insulin) and what to do when these occurred. The general protocol was to teach a patient one lesson per visit, and in line with that, we taught them how to take just one medicine each time we were with them.

**Me dressed for a home healthcare visit**

I covered several counties to begin with. One day as I was driving through the countryside, from one town to the next, and listening to a symphony from England on my radio, I thought, "Where else could I be enjoying a lovely drive with music like this and getting paid for it!" However, there were many other days when various difficulties arose and I thought that I had certainly earned my pay. As the number of patients we needed to care for increased, I concentrated on one town and county. Even though I had lived in this town for six years, I visited some patients who lived in parts of town or countryside I had never driven to before. We nurses had written directions for how to locate our patients, and sometimes they were difficult to find at first. There were patients who lived in the woods and had no electricity. I recall one male patient who needed an injection. It was so dark in the small wooden hut where he lived, with no electricity, that I had to use my flashlight to enable me to give him an injection. On the way back to the car, I had to step around a snake slithering through the woods.

It was up to us nurses to perform many procedures: inserting gastric tubes and catheters, starting intra-venous infusions, and adjusting pain pump infusions. We had to take turns being on call at night. When seeing patients whom we had never visited before, we hoped that the directions given to us were accurate!

Then the visits would have to be recorded accurately, and this took more than a little time. I worked for the agency for seven years, and for the most part enjoyed my work very much. It was a pleasure to help people stay in their homes as long as possible.

The following year I worked for hospice. This job also involved visits to people in their own homes, people who were terminally ill. One of these patients I remember especially. She was younger than I, and had emphysema and chronic obstructive pulmonary disease. She was using oxygen at two liters continually. She was living in the home of a niece who was married and had three small children two, four, and six years of age. The niece's husband was not happy to have her in their home, and his wife had to spend a good bit of time with her. My patient had a daughter in Texas from whom she was estranged and had no contact.

Our hospice team consisted of six people: nurse, chaplain, aide, and three others who helped in various ways. One of our team was employed at AT&T on the night shift. One night she sent out a notice to all of AT&T's night shift employees: "*Urgent*. Hospice patient. *Have a heart. Donations needed*. Older lady with very limited time left hasn't seen daughter in over ten years. We need airfare/expenses from Dallas Texas." The employees responded and raised the money needed for the round trip flight from Texas! I went to the airport to meet her daughter and drive her over to see her mother, and they had a time for reconciliation. Her mother died soon afterwards. There was a Catholic service for her at which I sang, "Ava Maria."

Later I received a note from her niece thanking me for caring for her aunt, and she especially mentioned how much she appreciated my family coming over and singing Christmas Carols to them on Christmas Eve. This was a tradition in our family. After attending Christmas Eve services at church, we would go as a family to the homes of patients wherever I was working as a nurse, whether in the hospital, home health or hospice. One time when we were singing in the hospital I worked at, a nurse from the maternity ward opened the door and asked us to sing "Away in a Manger." Then one of the visitors asked if we had a recording of our music, and we replied, "No, but we could make you one." We went home, and after experimenting discovered that the best place to make a recording was in the bathroom gathered around the sink!

One of the goals in hospice nursing is to help the patient realize that his or her life has been worthwhile. It makes hospice nursing worthwhile as well!

Home health and hospice nursing was what occupied my time during the week, but on Sundays I looked forward to attending worship at church. I enjoyed singing in the choir and ringing in the handbell choir.

The pastor of the church I was attending in Conyers accepted a new call and moved to another part of the country. A search committee was formed to work on the process used by the Presbyterian Church in securing another pastor, and I was elected to be on the search committee. There was a lot of paper work to be done, first describing what our congregation was like, and then what kind of a pastor we needed. In accordance with the Presbyterian denomination's procedure, we requested information about pastors who were looking for a call. The committee met weekly, and eventually we traveled to visit the churches where the pastors we were interested in would be preaching. We walked into the sanctuaries – one or two at a time – so that the congregation would hopefully not know our reason for attending. Thankfully, this committee completed their assignment, and we installed our new minister, Rev. Kirby Hill.

Some years later our church found it necessary to relocate. I was on the Session at that time and spent time with a few other members in trying to find a portion of land for sale that would be a possibility for a church site. There was nothing in our county available, so we had to look elsewhere. At last a site was chosen! Somehow I ended up on the building committee and was chosen to be the secretary. Other committee members, with more experience than I, spoke in terms I was not familiar with, and taking minutes was a difficult job, but I persevered. It was exciting to see the church building take shape. I remember when the pastor was hoisted up on a lift to place the pinnacle of the steeple in place!

We had to choose a new name for the church, and members of the church were asked to submit names. They did – many names! I wrote to our Presbyterian Church headquarters and asked for a publication that listed the names of all the Presbyterian Churches in the United States; I read through them all. The name chosen by us was "The Presbyterian Church of the Resurrection."

In addition to traveling in my work as home health nurse, other opportunities presented themselves. A group of friends from Monticello were driving to Mexico to help build a house for a Mexican family. I was able to join the group, many of them young people. The weather was very hot when we were there, and my main responsibility was to see that the younger workers did not get overheated. I would spray them on the back of their necks with water from a spray bottle and would pull them out of the work line if I felt they were getting over-tired. I was also a part of the line that passed bricks from one person to the next to move the bricks to a needed location. Yes, it was hot work! The Mexican family whom we were helping worked along with us, and they were overjoyed to have a new firm dwelling. When the house was completed, we held a dedication. We had a poster board on which everyone involved in the building drew an outline of their hands, which the homeowners put up in their new home as a remembrance.

Not long after Blake died, I was asked to serve on the mission committee of Greater Atlanta Presbytery, and I was happy to do so. At the second meeting of the Presbytery committee, I heard one of the members saying that she was going to Haiti to check on the health care workers she had trained there. I found myself walking over to her and asking, "Can I go with you?" I don't think that she knew that I was a nurse, but she agreed. A third person was also with us, a man who had retired from the Communicable Disease Center in Atlanta, who went along to check on the goat project. Being in Haiti with the folks out working in the fields reminded me of Blake's and my work in Taiwan and made me feel close to Blake. I was there on the first anniversary of his death. One afternoon we were walking out of a village into the countryside when we saw a double rainbow in the sky! God's benediction on our day!

In 1994, a group of Lutherans from Minnesota was going to Norway! My sister Bonnie and husband Milt from Seattle were going, and I couldn't pass up the opportunity to join them, so I took an early retirement from home health nursing. Bonnie and I were of 100% Norwegian background! Our dad was born in Lillehammer and came to America when he was 15 years old. Mother, though born in China, was also of Norwegian heritage. Our group of Lutherans flew to Amsterdam, and then traveled through Sweden and on to Norway, where the scenery was spectacular! I had contacted relatives who live in Norway, and after the tour group had returned to America, Bonnie, Milt and I rented a car and were able to visit with some of them. One visit happened to be at a family birthday celebration of a couple's one-year-old son, with uncles and aunts all gathered together! I had taken along Mother's photos of her Norwegian relatives, and as our hosts looked at the photos of themselves from a long time ago, there were many chuckles; this aided in our bonding together. We continued on and visited in some of the old stave churches built there. In one we listened as the guide told us about the church and worship. When finished, she led us up the hill to the home we had a picture of where one of our relatives had lived! We also visited Lillehammer, where Bonnie's and my father had been born, and we saw the church where he was baptized and confirmed.

The next year, in 1995, at a Mission Conference in Montreat, North Carolina, we attendees learned that mission volunteers were needed in many parts of the United States, including even Alaska! Two of us applied to go to Sheldon Jackson College in Alaska, and we were accepted! The college was in Sitka, which was on an island not too far from Juneau. Landing at the airport in Sitka required the skills of a good pilot, as the runway borders on the water. If visibility is less

Sheldon Jackson College in Sitka, Alaska

than 500 feet, the planes cannot land. The day we arrived was a beautiful sunny day, the snowcapped mountains clearly visible, and the water was shimmering, dancing in the sunlight.

We had to pay for our flight over there, and then were given free board and room. We each had a single room in a dormitory. There were 35 mission volunteers from 14 states working at various tasks that summer. Our task was with the housekeeping department, cleaning rooms and making up beds for conferees who were arriving. Our first task was to clean the rooms after the college students had left. Guess what shape they were in?! One time when my older friend Vivian was down on the floor scrubbing the floor and rugs, she said, "If only my kids could see me now!" We also had to pull a cartload of sheets and towels over to the commercial laundry, run them through, and then fold them after they were dry.

But our work had benefits, for we ended our workdays earlier than other workers and could go shopping in the stores nearby. The food in the school cafeteria was absolutely marvelous! Lots of fresh fruits and vegetables and delicious

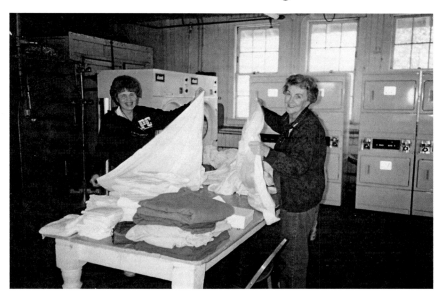

Vivian and me folding sheets and towels

food, best we had had in a college cafeteria! Another plus was attending the summer concerts by musicians from around the world! On days off we were free to hike up some of the mountains where we encountered hunters – and occasionally bears! It was a beautiful mountainous island. Vivian's and my days in Sitka remain with us as happy memories.

Being in Sitka had been such a great experience, that two years later, when I saw an ad in a Christian newspaper that read, "Scottish Conference Center now accepting volunteers from the United States for short term positions," I read on. This was at Carberry Tower, a Christian Conference Center outside Edinburgh, Scotland. Scotland! Blake and I had always hoped to go there one day but never made it. I knew no one over there, but I contacted the Scottish Conference Center, sent them a short biographical sketch – along with my statement of faith – a photo, and a physician's bill of health. I was accepted. When June arrived I flew to Scotland. I was the only American on staff that summer, and was one of three housekeepers who supervised the younger domestic workers who came from Brazil, Kenya, South Africa, Nigeria, Hungary, Germany, and Scotland. They cleaned the rooms for guests and served the meals in the dining hall. One of them, a young man from South Africa, asked me, "Apart from becoming a Christian, what was the most important decision you made in your Christian life?"

After a few minutes I responded, "Learning to trust the Lord at all times, in the good times and the bad, and letting Him guide me through life."

Carberry was the largest Christian Conference Center in Scotland, serving all churches and the general public. The castle tower there dated from 1480! The family of the late Lady

Elfinstone, sister of the Queen Mother, deeded the 30-acre wooded estate to the Church of Scotland in 1961. What beautiful grounds!

Inside the baronial mansion, it was challenging to find my way through the many stairways and halls. The language was also challenging! I enjoyed attending conference center lectures when not working. My last day at work I was shocked to hear that Princess Diana had been killed in a car accident the night before! Grief pervaded the entire country. I was able to watch the funeral procession on television and shared in the grief of all the people as we watched the two young sons walking behind the casket.

With a travel stipend, I was able to travel to many parts of the country, including the Isle of Iona, where Christianity first came to Scotland from Ireland in 563 A.D. The summer ended, and it was hard for me to say goodbye to my friends in Scotland and fly back home to America.

Five years later, I returned to Scotland on a tour of the Highlands and the Islands, which were so interesting and contained so much history! Skara Brae! This was a 5,000-year-old village from the Stone Age, built before the Pyramids and Stonehenge! It was engulfed by a sandstorm – buried for 4,500 years after being occupied for 500 years. In 1850 a hurricane devastated this area. When it had died down, the islanders discovered that the gale force winds had uncovered the remains of the prehistoric dwellings!

We saw Scapa Flow, a great natural harbor that was a strategic Royal Navy Base during both World Wars. Here the captured German fleet was anchored after the First World War, and here the fleet of 74 ships was scuttled. Only six of the ships remained when I saw them. Our tour bus drove us to the Ring of Brodgar, standing stones completed about 1200 B.C.

Originally there were 60 of them, but we saw some of the 27 still standing, the tallest at 14 feet.

As a climax to our tour, we had front row seats at the world renowned Military Tattoo on the Esplanade of Edinburgh Castle. The members of the military band were only some of the 1,200 performers from the British Commonwealth, Europe, and, for the first time, America. It was a fascinating evening of music, dance, horsemanship, and fireworks!

It was a miracle – the sun was shining that day, with blue skies overhead. Queen Elizabeth and Prince Philip were in attendance that night, as a final special celebration in honor of the Queen's 50th anniversary of ruling the United Kingdom! When they alighted from their car, I saw she was wearing a yellow coat as she walked up into the stands with us. What a fitting event to end my days in Scotland!

Other overseas travels I experience included a trip to Nicaragua in 1996 for two weeks, as a member of Greater Atlanta Presbytery Mission Committee. In 1998 I went on a trip to China to visit the area where my parents had worked when I was a child. I had a picture of the house on Kikungshan (Rooster Mountain) that had belonged to my grandmother, and I was sure I would be able to locate it. It wasn't that easy. One of the Chinese men we met while looking for the house had played with missionary children in his youth. He said, "I know where that house is." When he pointed it out to me, I was dubious, but he said it had been changed. Then I turned around and looked back and saw the high rocks I had played on as a five-year-old! It truly was the place! Nearby I found the small Lutheran Church where my parents had been married in 1922.

In 1999 I joined a three-week tour titled, "The Jewels of Eastern Europe," sponsored by The Friendship Force. People from all over the United States were to gather in Newark, New Jersey, and fly together to Berlin. A number of us were at the airport in Atlanta to fly to Newark; Hurricane Floyd blew in from Florida and disrupted our plans! We were at the airport all day. In the evening, some of us were still waiting for a flight. One of the airline clerks hurriedly made out tickets for those of us who remained, and said, "Run to see if you can board this plane!" We ran! The other passengers had already boarded. We gave our tickets to the agents, who looked at the tickets – and at us – and finally gave us permission to board! We found we had business elite tickets for our overseas trip direct to Barcelona, where we boarded another plane to Zurich and on to Berlin! Our baggage caught up with us four days later! We first had a five-night stay with a wonderful family in the eastern part of Germany close to the Polish border. When we left them, we went by coach to Dresden, Prague, Brno, Bratislava, Budapest, Vienna, Melk, Salzburg, and Munich.

Back home in December, I received a phone call from my sister-in-law, Lila, saying that my older brother John had died. He suffered from Alzheimers, but his death was very unexpected. He had gotten up that morning, walked to a chair in the living room and asked Lila's daughter-in-law with whom he was staying, "Is breakfast ready yet?"

Lila's daughter-in-law replied "No, not yet." When breakfast was ready, she went to call him, and he had gone to his Eternal Home. I flew out to Los Angeles, spoke for the family at his service, and stayed on to help Lila with her adjustments to John's passing and her own knee surgery.

2001 was special! I remember my tour to the Holy Land on a Pilgrimage in May…to walk in the footsteps of Jesus, to see where He fed the 5,000, walked on the Sea of Galilee, shared the Beatitudes with His followers, healed the sick, and called us to be His disciples. Since then, when I read the Gospels – Matthew, Mark, Luke, and John – I can visualize where the events happened, and it makes the Scriptures so meaningful! When the tour group returned home, I stayed on and joined with two members of Greater Atlanta Presbytery representing the PCUSA (Presbyterian Church USA) who flew in to meet me. We were a part of a hunger program pilot project that partnered Greater Atlanta Presbytery with the Palestinians. The three of us returned to America as advocates of justice, knowing we needed to make Americans aware of the unbalanced picture presented by the media.

Me in front of the Blue Mosque
in Istanbul, Turkey

In April of 2004 I was one of 20 travelers from around the United States who embarked on a 15-day tour to Turkey – the land bridge between Asia and Europe, and site of one of the great cradles of civilization. "Two Thousand Years of Christianity in Turkey" was the title of – and the reason for – our tour, which allowed us to walk in the footsteps of the New Testament Apostles, especially Paul and John. We visited five of the sites of the Seven Churches of Revelation and sailed in a private boat to the Greek Isle of Patmos, where John was imprisoned and received and recorded the Vision of the Book of Revelation. Antalya, on the Mediterranean Coast with its beautiful view of the snowcapped mountains, is a center for the Presbyterian Church's work in Turkey now. Cappadocia country with its bewitching landscape of hardened eroded volcanic ash fascinated us all! Of interest to us was that St. Paul was the first person to bring Christianity to this area, and the "Cappadocian Fathers" gave our church the Nicene Creed, which we still use today.

In 2005, I was especially fortunate to take two trips overseas. In July I was able to join a presbytery mission trip out of Louisville, Kentucky. My son David, who was my only child who had never been in Taiwan, and who was recently married, was able to come and see where his parents had worked over 39 years ago! Most of our time was spent with the mission trip on the west coast, and then we had two extra days to travel to the east coast. A typhoon wiped out one of those days, but we had 24 hours to spend over there. Missionaries of the PCUSA, Rev. Choon and Yen Hee Lim, met our train in Hualien, and after a quick meal at a restaurant, they drove us down the coast to Yuli, where there were 30 folk waiting to welcome us! We were able to visit the house we had lived in, now being used by a Christian dentist, then continued on to visit two more mountain churches. The pastor of one of the very large Bunun churches had worked with our family as a high school student. How great it was to see him now! So much had been modernized in Taiwan since the days we were there.

Then later in the year, I *had* to accept an invitation from China to attend the 100th anniversary of the hospital that Blake's grandfather, Dr. John Wilson Bradley, had raised money for and built in Suqian, Jiangsu in 1905! Not only I, but John and Anne, were able to attend. Anne's passport arrived, thanks to the assistance of two senators, two days before we were to leave. A moment of grace! Altogether only 12 accepted the invitation to attend the anniversary, including two other granddaughters of Dr. Bradley, Sujean and Mardia Bradley, who were our cousins.

The medical director of the hospital met us in Shanghai! A bus ride took us to many places, including the home where Pearl S. Buck had grown up. Her parents were Presbyterian missionaries. In Nanjing, we walked up the 392 steps to see Sun Yat Sen's Mausoleum.

As we approached Suqian, a police car with flashing lights escorted us into the city. What a welcome our group had. Nurses presented us with sprays of colored flowers, and the mayor personally welcomed us. We were in Suqian a number of days, touring in the hospital and visiting with the staff. We planted a ginko biloba tree in memory of Dr. Bradley. We met a man who was the son of the first Chinese to be trained to be a doctor by Dr. Bradley. We surely felt welcome, and returned home with many good memories of the mission work that had been done in China over the years.

Other trips I made were to Nova Scotia and the Maritime areas, and later, a cruise from Seattle to Alaska and back. My last overseas trip was to Germany in 2010 to see the Passion Play in Oberammergau. As it is given only once every ten years, I knew this was my last opportunity to see it. A friend and I signed up for a Lutheran tour and flew to Berlin, then took a bus through Martin Luther country, visiting the cities in which he was born and had worked, and saw where he nailed the 95 Theses on the door in Wittenberg. The tour ended in Oberammergau where the Passion Play was presented. A partially open-air stage on which 800 actors could be present at one time, an auditorium filled with 4,600 people, and no vacant seats! The play was spoken in German, but we were given an English translation! It was unforgettable, the scene of the crucified Christ, our Redeemer!

Our flight home was from Munich, scheduled for 9 a.m; to get there in time for the flight we had to be up at 2:30 a.m., to pack and leave by bus. The flight was delayed, as the airplane had no radar working. Germany didn't have a replacement radar; one had to be ordered from outside the country. Then it was held up in customs! It was well into the afternoon before we were able to fly, but it was non-stop to the United States. We were safely home!

With all my family grown and in homes of their own, I found myself living alone in my three-bedroom home in Conyers. It had served me well, but I was thinking about retirement, and I decided to visit some of my friends living in a Presbyterian Retirement Community on the edge of Atlanta. Nice as it was, I knew I didn't want to stay in Atlanta with all the busy traffic, six lanes in one direction on the interstate in some areas!

My thoughts turned to the mountains of North Carolina. The family has a two-bedroom cottage in Montreat, but I didn't plan to move there because I wanted to live in a retirement community. In Asheville, I looked at several retirement communities, one Methodist and the other Episcopalian. Both were very large and had high-rise buildings and a large population. Then I visited Highland Farms Retirement Community in Black Mountain. No buildings were higher than two stories, and as I remember, it was the least costly of the three. This would be my choice. I applied for a one-bedroom cluster home. There weren't too many of them, and I had to wait two-and-a-half years before one was available, so I remained in Conyers.

In those two years I had time to downsize. My children had helped me measure the length of the walls and the contour of the rooms at Highland Farms, and so I was able to decide which pieces of furniture I would be taking along, and which items were available to my four children to have. In Conyers (Atlanta) I had a double garage but was never able to get my car in. It was filled with bookcases and lots of books, file cabinets with lots of sermons, and other items and boxes that had to be gone through.

I had put my house on the market months before I was notified that I could move into my new cluster home at 31 Wagon Trail at Highland Farms. My four children and their spouses helped me with the move. On the morning of Thursday, April 6, 2006, we picked up our reserved Penske truck – and the loading began – large furniture first. We all were involved in loading up the truck and tying down the items. My son-in-law drove the truck with another person traveling with him. Some of us followed in my car, and the rest in several other cars. The weather was clear and we made good progress, stopping to eat on the way.

When we arrived, I went inside the cluster home, and as the furniture was brought in, directed where it was to be placed. During this process, a gentleman who lived in one of the six homes in the cluster came over to welcome me and brought a delicious cake for us to enjoy. That evening our family all went out to enjoy a good meal together! We were most grateful to the Lord that the move had been accomplished safely, and no one had been hurt lifting the furniture and boxes.

Some of the items in the truck were to be taken to my cottage in Montreat, a 15-minute drive away, and that was done the following day.

Highland Farms has a capacity for about 300 occupants, in apartments, cluster homes, or in four individual houses, plus about 30 in health care. The retirement community has the ability to see one through retirement all the way to the end of life. Many paths wind along a beautiful campus, around the lake, beside a stream, with the most scenic views of the western North Carolina mountains! Many friendly folks walk around the campus daily, some of them with dogs on a leash.

Meals are served in the dining room at noon and in the evening from 5 p.m. to 6:30 p.m. Breakfast can be purchased in the Deli in the morning, and at noon such things as sandwiches and salads are available. Those of us living in cluster homes, condos, or houses receive meal credit for $100 to be spent monthly. Those in apartments receive either a noon or evening meal daily.

The retirement community provides many activities, and trips scheduled with sign up sheets, including the bus ride to the Asheville Symphony. Some are overnight trips, and the charges are added to one's monthly bill. Free exercise classes are held three times a week.

My home has a living room, dining room, kitchen, bedroom and bathroom, and also a sunroom. The living room has a number of my paintings of scenes in Taiwan hanging on the wall, and above the buffet in the dining room is a large Japanese screen with cherry blossoms and a stream of water flowing down an angled split bamboo branch with a bird perched on it.

I have never wished to be any other place at this time of my life!! Our residents are people who have traveled around the world in their work or leisure, are well educated and are very friendly folk.

Music is one of my main joys in life. Soon after my move to Highland Farms I heard about the Asheville Choral Society and made arrangements for an audition. The song I sang at the audition was, "Oh, My Lover Is a Fisherman," a song I had sung at St. Olaf College in Northfield, Minnesota when taking singing lessons. Afterward, the director asked me if I knew German, and I replied I had had two years of German in high school and one in college, as well as two years of Latin. She reached out her hand to congratulate me, and I was in!

We had practice every Monday evening at a church in Asheville. I had attended every practice, and we were soon going to give our Christmas Concert in a large church in Asheville. I had been losing weight and strength but was determined to sing at the concert. My son David walked me up to the place where I stood in the back row before the other singers filed in, and I sang! We had a second concert on Sunday afternoon, but I was so exhausted I couldn't get out of bed in the morning. Soon afterwards I was taken to the hospital with temporal arteritis (inflammation of the temporal artery), diabetes secondary to high doses of prednisone prescribed for me, and bilateral pneumonia!

I did not try to sing with the Asheville Choral Society during the winter term, but by spring I was able to do so. And for three years I thoroughly enjoyed practicing and singing with them in concert. We had an exceptional director, an accompanist when needed at the piano, and a very talented group of singers. Then I was diagnosed with asthma and did not return, but I often attended their concerts.

When I first moved to Black Mountain, the family members who lived nearest to me – David and family – were living in Winston-Salem, a two-hour drive away. Several years later they moved to Montreat with their son Blake who was about six months old. Now they were only 15 minutes away. I loved baby sitting for them! Blake is now seven years old and in second grade! He loves school, loves sports, and is playing on a soccer team, so on Saturdays you will find me on the soccer field sidelines cheering his team on.

My eldest child Karen is married to Ricky Nelson, and they live in Georgia, a three-hour drive away. John is married to Linda Golson and they have two adorable daughters, Teri Anne, a four-and-a-half year old, and Emily, two years old, living in Milledgeville, Georgia. Anne is married to Rev. Reed Wilbanks and is living and serving in Wilmore, Kentucky. We are able to all get together on special occasions.

When I first arrived in Black Mountain, I joined the First Presbyterian Church in Swannanoa, a lovely church high up on a hill overlooking the valley. It was the first Presbyterian Church in this part of North Carolina. The minister there was a Columbia Seminary classmate of David's, and an excellent preacher. When her six-month term was up, I decided I wanted to attend a church closer to home, and after visiting Black Mountain Presbyterian Church in town for weeks, I joined this church. Soon I was singing in the choir and playing in the bell choir – and continue to do so. Our organist and choir director are fulltime at the church, and the music during the services is so uplifting! Our pastor's sermons spoke straight to the congregation, and all attention was on her when she preached. She has since been called to a much larger church, and we now have an interim preacher – who is also an excellent preacher!

I have also chaired a "circle" for four years and am serving on the Mission Committee. We are a very active church, serving the community in many ways. There are classes for pre-school children during the week. On Sundays, if you want a good seat in church, I suggest you come early!

Many of us attend reunions of schools that we attended in the past. Twice I have planned reunions for those of us missionary kids who went to ASK, the boarding school I went to in China during the war with Japan. The Blue Ridge Assembly, about a 15-minute drive away from my home, has wonderful facilities, and they were so cooperative in helping me to plan these reunions. We held one in 2008, when 23 students came to participate – from California to New Hampshire, Minnesota to North Carolina. Again in 2012 we gathered in the same location, and 13 students were able to attend, the oldest being ninety years old! I have also traveled to reunions of Morrison Academy students in Oregon, Fairview Hospital nurses in Albuquerque, New Mexico, and hosted one for them near Hendersonville, North Carolina. My most recent reunion was last year (2014) when I flew to Minnesota to attend my 60th anniversary at St. Olaf College.

Living so close to Montreat is also a blessing. It is one of our Presbyterian Church USA's three conference centers in the United States. In the spring, summer, and fall, there are conferences held continuously, with many in the winter as well. In the summer, six youth conferences are held with 1,000 young people coming from many places in the United States. Wonderful music conferences on two consecutive weeks bring outstanding directors for adult, senior high, junior high, and children's choirs from many places. Members of bell choirs can update their skills, and there is an organ recital as well! Each Friday evening a concert is held in Anderson Auditorium, with folks in the audience filling every available seat!

The other day several of us residents were talking about our Givens Highland Farms Retirement Community. (It was taken over by Givens several years ago.) We had talked with many other residents who came from different parts of the United States and knew of retirement homes there. We all agreed that we are in the best possible location, in this beautiful part of western North Carolina, in view of the mountain ranges around us, and we would never choose to look for another retirement home. We like it *here*!

My heart is filled to overflowing with gratitude to the Lord for His call, guidance, protection, His grace and forgiveness, and His love for me and our family, through all the days of my life, and for the days to come, as I walk through these sunset days of my life…with God's song in my heart!

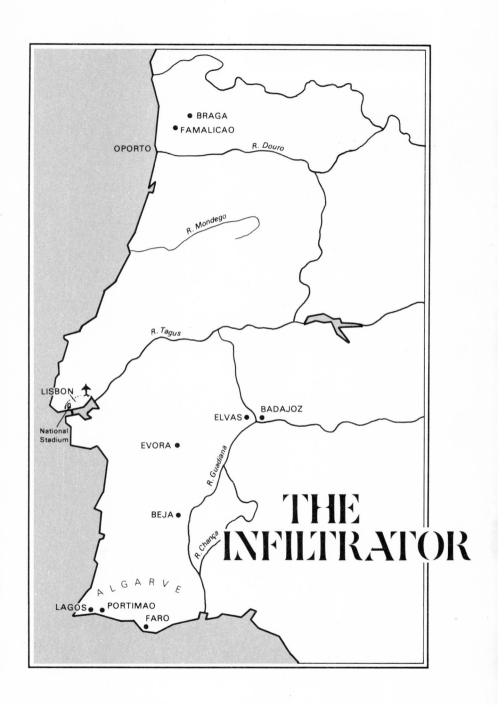

THE
INFILTRATOR

# THE
# INFILTRATOR

## Martin Walker

The Dial Press/James Wade
New York

Published by ·
The Dial Press/James Wade
1 Dag Hammarskjold Plaza · New York, New York 10017

Originally published in Great Britain by Hart-Davis MacGibbon Limited,
London, a division of Granada Publishing Limited.

Manufactured in the United States of America · First U.S.A. Printing

Library of Congress Cataloging in Publication Data
Walker, Martin, 1947–
The infiltrator.

I.  Title.
PZ4.W1817In   1978   [PR6073.A413]      823'.9'14      78–19042
ISBN 0–8037–4004–2

For Louis, Maria, Joao, and Carlos.

*Obrigad'*

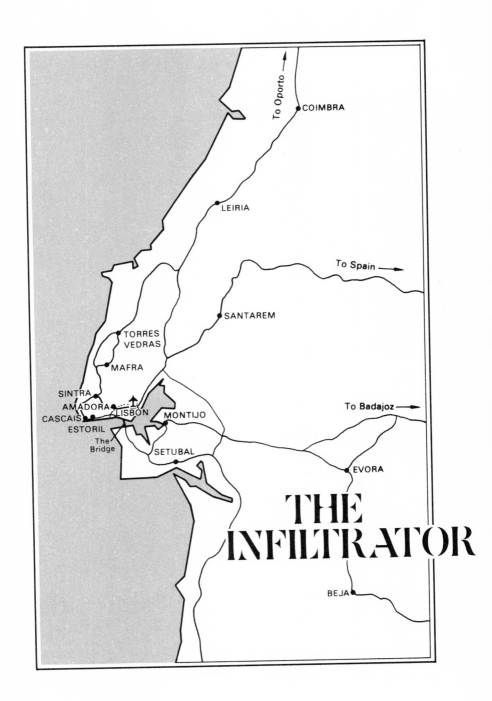

THE
INFILTRATOR

# 1

The fat man looked uncomfortable. It may have been the budget, which only ran to the cheap seats on the Sol side of the bullring, and the late afternoon sun of Madrid was still cruel. But mostly it was the package.

It lay on the stone seat between us, carelessly wrapped in a copy of yesterday's *ABC*, the Spanish newspaper that looks like a magazine. Both of us were trying very hard not to look at it. It

1

was easier to look at the bullfight. The fat man liked bullfights. He had been the Resident in Madrid since the war and he had invented the rendezvous system. He told London that it was best to send a man into Spain on a Sunday, when all the ambitious and careful Spanish spooks who staked out the airport would be at church. An ambitious spook was a good Catholic, he had observed. So send them in on Sunday and meet at the bullfight. London bought the idea, but insisted on the cheap seats.

Ruiz was getting ready to kill, one side of his suit of lights still dusty from the tumble he had taken when the bull veered. Ruiz was a dandy and hated to tumble, so he had punished the bull with too many close *muletas*, wrapping the bull tightly around his body so that its shoulders sprained and its neck fell. There was no need for it. He went in, sighting down the curved blade of the sword, his left hand drifting the red cape away with the bull and the sword swooping. There was a gleam of tumbling light as the blade bit bone and bounced from the bull's back. Now it would have to be butchered. The crowd hurled jeers and cushions into the ring. Ruiz stalked away as if it were nothing to do with him.

"The border at Badajoz is easy," the fat man said. "Pick up a girl tonight and take her with you. Use a hired car. American chick. Buckets and spades on the back seat. Suntan lotion and *Newsweek* and duty-free cigarettes. The border won't bother you. Then you deliver the stuff and help them reestablish the network. They shouldn't need you too much. They were very good in Angola."

The mules were dragging the dead bull from the ring and the fat man bought a beer from the vendor. I had to call him back to get one for myself. He couldn't be that cautious. We'd already been seen talking together. We drank some beer and the horns blew and another bull, fresh and confused, charged into the ring.

"Of course they were good in Angola. They didn't like the Rhodesians either and the army was on our side. I think it could be different here. They were born in Angola. Portugal is a foreign country for them."

2

I spoke calmly enough, but he knew I was angry. London had probably told him that I didn't like the idea of transplanting a network from Africa to Europe, particularly a network whose major job had been commercial espionage. It's one thing to have a group of colonial traders watching trade with Rhodesia; it's quite another to send the merchant bastards back home and expect them to operate politically.

"Look, they are still Portuguese," the fat man said wearily. The bull was standing below us, claiming the little piece of the ring that would become his ground for the fifteen minutes or so his life had left. The Colombian matador, his first season in Spain, was gingerly probing the limits of the bull's ground, trailing his purple and yellow cape.

"They all have families back here in Portugal. They are all angry. They've lost homes and money and status in Africa. They'll operate politically in any case. We might as well use them. And our old networks in Portugal were not constructed for a revolution. I know they should have been, but London didn't see it coming. Blame London—blame yourself."

"Very simple. Very nice." I had some more beer. "I come in with enough heroin to get me a life sentence, set up some bewildered little tradesmen as big-time hoods dealing heroin, and expect them to run the revolution for us. And we don't even know how much of a market there is for the stuff in Lisbon. They'll probably deal it to some sailors for peanuts and sit back and drink the money and reminisce about Angola."

"That is why we are sending you there. You needn't give it to them all at once. We can always get you some more. And you keep on their tails. You stop them sitting back and thinking about Africa. You get them to organize. A returned Angolans' society. Political meetings. Alliances with other parties. Build up the Angolan vote—you get your finger out and you can deliver a block vote of half a million. You'll be on the inside, running two cabinet members, the dope trade, and half the hoodlums in Portugal. And meanwhile the old networks run the other half. Revolutions make for dispossessed people. That's what the old networks will be doing. They'll make those dispossessed into a right-wing party, and we can run that too. Now shut up. I want to watch the pics."

"What about the opposition? What are they doing?"

The fat man brushed me away, his eyes on the bull who had lifted his head for this horse, in spite of the pain wrenching at his savaged back. He had the horse in the ribs, thrusting it bodily into the barrier. The pic could not manage a proper thrust. The capes taunted the bull away, to try another charge.

"As often as not, these days, they only let them be piced twice. They can have four, but ever since that idiot Cordobés they all think they can handle half-piced bulls." The fat man was proud of his knowledge of the bulls and used to hang around the cafes in the Calle Vittoria where the old bullfighters drank. Once he had asked London for permission to buy a partnership in a bull-breeding farm in Estremadura.

"What about the opposition?" I said again. How much had London told him?

"That's for the home front to tell you," he muttered. "I'm Madrid. I'm not your fucking Portugal. I'm supposed to rebuild my entire network here because London has only just realized that Franco's dying and we could have a revolution here. I've got to have the bloody Communists and the Socialists and the unions and the armed forces sewn up, and I'm supposed to do it over-night. Years ago I begged them to give me some money for it. It would have been cheap then. Now Portugal catches them with their pants down and they start seeing revolutions everywhere and want to have their fat little hands in it. Fuck 'em."

Chisholm had warned me that the fat man was a grumbler. Like most of the Residents. Too long out of touch with London, too long in place, too ready to blame the head office for ignoring them, for not taking the local Resident's advice. Always complaining they were never told enough, and that would be Chisholm's fault too. If the faceless little bureaucrats who worked around his office had dared to invent him a nickname, they'd have called him "Need-to-know" Chisholm. The principle governed his entire life. From the occasional gossip, I was pretty

4

sure it governed his marriage too. The only evidence we had ever seen of her was the hand-knitted tea cosy in his second office, the one behind Goodge Street.

"Madrid isn't my problem," I told him, no comfort in my voice. "You know I'm only concerned with Portugal."

"So are the Spanish, dear boy. And I know a lot about the Spanish. Portugal is on their doorstep. The Spaniards were worried enough last year, when the soldiers pulled their coup and put an end to forty years of cosy, neighborly dictatorship." His voice was offhand, his eyes on the ring.

"And now the Communists are starting to take over, I suppose the Spaniards are wetting their pants." I shrugged as I spoke. I didn't expect to run across any Spaniards.

"Don't underestimate the Spaniards," said the fat man, quick to the defense of his adopted land. "They've run a police state here for a long time, with very few ball-ups. That means a very efficient security service. And Portugal is their backyard."

"I know a little about them. The DGS. Very efficient, I'm told." I was almost humoring the old man. Not so old. Maybe fifty. Fifty-five. I hadn't checked.

The bull was tiring now. The *banderillas* had been stuck a little to the left, to cure his tendency to hook that way. That would pose problems at the kill. He had to charge straight then. A little hook to the right and the Colombian would never make his triumph in Madrid. The red cape fluttered.

"Did Chisholm tell you to watch the Yanks?" the fat man asked. He kept his eyes on the ring. The bull was back in his ground, watchful and hurt, intent on staying in the tiny patch of the ring he had staked out as his own. The Colombian inched over the invisible frontier. The bull's head rose, his eyes on the cape or on the man—only the Colombian would know, and his life depended on it.

"Yes, Chisholm said to watch the Yanks. He always does. He's got Yanks on the brain." The bull charged for the cape, which rose before him. A high pass, the horns grazing the man at the height of his shoulder. A high pass to give the bull some confidence again. The Colombian was very keen to do well.

5

"Do you know why he hates the Yanks? Did you know about his wife?" The fat man had leaned forward as the Colombian wrapped the bull around himself, but slowly, so as not to tire or stretch that bloodied back where the bull kept his courage; the Colombian was taking a chance. A bull learns more in his few minutes in the ring than a man learns in a lifetime.

"I thought Chisholm was happily married. A sweet little lady in Pinner who knits tea cosies and likes Bournemouth for her holidays." As the bull tired, the unmarked territory that was his ground shrank around him. Only he knew where the line was that forced him to charge. The Colombian deliberately strode into it, jeering at the bull, his wrist twitching the heavy cape. His senior *banderillero* was at the barrier, shouting something. The crowd yelled at him to shut up.

"That's his second wife. She was his secretary when he was in Military Intelligence in Berlin. His first wife was something else. She was Belgian and very beautiful. She left him for a Yank in Berlin. He's hated them ever since." The *banderillero* called again, a forlorn voice at the barrier.

"What's he saying?"

"It's South American Spanish," the fat man said. "He says the bull's a quick learner. He should know. The bull turned very fast for the second pair of *banderillas*. The Colombian won't listen. He wants a triumph."

This time the Colombian kept the cape low, trailing it slowly over the ground so the bull's nose plowed a furrow in the dirt. He spun inside the bull, offering his back and the drooping cape. The bull wheeled, still too angry to think, and again charged the cape, which flirted across his eyes, wheeling him until his haunches locked. The Colombian strode away, leaving the bull in place, confident of his dominance.

"I knew her—the first wife. I knew Chisholm too. He was never on operations, did you know that? He went straight from Military into running networks in Berlin. We were losing so many then that he got promoted several grades. We needed every network man we could get. We used Germans, of course. They

6

were expendable. Chisholm came up with the best idea to recruit them. They all had to go through a clearance procedure before we freed them. We called it de-Nazification. Chisholm went into the camps, checked the records for the naughty boys, and told them they could be free if they worked for us. They were amateurs, but they were expendable. We lost hundreds. That's what Chisholm called cooperating with our fellow Europeans. Bloody butcher. Bournemouth for his holidays. Christ she was a stunner, that first wife. She saw through him fast enough."

It was time for the kill. Two more passes, perhaps four. The Colombian had done well. He would be awarded the ears. The fat man pulled out a white handkerchief.

"I'll be surprised if you find many Yanks there. Not of our kind, anyway," the fat man said. "They'll all be too busy at home with those congressional investigations. They'll work through their military boys, through NATO intelligence. Christ knows they've trained enough Portuguese officers to build up a network there. That's where this summer will be decided. In the Portuguese army. They started this revolution and they've got to finish it. Nobody else has the guns."

The first pass was very close, the tip of the horn almost flicking the open mass of silk and sequins that made up the Colombian's suit of lights. The second was safer. There was space between the horn and the man.

Around us, men began to chat among themselves. The beer vendors began to walk up the aisles. The bull was still alive, still dangerous, the sword yet to enter. But the fight was over. The bull had tried his last weapon, a last hook, and the cape had forced the neck to flick the other way. He was as good as dead. This time, the fat man bought two beers.

The Colombian was now certain of the kill, so certain he was going to kill in the old and dangerous way of Navarre. This was how they killed two centuries ago. *Recibiendo*. The killer standing silent, the sword poised, inciting the bull to one last, low charge at the cape and hurling himself onto the sword. The feet immobile, the elbow cocked to drop the blade into the neck as

7

the bull went past. The Colombian stood straight, his head peering over the sword, the cape flicking sand at the immobile bull. The crowd was silent again.

The bull had done enough. There was no drive in him, hardly the energy, for a last charge. He too knew it was ended. The sand flicked into his eyes again. That cape. That taunting cape. His hind hooves inched together. His haunches gathered and he came, still following the cape as it drifted low and the Colombian pivoted and dropped the point of the sword so it slipped easily into the back, driving down through the muscle to the heart. The bull took the cape, the sword was placed to the hilt, the Colombian as still as a tree on a windless day. The bull lurched on, the front hooves beginning to buckle. He was already dead. The cape hung from a horn, and around the bullring the white handkerchiefs waved. The bull fell. The Colombian had made his triumph. The fat man tore his fight ticket in half and gave me one of the pieces.

"There's a bar in Estoril called the Navigator. Be there on Tuesday night. There'll be a little photographer called Joao who will ask you about freelance work. Tell him you're interested, that your newspaper might need a photographer. If he has the other half of the ticket, give him the heroin, or as much of it as you see fit. He's your contact with the Angolans. And there's a kid. English and crazy and very close to the far Left. He's a Trotskyite or something. He thinks you're really a journalist. I'll put him in touch with you. He's my son."

The fat man walked down the stone seats to the exit. He left his cushion behind. I hadn't thought to hire one. I put the half-ticket in my hip pocket and left by another exit and took the Metro to Puerta del Sol.

*Un kilo*, even of heroin, doesn't weigh very much. It was still wrapped in the newspaper. Pity. I would have liked something to read on the Metro.

# 2

A lot of things the instructors told us never made sense until you thought about them. Like being followed. The first reaction when you think you are being followed is to lose the tail. Wrong, said the instructors. If somebody is following you, then they are interested in you. So you are interested in them. Let them follow. See how hard they'll try to keep on your trail. If you have time, see what kind of approach they make.

I still wasn't sure about the girl. She had been at the bullfight, somewhere behind us. I first spotted her as we left. She was standing uncertainly on the edge of her stone seat, looking after the fat man but her eyes darting toward the exit I was taking. I had loitered a little to make it easier for her. Mid-twenties, long and straight dark hair and large sunglasses with a pretty mouth. She was wearing jeans and a T-shirt with a canvas shoulder bag. That made her non-Spanish. Spanish girls with the style to wear jeans have to show they can afford expensive leather handbags. The bag was bulky enough to hide a light coat or sweater, and she had a long silk scarf knotted around her neck. She could change her silhouette and her shape in a crowd in seconds.

I didn't see her on the Metro, but I took the exit on the far side of the Sol Square, toward the security police headquarters. I then walked back across the square toward the Calle del Carmen, and when I stopped to browse at a news kiosk I saw her fifty yards away. This time the scarf was knotted around her head, the long ends trailing behind her. It looked very fetching. I bought a copy of *Cambio* and sat at a cafe table, watching the last of the sun on the red brick of the DGS building. I put the package on the next seat and read the *Cambio* cover story on the Communists in Portgual. "The Red Neighbor," said the headline. The girl had settled in another cafe. She was reading the Barcelona paper *Vanguardia*.

I called the waiter and asked him for another coffee, with a cognac to keep it company. I also asked him if he had any friends in the cafe across the street. He said he used to work there, so I gave him 100 pesetas and told him to see what the waiters said about the girl. He went to the phone and came back with the *café*-cognac. She spoke Spanish like a Mexican bargirl, and there were American Express checks in her wallet. She was smoking duty-free Marlboros. She was a Yank.

She had taken her sunglasses off, and she looked pretty, in a clean, California way. It was hard to tell at this distance. Her legs were propped up on a chair. She was wearing high-heeled sandals, so she couldn't run if I moved fast. Nice ankles. A light tan on her arms, her hair very sleek. She picked up her cup, wiped her finger around its base, and licked her finger clean. As fastidious and self-indulgent as a cat. She sucked on the end of her finger a moment, lapping up all the sugar that had been left in the cup. I began to like her. I must have been grinning because she suddenly turned to look at me and grinned right back. I raised the cognac glass to her and drank it, letting what drops were left trickle into my coffee. I drank that to her as well and picked up the heroin, took the back exit, and went back to the pension where I was staying. If she was following, she could find me again.

I had a room in one of the cheap semi-brothels around the theaters in the Calle del Carmen. Two quid a night and they don't bother to ask for passports or make records of the guests. For another 100 pesetas you could take a woman in, or as many women as you want. A hundred pesetas for each one. The whores charge their own price.

I took a shower in the communal bathroom, some guy banging on the door who wanted a crap. Dried, I walked out in a towel, nodding at him. He darted inside. I thought about the fat man's advice. A nice, old-fashioned idea, just like the fat man, but it might make sense. Except that I'd have to lose the girl as soon as I reached Lisbon and she might complain to the police about the nasty British tourist who had used her and left her . . . complications. The last thing I needed were complications.

As far as London was concerned, I was an experiment. They had trained me for eighteen months for this job. Me and eight others, on an intensive course in how to break a country apart and rebuild it in their way. Even Chisholm finally gave in and approved. Maybe he was sick and tired of hearing the Americans brag about how well they had done with the idea in Chile. When Chisholm had come down for one of the weekends, he had rambled on about Chile being a crude early experiment, and how he could always shut the Yanks up by talking about Vietnam, but even he saw how the idea made sense.

It was one of those courses where they tell you from the beginning that there will be no cowboy stuff, which means that

11

barring street accidents and heart attacks, we would all live through it. We did have one casualty, a nervous breakdown. It might have been the pressure of work or it might have been the awesome beauty of what we were learning to do. Anybody can learn to kill a man, but to kill a country is different. He was the only one in the course none of us knew. All the rest of us were SAS.

It has become very difficult to recruit people for intelligence. At about the same time that people started to phase out the idea of the manned bomber, on the principle that missiles were more accurate and less inclined to turn back when the going got tough, Whitehall suggested that we start phasing out the recruitment of intelligence "actives." They had a brave new world of all the intelligence they wanted coming from spy-planes and spy satellites that could photograph car number-plates from a hundred miles up. They were right; 95 percent of intelligence on the Soviet bloc gets done that way, with teams of highly-trained specialists poring over every word the Russians and East Germans publish about science.

People like Chisholm hung on, pointing out that a lot of intelligence still had to be done in Africa and Asia in the old fashioned way. We'd always need actives for jobs like that. Whitehall accepted that, but insisted that they be recruited as civil servants, or get transfers from Scotland Yard's Special Branch or Military Intelligence in the usual way.

Everything changed with Ulster. As soon as the IRA got started again and killed off the twenty-odd Special Branch men who knew Northern Ireland and its hard men, Whitehall suddenly found itself bereft of all intelligence. There was a period of about two years, between 1969 and 1971, when London knew almost nothing about Ireland except what they read in the papers. So they tried to hire some journalists, and that didn't work. And they asked Dublin for assistance, and that didn't work. And then Whitehall suddenly realized that it wasn't just the Catholics who were shooting at the army, but the Protestants too. That was when Whitehall gave in and gave the okay to use the SAS.

12

There are a lot of myths about the SAS. At that time, we were simply highly-trained soldiers, accustomed to working in groups of three or four, and trained specifically to be dropped behind enemy lines and cause havoc. We all had a working knowledge of explosives, sabotage, radio communications, small arms weaponry, and unarmed combat. We were good but we were not built up as some kind of lethal supermen like the American Green Berets. We were all very fit, accustomed to living off the country, to hard marching and all that went with it. But in 1971 they started to put us into Belfast and people like Chisholm suddenly realized that they had perfect material for active agents. They worked us till we dropped. Some of us got killed at first, by trying stupid things like Belfast accents. They spent weeks teaching us to speak like someone who had been born and bred on the Creggan estate, but in a country as small as Ulster, that just isn't enough. If you claim to come from those back streets, then a dozen people would have been to school with you, would have started smoking cigarettes behind the school toilets with you, would have dated the same girls and been belted by your man. In Ulster, cover did not come with an accent.

They eventually eased us into Ulster in all sorts of ways. I spent six months working in a local government housing office as a "seconded" English expert. That was good enough. Some even went in as journalists. Once it was accepted that we would not get away with pretending to be Ulstermen it was simple enough.

We worked as a series of self-contained units. We would spot the hard men, the ones who could organize supplies of explosives, and then get hold of detonators and train others to make bombs. Or the man who had British Army training and then taught the kids from his street how to lay an ambush for British troops and get away after a quick volley. We found out who they were and we started to kill them. Those were the orders. Chisholm first got interested in us when we stopped just killing them and started to make the killings look as though they were done by the Catholics. Or the Protestants. Chisholm liked the economy of that. It meant that the UDA and the UVF would start taking on the Provos, and the Provos would start taking on the

UDA, and with any luck, the British Army could have a quiet life.

After Oman, it was first nature to us. The rule in Oman and in Aden had been that if we had to kill, it had to look as though it wasn't us who did it. We brought the principle to Belfast. Chisholm claimed it as his own idea. Army HQ at Lisburn started feeding our information about who was who and who lived where and what car they drove into the big computer that was already programmed with the electoral register. Then all the army patrols on the streets were ordered to keep an intelligence log of unusual car numbers in their streets, and the kind of furniture people had in their parlors, and which pub they used, and it all fell into place.

We knew who was visiting whom, who was having an affair with whom, and who was the latest recruit into the paramilitaries. It was never perfect. Stolen cars could put us off, and the social security fiddles could put us off, getting us chasing men who never existed but who were drawing the dole every week. But we started to make the arrests, and the house searches for guns started to yield results, and if the politicians had ever had the balls to arrest everybody we said could have been arrested, we'd have stopped the violence. But that would have meant arresting about one person in six all over Northern Ireland. It was when that figure flicked out of the computer that we knew we would never win. The IRA was a joke, made up of some aged alcoholics and a load of teenage cowboys. The UDA was a sick joke. But the community as a whole was too big to handle.

There was still a lot of fun. We opened a massage parlor with saunas, and we had the girls flown over from London. We bugged the couches and the sauna and it became the classiest brothel in town and a very good source of high-level intelligence. We used to get assemblymen, politicians, councillors, and industrialists. The operation even made money. We helped start a food cooperative in Andersontown, and started to employ detainees who had just come out of the internment camp at the Maze. We even helped organize collections for the families of detainees.

Within two years we were bringing in more intelligence than the analysts at Lisburn could handle.

It was then that they started to pull some of us out for the special course. Chisholm briefed each of us at Leconfield House before we went down to Somerset. The word he used was "destabilization," and he told us about the political scientists, the behavioral psychologists, the trade union officials, the journalists, and the sociologists who would be waiting to train us in Somerset. He made it sound like a university for intelligence agents, which I suppose is just what it was.

We learned in classrooms and in lecture halls and in the tiny film projection room just what makes a country work. Its industry, its communications, its political organizations, its private clubs, and the links between all the power bases. And we learned where the weak points were. We were taught how to organize a strike committee, how to set up a dummy company in a tax haven to launder money, how to disrupt an industry, and how to make a nation panic.

A lot of the cases we studied were British. They showed us from British examples how a strike at a components factory can disrupt the entire car industry; how packing three trade union branches can get rid of one Labour MP and replace him with another. How to use the press, how to run a print shop, how to disrupt a demonstration. The trade union officials showed us how a branch was built, and then how it could be manipulated by a handful of men who knew what they were doing. We played roles as trade union negotiators bargaining for more pay. The next day we would act the part of the employer. The day after that we would learn how to provoke a wildcat strike and keep the official union men out of the factory.

Occasionally, specialists would come down to teach us their arcane arts. We had a graphic designer one day, to teach us how to design leaflets and posters; an advertising executive to show us how to draft leaflets and how to write slogans. Some of it we knew already, like the old trick of cement in railway points to derail a train, but the instructors were leaving nothing to chance.

15

Chisholm even brought a police superintendent down to tell us what the Yanks had taught him about interrogation techniques at the International Police Academy.

The staff instructors stayed with us throughout the course, but only during the formal teaching hours. There was no social mixing, not even with the other students. The normal SAS refresher training was maintained; the regular three- and ten-day survival exercises in Norway and Scotland, weapons drill at Pirbright, and so on. But there were no days off, no convivial evenings. Women were brought up to Somerset for us once a week, and there was a library and video film stock for us to use, and the food was good. The only times we relaxed were when they brought down our cover nurses—people who were already professionals in our own specialty. Mine was a journalist on the Arena Agency, one that we regularly used for cover purposes. He took me through the day's stock of newspapers, showing how stories were written and how they got processed into print. I learned how to lay out a newspaper, how to run a telex machine and write a cable in the odd, truncated language of press telegrams.

Four of us were trained in purely journalistic cover techniques, and all four of us had been given press cards at some time in Northern Ireland. The rest were trained for business cover, and they learned much more than we did about setting up import-export agencies, accountancy, and how to make money. Once a month, they let us all loose on the fictitious country they had invented for us to practice on.

We designed it as a Communist state and developed a counterrevolution to destroy it. We built it up as a parliamentary democracy and then built up trade unions to challenge parliament and forced a confrontation. We played it as a military dictatorship and then propagandized the troops. It was a logical extension of the war games theory that armies use all the time. We simply extended it into a civilian and economic framework. By the end of the first six months, we could replay the basic political models on our own, using the computer terminal they had installed for us. One of the exercises was to build a Chilean model on the computer and replay the American destabilization plan there. We looked for the weaknesses and found most of them not in Chile but back in the United States, where political and press opposition inhibited American policy. Chisholm liked that.

I tried to build a computer model of Northern Ireland, but no matter how I spread the variables, the model would not work. The same thing that had kept the IRA and the UDA alive on the ground, that civilian community whose loyalties to their neighbors overcame their loyalties to the British Army, just would not fit. We tinkered with the program for weeks, in our spare time, but we never got the model right. No matter how we ran the program, the British Army always wound up controlling the violence, which failed to happen in real life. It was shortly after that incident that our group had its first mental breakdown. The psychologist called a group session and argued that the breakdown had been a positive sign. For the next two weeks we were taken by bus away from Somerset and put through one of the Royal Marine courses at the Shetlands base. The wind blew the worries from our minds, and we felt fit again. The second week we trained with live ammunition, firing on fixed lines. Then they took us back to the computer.

Chisholm swallowed his pride and brought an American instructor in for a week to lecture to us about how the program had worked in Chile. He was very enthusiastic, but even he couldn't make the Ulster model work.

The last outside expert they brought in was a man from Dartmoor. He still had the prison pallor and the haircut. He was American too, one of the hoodlums who got arrested after the Mafia's abortive reconnaissance into the British gambling clubs in the 1960s. He was of little use, but somebody must have told him he would get a shorter sentence if he cooperated, so he tried very hard to tell us how organized crime organized itself.

By the end of the course, nobody seemed certain whether the project had worked or not. We were all worried about the failure of the computer model on Northern Ireland, and three of us wrote a report to Chisholm on the need for an unprecedented authority to give individual agents the right to stop major international loans and credits. The one thing that had emerged clearly from the American experience in Chile was that the economy was the most fragile and responsive element in the state. The Americans had been able to block all World Bank and inter-American bank credits to Chile, pulling something like 100 million dollars out of the economy each year. Our report concluded: "With that kind of economic muscle, agents like ourselves are redundant; without it agents like ourselves are impotent." That made Chisholm very thoughtful.

Then the Cyprus crisis blew up, and Chisholm sent one of us into the island. The original orders called for a reconnaissance job, a simple scouting operation. But he managed to win the confidence of some of Sampson's goons and got the tip-off on the planned assassination of Makarios, which is how the RAF helicopter happened to be near enough to rescue the Archbishop. Chisholm was even more pleased by a final report that said Sampson had only launched his coup after receiving assurances of benign neutrality, if not support, from the Americans. The Somerset graduates could thenceforth do no wrong. Chisholm didn't seem to mind when Whitehall had to tag along with American policy in Cyprus, even after the report of their complicity. Chisholm had made his point. The man who got the information was less pleased; Chisholm made him an instructor.

They had moved us all around since. Two of the blokes were settled in Scotland, waiting for the oil bonanza to brew up a new Ulster and then somehow control it. There was the nervous breakdown, and there was a death of one of the best of us, another SAS man, in Nigeria. We heard of his death after the coup that toppled Gowon, but Chisholm refused to let us put the Nigeria game plan into the computer. One man was sent to Canada, to Montreal, where he infiltrated the Parti Québequois, and another was in East Africa, sniffing around the rotting country misruled by Idi Amin. One stayed in Northern Ireland, in spite of the computer's dire prediction, which left me for Portugal. I

18

know Chisholm had been thinking of sending me to India, but Portugal blew up faster. And he had his dream of a Euro-operation to keep the Americans out.

It was funny how the rule of no socializing during the course had served to keep us apart from each other. I had known the SAS lads for seven tough years, not always on the same jobs and not always even in the same country, but we were still part of a unit when we got back to the SAS camp in Herefordshire at Banbury Lines. I'd done the parachute training course at Abingdon with the one who died in Nigeria, but after the Somerset course there were no more friendships. There was everything else we needed. We all drew a major's pay, tax free, and expenses were generous, but that wasn't the attraction. It was mainly that apart from some Americans and probably some Russians, we were the only men in the world trained to pull countries apart and rebuild them by pure manipulation, and Chisholm played upon that.

There was one time that Chisholm protected us. It was early in 1974, long before the course was finished, and the days were filled with the chugging of a generator to keep the heating and lights going. The country was blacked out, area after area, by the miners' strike, and the pay-instructor told us we were going to be used in Britain. He told us at the end of a lecture and I remember us falling silent as we left for the next class. We hadn't been prepared for it.

We were all very tense for a couple of days, until Chisholm came down and said the flap was over. There was going to be an election. The pay-instructor was replaced shortly afterward. We later heard he had proposed that we be used to check on suspicions that some other agents were doing the very job we had been trained to do, but doing it in Britain. Somehow Chisholm scotched the whole idea, and although we never worked out quite how or why, we were all grateful to him. It was the same odd shock that the army got when it first went into Northern Ireland and realized that it was fighting and being shot at, not in some Persian Gulf village but in the same kind of back street where the soldiers had grown up. They were diving for cover in the doorways of shops like Boots and Woolworth's, just like the ones their mums used back in Liverpool and Sheffield. It was like being in a play where the scenery was set for civil war. The ground was too familiar. Even the swear words the women used at us in Belfast were the same ones we exchanged in the army canteens at night. I remember hearing one of the snatch squads being briefed on how to handle the schoolkids who were throwing rocks and Molotovs at the patrols. "Think of them as your kid brother who needs a belting," the old warrant officer had said. A nasty kind of war.

Down the hall, the old Spanish plumbing gurgled. I took a drink from the bottle of duty-free scotch I had got on the aircraft and rolled myself a cigarette. The match flared in the mirror, its silvering so old that I and the room looked like we had been washed in sepia, in the gentle brown of old photographs. I looked at myself; a soldier of the queen. No redcoats these days, and none of that comforting camouflage gear I had got used to in the Paras. Blue denim everywhere, and not a gun, not a trick suitcase, not a radio-transmitter to be seen. Just two neat bricks of smack, credit cards, press credentials, and a typewriter. A cassette tape-recorder on the chair. Even Castro had started his revolution in Cuba with more than that. I pocketed the cigarette papers and my tobacco and strolled down the hill to the Sol Square to see if the American girl was still reading her paper. Or whether she would reappear.

# 3

She had left the cafe. I went back to the one I had used and gave
the waiter another 100 pesetas and asked him if his friends had
noticed anything more about the girl. He told me to wait and
darted across to the other cafe. He came back with a book of
matches she had left at her table. They advertized the Castellana
Hotel, one of the plush five-star places across town. I thanked
him and strolled down to the Plaza Mayor, past the stamp shops

with the old collectors arguing prices as they did their deals. I had never understood the charm of stamp-collecting, until Chisholm had sent us all a memo on how stamps were even better than heroin for instant money.

I skirted the philatelists, walking across the cobbles of the central square and going down the steps to the street of the knife-grinders and into the network of tiny streets and tinier bars, drinking weak beer and looking at the tourists. The season was getting late. Older people, couples with families and people from Northern Europe mixed with the American students whose early holidays made them dominate the tourist trade in the early summer. I wondered how many of them had come to Spain because they were worried about trouble in Portugal, or who had canceled holidays in Cyprus because of the war. Every summer, the Mediterranean lands saw the largest mass migration in history, more vast than the shifting of the tribes that had toppled ancient Rome, more costly than the Anglo-American invasion of Europe in 1944, and yet with an instinct to avoid trouble. I wondered what the decline of the tourist trade was doing to the Portuguese economy. The tourists could kill a country by voting with their feet.

Idly, I wondered if Chisholm had ever thought of that. It would be easily done: some well-timed bombs in air terminals or in some resorts, with leaflets from some imaginary liberation front claiming the credit. Maybe even fly in a couple of typhoid cases, give the story to the press, and watch the economy crumble as the supply of travelers' checks and deutsche marks and dollars began to freeze up.

There was a lot of foreign money crossing the counters of the Madrid bars that evening, tourists being short-changed in the fashionably dark little bars redesigned just for them. The average Spanish bar is all bright neon light and tiled walls and pink and green prints, but that wasn't what the tourists expected. So the barmen got their names in the tourist guidebooks with their redecorated places, cork on the walls and fashionable spotlights and some broken-down old rustic hired to imitate an old bull-

22

fighter. That was how the guidebooks said it should be and that was how it became, with prices to match.

I strolled back to the Plaza Mayor, visible enough if anyone wanted to follow me. I changed direction to walk toward a plate-glass window, looking at the reflections of the people in the square behind me. Drifting back into the Sol Square, I knew I was clear. For a second or so, I mused on crossing the city to the Castellana and bribing the porter to give me the name of the American girl, but I was already putting her down to coincidence. Tourists go to bullfights, and they go somewhere central like the Sol Square for a drink, and if they have any sense they go by Metro. The fat man reckoned the bullfight rendezvous was secure enough, and the few hours I had been in Madrid had not been long enough for my face to be known. With the Somerset course I had been out of circulation long enough. I decided to forget about the girl and eat some dinner. The fat man had recommended a couple of restaurants, but I wasn't that hungry. I would stay near the center and eat *tapas*, the little snacks the bars serve.

They all had their own speciality. Some places did stuffed mushrooms, others had seafood, but they all did the basic things like soup and fresh smoked ham carved off huge legs that hung on hooks from the ceiling. A *ración* of ham, some bread, and maybe a bowl of the tiny shrimps fried in olive oil and garlic with a glass of wine from La Mancha—I was starting to salivate as I went up the hill toward the main street of José Antonio when I saw the American girl rummaging in one of the open-air book-stalls in the dark little arcades that lead through the Plaza del Carmen.

The stall was full of old Spanish books, with a tiny section of secondhand paperbacks in French and English. She was leafing through a Vonnegut and had just dropped it on a pile of three others she had selected when I edged alongside her and picked up the book as if to buy it. It was *Sirens of Titan*, one of the science fiction titles they used to offer the troops in Belfast. They always offered science fiction and westerns in the unit libraries.

They must have thought it would take our minds off Belfast.

"I'm sorry . . ." she began. "Pardon, *senor* . . ." She smiled and made sign language that she was going to buy the book. Then she recognized me.

"Enjoy the bullfight?" I asked. The old man who ran the bookstore sidled toward us to make the sale.

"Yes," she said. "Thank you." She gave the man a 100 peseta note. He drifted off to get some change.

"When I saw you at the cafe this afternoon I was thinking of calling a policeman," I said. She looked blank. "I'd seen you at the bullfight and then at the cafe. I thought I was being followed by a strange woman. We British get nervous." She grinned wider. "You won't find the policemen here too wonderful," she said. "I like the way they polish their hats," I said. "It inspires confidence."

She put her change away and looked at me speculatively. She had wide-set, very clear eyes. The canvas jacket was draped over her shoulders and it began to slide from her as she put the paperbacks into her bag. I grabbed the shoulder and re-settled it. "Come on," I said. "I'll buy you a drink and tell you about Spanish policemen."

"What about them?" she said, staying put. "Did you know that the only time Franco's paramilitary police were beaten in battle was by British football fans?" I asked her. She grinned again. "Okay," she said. "Buy me a drink and tell me the story."

So we strolled back down to the Sol Square and past the Plaza Mayor while I told her about the Glasgow fans who flew out to Barcelona for the European cup match. They didn't like the referee and they didn't like the Guardia Civil everywhere but they had developed a considerable affection for the local wine. They called it Electric Soup. When enough of the soup had gone down and the referee had made enough bad decisions and the Guardia Civil had started to assert themselves, the Glaswegians went for the police with bottles. The police reserves went in with riot shields and tear gas, so the Scots responded with a volley of bottles, ripped up the wooden seats they were supposed to sit on, and charged the Guardia. The Guardia broke under the first charge, counterattacked.

We got to one of the Galician bars where the counter is heaped with fat, muddy snails, and I ordered two *tintos* and told her about the Scottish charge that drove the police out of the stadium, while the Barcelona crowd cheered them to the skies. Franco had never been too popular with Barcelona, and very few Scotsmen had to buy themselves a drink that night.

"I'm not too sure I believe that," she said. "But it's a nice story." She smiled encouragingly.

"That means you can't have any Scottish blood," I protested. I wondered if she would keep the conversation going if I let it die.

"My grandmother used to claim there was Indian blood in her family."

"I'm not too sure I believe that," I said. "All the Yanks I've ever met have bragged about their Indian blood. I always thought you killed them off too fast to give them the chance." I ordered some more snails and two of the sailors' coffees, laced with *aguardiente* from Portugal. I set fire to the spirit with a match and showed her how to drink from the far side of the rim, through the blue flame.

"I saw bullfights in Mexico," she said. "I liked them. But the bulls are much bigger here. It's more stately, more of a ritual. Crueler." She shrugged. "Maybe I don't know enough about it."

"Are you on holiday alone?" I asked.

She shook her head, the hair rippling silkily. She was a living testimony to American cosmetics. "I've been with two girl-friends, but they have to go back. I'll stay awhile. I have some money left. Back in the States, I'll have to find a job. Not yet."

I thought about how much it would cost her each night, staying at the Castellana, and then she said, "If I keep staying at the cheap pensions, I have enough money for the rest of the year."

I thought about that. Just having a matchbook from a luxury hotel didn't mean she had to be staying there, but it nagged at me. We chatted about Madrid and France and London, where she had been before and where she might go next. I said I was heading for Portugal and she said that sounded good. I told her I was a journalist, heading off to cover the Portuguese revolution, and she talked about working on a student newspaper at Berkeley. She had been born in California, she said, so she went to Berkeley. She had been there six years, getting one general arts degree and a master's in political science. She thought she might try and work for a Congressman when she got back to the States.

She asked about my journalism, I muttered vaguely about a lot of time in Northern Ireland. She asked if it had been dangerous, so I told her the story about the Fleet Street man who had checked into the Europa, put his suitcase on the bed, and gone down for a drink at the bar when the bomb went off in the bus station behind the hotel. It blew in the windows of his room so they shifted him to a room at the front of the hotel, and he left his case on the bed and went back to his drink. He had just taken a sip when the bomb went off in the pub across the street, blowing in the windows of the new room. He'd taken the next plane back to London, never unpacking the suitcase.

I asked her how long she had been in Madrid. Three days. She had done the usual museums, taken a day trip to Toledo, seen a flamenco dance and a bullfight. She lit herself a cigarette with a match from another little book advertising the Castellana. I asked where she had got it. She laughed and said she and her friends had gone there for a drink and stolen some matchbooks. I believed her.

She went off to the tiny toilet at the back of the bar, while I rolled myself a cigarette. She had left her canvas bag at the table, so I looked inside and quickly skimmed through her passport. Marianne Thayer, twenty-four, born in Whittier, California. An entry stamp for Madrid airport three days ago. Stamps for France and Britain. Earlier stamps for Mexico and Chile. No special distinguishing marks. Cigarettes and a little heap of matchbooks in the bottom of the bag. A heavy room key with a metal tag that read Pension Lis. A map of Madrid, a plastic bottle of skin lotion. Paperbacks, a little bottle of vitamin pills, some nail varnish. She had taken the handbag to the toilet with her. Some museum admission stubs and some sunglasses. I heard the toilet flush, so I shoved the bag back under her chair and lit my cigarette and signaled to the barman for two more of the sailors' coffees and a bowl of the garlic-fried shrimp.

When she came back to the table I offered her a shrimp. She opened her mouth and I popped it in. "More," she said. I ordered another bowl and said it was good that she liked them. She raised her eyebrows. I explained that I loved them, but the garlic was strong and as long as she tasted the same way everything would be fine. She said she liked the smell of garlic but she was getting sick of the sailors' coffees, and why didn't we have some more wine.

"Have you traveled much?" I asked her. "Apart from this trip?" I was feeling mellow, relaxed, enjoying the sight of her. But I wanted to see if what she told me matched the entries in her passport. Unless she had left the bag behind deliberately.

"Just in South America—Mexico, Panama. My father's in the military. I went down to visit him, where he was based. The army paid for the flights—I saw more of the PX and the beaches than the sights." She smiled lazily, and I imagined her on beaches.

"Are you close to him—your father?"

"We used to argue a lot," she was shaking her head. The *aguardiente* was making her talk. "Vietnam mostly. He was over in 'Nam when I was at college. Going on the peace demos, and he used to write pompous letters back to me about not betraying the flag." She shrugged. "As though I was betraying him. Him personally. There was a big fight when we came back. My mother too. She was against the war, but she died." She looked up at me, watching for my reactions, to see which side I'd been on. "Vietnam caused a lot of fights in families."

"Northern Ireland did the same in Britain," I said. "Still doing it." I kept my voice neutral.

"Yeah," she said over the rim of her glass, drinking the wine that had come. "Yeah, the war goes on." She said it lightly, but her eyes were sad. They were well made up. No great smear of eye shadow on the lids, just the thin pencil lines and mascara, and she used that actors' trick of putting a tiny blob of red in

27

the corner of each eye to make them look bigger. I thought how long it had been since I had just sat and chatted with a girl. It reminded me of being on leave, two weeks away from Belfast on one of the package tours the army gave us discounts for. It was always a little like this, foreign food, Mediterranean summer, wine rather than beer, putting your best shirt onto skin that was tender from the sun, going to a disco and picking up a girl and later asking her not to scratch my sunburn. Remembering more clearly, there hadn't been much talking with those girls. Dancing, drinks, laughs, and bed, but not much talking. I knew her name was Marianne but she didn't know I knew. I asked what her name was. She said Marianne. I said that was a nice name and I was David. We finished the shrimp and had some cheese and I said I wasn't a great flamenco fan so why didn't we just stroll the streets and explore.

"Is there a red light district?" she wanted to know. I said there had to be and I thought I knew where it was. She said she liked them, the arrogant way the girls lounged and the looks on the men's faces and watching the cops go inside to collect their rake-offs. I asked if that was how it was in California, and she said she knew it best in Tijuana but she reckoned it was the same all over the world. I told her about the one in Amsterdam where the girls sit on chairs in the windows with the bed behind them, and how the ones on the second floor had mirrors positioned beside the window so you could still see their faces. She asked if that meant the girls were independent, without pimps, and I said I thought there were always pimps. I had known one or two in Ulster, and the girls always seemed to be in love with them. The girls needed a regular man. She said I was a chauvinist. I said I thought she was a name-caller and she grinned and we went off to look for the red light district.

We found it on the far side of José Antonio, down past the Fuencarral. It began with strip joints, faded color pictures of enormous breasts in the windows, rock music blaring out, and tough guys on the door. A lot of cops, a few girls in the bars, not many clients.

"I suppose it's because of Sunday," she said. "In a Catholic

28

country, people go to Mass and feel pure again." I said it would probably wear off by tomorrow and the streets would be full. We strolled on, in silence, a little depressed. She said she had really liked those shrimp, so we stopped at the next bar and had another bowl and I suggested we find a discotheque. I liked dancing. She said fine, not too enthusiastic, but we hailed a cab and left the choice to the driver. The evening was fading and the conversation was drying up as fast as one of the river beds in Oman. I remembered those two degrees of hers and all the small talk I knew felt foolish. So it goes, I thought, and she murmured, "So it starts." I hadn't realized I had thought aloud.

I turned to study her, the profile in alternate light and shadow as we passed the street lamps. Her eyelashes were long and real, the lips full, the jaw firm and her eyes nervous as she turned to meet my gaze. "What is it, David?" She sounded solemn. I was going to be flip and say "Just browsing," but I shook my head. "You were miles away," I said, "and I was wondering where. Did that street upset you?"

"A little. It was none of my business, but hookers interest me. I was thinking of a time when I felt like one. I remembered something my mother told me once, the last time I saw her before she died. I'd been through a bad affair at Berkeley, a guy who was about to be drafted for Vietnam. He didn't want to go, but his father was a lawyer and he was reading law and there was a whole future waiting for him if he did it the right way, the American way. He could have gone into his father's law firm and been rich and prosperous and comfortable. His father could have fixed it so that he didn't have to go to Vietnam. He could have had a safe, honorable berth in the States for two years, or maybe Germany.

"We used to talk and talk about what he should do. He could have gone to Canada, just skipped the draft and gone to college there and waited for an amnesty or something. Or he could have gone to a pricey shrink who would have certified him too delicate for the army, or he could have volunteered for the navy and been safe enough that way. I wanted him to go to Canada, because I knew he'd never enjoy going into daddy's law firm and becoming

29

rich and venal like his old man. He was a nice guy, very confused but very nice—too nice to make the decision. I kept on sleeping with him even when I knew he was too weak to decide. Even when I knew he was so weak he would get drafted and go to Vietnam and probably get killed out of pure inertia. We were making it together one night when I realized I had no respect, no belief, no anything for him anymore. I didn't even like him, but it was one of the best nights we ever had together. I woke up knowing it was over but I still didn't leave him. It was like screwing a different man, an anonymous man. I guess it was like being a hooker, only in some way I used to enjoy it."

We had stopped at a traffic light. She reached for a cigarette and lit it. I took her pack and lit one for myself as she leaned far back in the seat and blew smoke straight up to the car roof. I asked what her mother had told her.

"I was coming to that. My father was in Washington, not long back from Vietnam, and my mother was staying at her mother's home in Whittier. It was Thanksgiving. All the family were there except father, and we all got a little loaded. She and I sat up talking pretty late and I told her about Jeff—that was the guy. And she told me that she felt that way a lot of times with my father. There wasn't much affection left, there wasn't much of anything, but they shared a bedroom so they screwed from time to time. No matter who the guy is, or how long it lasts, she said, there are times when you'll feel like a hooker. You'll want him to leave the money and go."

The cab pulled up at the disco. The driver turned around. I hardly noticed him. Marianne was looking at me, and there was something not challenging, not defiant in her eyes, but close to both those moods. She looked a bit like one of the kids the snatch squads used to grab in Belfast for throwing rocks. Proud of having done something without knowing what it was.

"I've often felt like a customer, Marianne. That's just the way people are. But I've never felt like a pimp. And I don't think you've ever felt like a madame. That gives us both a whole new perversion to look forward to. Now do you want to come and dance it out of your system or do you want to go back to your hotel? I'd rather you stayed."

She wound down the window and threw out her cigarette. "Pay the man. Let's see how a Limey shakes ass." She opened the cab door with a flourish but it scraped on the high curb with an obscene sound and she giggled and stuck her thumb in her mouth and looked at me in mock remorse. I paid the man and gave him a tip to shut him up about his scraped door and then I paid the doorman because we weren't members and we went down the stairs holding hands.

I have a theory that people dance in much the same way they make love. You either know your body and like it and are confident about it or you aren't. It doesn't much matter what shape it's in, just so long as you and your body aren't strangers. Marianne was very, very sure of hers. We had a DJ who was in love with heavy soul, and she moved to it with a flowing rhythm, her feet locked to the floor, all the movement from her hips and shoulders. She saw me watching and bit her lip and slid her hands up the back of her head to lift her hair and thrust her hips forward and back like a piledriver before dropping her hair and looking demure again. I could have hugged her.

The place was expensively furnished, with dark green velvet seats and tables in glass and chrome, lit by high spotlights that threw tiny cones of light onto our drinks, while red and green and blue spots flared in time to the beat of the music. The dance floor itself was the usual truncated size, but the other couples moved back a little to watch Marianne as the music slowed and all the other dancers moved together. I was moving forward to dance closely with her but she just slowed her rhythm and moved alone, her feet sliding and her arms moving low as the Otis Redding lased heavily from the speakers. I stepped to her and around her, making a frame for her to sway in, moving to her left to match her and edging back as she came forward. We got it right, her arms whirling outspread as I locked my hands before me, my arms rising as hers fell. As the music faded out she eased forward, her trunk circling gently until her breasts were flicking

31

my chest. I held her tight to me as the DJ turned up the volume for the harsh chords of "Satisfaction."

This was my music. I had my first long leave from the army after doing the Para course and I stayed with a mate from the Paras at his parents' place in Hendon. We were both eighteen, and we used to spend most nights at a pub in Wealdstone called the Railway Tavern. It shook every night, partly from the trains plunging through below the bridge but mainly because the landlord was a rhythm and blues man and he used to hire a new group called the Rolling Stones. In those days, before the first record, Mick Jagger used to collect your five shillings at the door before clambering onto the tiny stage and belting the numbers through a Woolworth's amplifier. They were great nights, and though he never sang "Satisfaction" he sang all the rest, and the way he moved on the five square feet of stage was all the dancing lessons I ever needed.

It's a tricky rhythm for dancing, the vocal line as slow and majestic as the beat itself, and you either move slow and heavy, dancing like a bass man plays, or you trick out and weave your own movements on the stately foundation of the thudding drum.

I went the slow route, rocking up from the knees and slamming my fists together for the beat, letting my head jerk with Keith Richard's guitar line as I sang out with the words I knew by heart. Marianne moved like Jagger, her knees arcing proud and high, her hands clapping a rhythm clear above her head into a pirouette and a second's mean stance before she stomped her feet to the floor for "Maybe next week/can't you see I'm on a losing streak" and we leaned forward, our foreheads touching, to roar at each other "I can't get no . . . Nonono," and I was swaying back again when her hands locked behind my head and she licked my throat from the groove where the collarbones meet up to the rasp of my chin. I put my arms behind her back and slid my fingers down the waistband of her jeans, feeling the rising curve of her buttocks and pulling her urgently to me. Her hands drifted to my hair and trailed over the top of my skull until I felt her fingertips on my closed eyelids. I felt her tongue flick lightly

32

at my lips and then she had whirled proudly away and we finished the song.

Every time in my life when I knew I was going to pull a girl I wanted, there had been a long relaxation trickling into my nerves. Whatever signal a woman gives, a smile or a touch or a kiss or a welcomed caress, there was the second to realize that her decision was made and everything after that instant was set, predestined, the future fixed. But this time there was no relaxation. There was Marianne, arching her back for the music as Eric Clapton drove into the opening bars of "Layla," and then me, shoulders churning from my waist as the first rippling riff of the guitar flooded the dance floor, and then there were both of us, wheeling and weaving together as the chords babbled on into a race of sound that we were running together. There was no fatigue in this music, no progression and no end until that stunning moment when the hidden bass surges over the guitar and the key changes and the pace changes and the piano drifts in and the dervish madness ends and the music mocks at its own pomposity and all the dancers sway to a halt.

"Enough," I said, and we finished our drinks and picked up our coats and climbed up the stairs to the night. We walked, almost aimlessly, and we had barely begun to wonder where we were when a cab cruised into the street and we drove back to Plaza del Carmen. In the back seat, Marianne lay back into my shoulder and I stroked her hair in silence.

We left the cab and she held my waist as we walked very slowly back through the dark arcade. We did not have to ask or say or wonder where we were going. It was all unspoken and as certain as the rhythm of her thigh pressed to the side of mine.

"Do you feel like a customer?" she said, muffled and low against my chest. I felt her breath through my shirt.

"Maybe I feel like a very old and very favorite customer might feel," I said after a while. "Do you think you showed a Limey how to shake ass?"

I felt the sharp bite of her teeth just above my nipples. Her mouth nuzzled further to the open neck of my shirt and she kissed me and worried my chest hairs with her teeth. "I think I'm going to show him more than that," she said. "Big mouth Yank," I said. She giggled and the length of her shook all down my side. "You should be so lucky," she said, and we were at my place.

I slipped 100 pesetas to the grinning landlord and followed her into the room. I pressed the button on the cassette and we had Stevie Wonder. She pulled a joint out of her purse and I gave her a light. She said she had brought some grass through Customs in her shoe. She passed it to me and I pulled a toke. It was reasonable Mexican, well dried and rolled thin in the American way. There was no roach and the smoke was hot in my mouth. I passed it back. "Far out, Marianne," I said. She smiled, her face reddening and a little swollen from holding in the smoke.

I had a red sweat shirt in my case that I draped over the table lamp by the bed. The room went darker, a deep red on the walls and marking her features with sudden shadow. Her eyes were very large as she lay back on the bed, her jeans dark and long on the white cover.

"Don't breathe it out," I said, and pushed all the air out of my lungs. "Now breathe it into me."

I leaned to her and put my mouth onto her and she breathed out very slowly and easily into my lungs. I held it, took the joint and pulled a stiff toke into my mouth. I signaled to her to breathe out. She did and put her mouth on mine and kissed me, her tongue tracing the shape of my lips, and then I gave her the smoke.

We did this as the joint burned, slipping my tongue into her mouth as she held the smoke, running it along the inside of her lips, swirling at the corners of her mouth, my hand stroking gently with one finger along her side. We finished the joint, and her tongue found mine and made its own slow journey from the roof of my mouth to the lips, her fingers tickling at my throat and mine slipping under the cotton of her T-shirt.

I inched forward on the bed, to raise the other hand to her face, the fingers scratching gently at the back of her neck. She eased under me, the blouse riding up, my hand smoothing the softness of the curve of her breast, and her thigh pressing warm against my groin. She began to unbutton my shirt, her fingers teasing, tugging at the hairs on my belly. We slipped off her shirt and she pulled my head down to her breasts, my tongue trailing down the hollow of her neck to the cleavage between her breasts. They were small and neat and warm on my cheeks, the nipples rising as my tongue zig-zagged from one to the other. My hand traced formless words, one finger trailing the other, over the softness of her belly, and I used my feet to worm off my shoes.

I took my mouth lower, gently licking the soft crease where the base of her breast thrust from her, nipping softly as my lips traced down to the top of her jeans. I licked at her fingers as they scurried to unzip and my teeth met at the flat rim of her hair, tugging gently as she worked the jeans over her hips. My mouth moved quickly back to hers and I rose to my knees, pulling off my shirt as she, newly naked, worked my jeans and pants down. Her hands came up to my shoulders, the nails scratching down over my chest and stomach as she kissed the sides of my thighs. Her hands cupped my balls as her tongue began to glisten at the base of my cock. I leaned to take her head in my hands and raise her mouth to mine. I stood beside the bed, throwing my jeans onto hers, and climbed back to her, diving my head to the warmth of her hips and bringing my groin to her mouth. Looking up, I saw her grasp me and raise the head to her mouth. Her eyes were closed. My tongue tickled to the moistness of her.

Outside the door, there was the sound of argument. I grinned as I tongued her. I had found the tiny hole earlier in the afternoon, and hung my shirt over it as I stripped. The man behind the desk would charge 100 pesetas to use the peephole.

I pulled away from her mouth, whispering that I wanted to screw. She still clutched me as I lay beside her, easing her body above. She rose on her knees, still holding my cock, to run it along the groove of her as my hands rose to pinch and caress her nipples. Her hips sank onto me and my throat locked into a long groan of delight. She bent to kiss me, her hands at my shoulders. My feet rose to touch her buttocks, to rock them into the rhythm of her moving as my own hips rose and fell. My fingers slid from her breasts to her back, creeping down the backbone to the crease of her thighs where they nipped at the hand-smooth mounds of her, sliding to the last hole, the tiny wrinkled spot that never had its due. Just one finger, nail-deep, probing her arse as her thighs locked.

I thrust her very high, following with my body, forcing her back so she sat on my thighs, still hips bucking now beyond control. I leaned forward, my hand under her back, laying her down as her head tossed from side to side, my weight on her, my hands flat on the bed, rising up onto my arms to drive my body high over hers. Her hips rocked from side to side as I probed as deep as I could go, pushing my hands behind her thighs to open her deeper, her legs right back beside her head, my chest on her calves and pumping like fury as we crashed and crashed onto the old but valiant Spanish bed, my cries as loud as hers as her legs sloped down to wrap around me and her damp face crushed into my neck. An hour, or four, we lay, my cock limp inside her, our hips shivering at each other, the sweat cooling on my back. We slept. At times I felt her tongue in my ear. At times I squeezed the breast where my hand had stayed. We slept.

# 4

I left her in the car at the border post outside Badajoz, taking her passport and mine for the guards to stamp, trying hard not to remember that I had enough heroin to addict a regiment in the little hired car. Marianne had picked up her case from the cheap hotel where she and her friends had been staying. I had woken early and slowly that morning, barely opening my eyes and seeing the hump of her shoulder and breast and hips stretching down under the sheet beside me like a row of little Alps. I thought first of the excuse I could use—the fat man had advised me to cross the border with a girl. In a way I was following official advice. I could claim she helped my cover, and call her my photographer or something. I knew she would not take kindly to being called my secretary.

Then I thought about the job I was going to do, not dangerous in itself but dangerous if the security got broken. And it's hard to run an operation from a hotel room with a woman in it. Then I remembered back to the bullfight and the trip on the Metro and the sight of her following me to the cafe, and I wondered who had picked up whom. I picked my way through the memories of the evening as if they were a minefield. The coincidence of meeting her at the old bookstall—when it was still in the tiny area of streets where she had last seen me. The happy way she let herself be bought a drink, and then the casual leaving of her passport in the shoulder bag when she went to the toilet. That innocent passport and those big, wide eyes. I looked up at the ceiling and knew that I didn't believe she was a plant. And then I thought it through all over again and knew that if she were a plant then she would want to stay with me. And that I would have to take her along, and watch what she did and find out who had planted her and why. I looked down at her again and knew I wanted to take her along anyway.

She asked if she could come with me over breakfast, standing dipping our *churros* into our coffee at a street kiosk. She said she had planned to move on anyway.

There was no way I could hear her say that and not be happy, but I gave her the warnings: I would be busy a lot of the time. I might have to move around fast, the deadlines and the stories had to come first. She said she could help, and she could share some of the bills and she wanted to stay with me anyway. The morning was full of anyways, each of us manufacturing reasons to do what we wanted to do. Anyway.

We stopped for petrol in Talavera and I bought her an ashtray from the local pottery. It had Wellington's face and 1809, the date of his battle there, painted on the inside. She kissed me thank you and asked if the British always bragged about their conquests. I told her we only bragged about beating the French. The rest didn't count. She knew nothing of the great campaign when Wellington clawed his way from Lisbon across Spain to the belly of France in seven long years of fighting. We drove on to the border country, the hard land they called Estremadura, its passes so long and steep that the car groaned and the memories of the military schoolroom came back. Napoleon saying that in Spain, a small army is beaten and a large army starves. Looking back at the ridges we had climbed and the dry land stretching behind she said she knew what Napoleon meant. I told her about the guerrilla war the Spaniards had fought against the French and she said it sounded like Vietnam.

It became a game for her, seeing a castle and asking me to tell her about another army, another campaign. Between castles I would describe battles to her. I showed her the pass in the north at Salamanca, where Wellington waited until Marmont's line was too extended and then charged the gap the French had opened in their front. She pored over the map for the little crossed swords that marked a battle and asked about them all—Albuera, where Beresford had marched his men into a gully and they volleyed it out with the French, to the point where whole companies were commanded by corporals and the British had taken 60 percent casualties before the French broke.

She wanted to know where I had learned all this, so I told her about the army school I had attended after my parents were shot in Cyprus, where history was a long list of British generals and military victories on land and sea. She talked about school in the States, with the oath of allegiance every morning and a long list of American victories in the history class.

"That was part of the whole Vietnam fuck-up," she said. "We had always won before and we had always been right before and we all had to learn that we were losing and that we were wrong too. Most of us cared more about losing than being wrong. Those schools did a good job."

"Be fair, Marianne. There is no other known instance in history of a great power pulling out from a war that it could have won, in a purely military sense, just because its own people made the generals withdraw. I'd call it the first known victory for public opinion, and if I were a Yank I'd be proud of that." I half expected her to tell me how Nixon and his gang had tried to browbeat and burgle and repress public opinion when she said, "Don't be a God-on-our-sider, Dave. Not you."

"A what?"

"A God-on-our-side man. We always learned that America never loses because God's on our side. The ones who took us into Vietnam did it because God was on our side. Then we get rid of Nixon and that was because God was on our side too. I can't stand people who are that complacent about it, so don't tell me you are."

"You can't say God's on anybody's side after you've seen the Christian tribes blowing hell out of each other in Northern Ireland. And when they hanged one of the guerrillas who helped shoot my parents in the back, the Greeks held a memorial service for him."

"You're being obtuse, Dave. I'm not talking about God. I'm talking about attitudes. Complacencies. And whose side are you on anyway?"

I pointed ahead to where the huge fortress of Elvas dominated the plain that opened out from the passes into Spain. We coasted down beside the castle and brought out the salami and cheese and wine she had bought in Talavera and sat in the stubble of the field looking up at the huge curtain walls and the cleared ground before them. She didn't say anything as we ate, and she didn't have any crockery to slam around to make her point, but it was clear she wanted an answer. I wasn't sure I had an honest one. The flip answer was to say that I was on my own side, and on hers, and on the side of the few people I cared for, and that was true enough. I thought back to the course I had gone through in Somerset, the number of times they told us we were really being trained to defend free institutions. When they told it to us I knew most of us were remembering the dirty jobs south of the Irish border, kill teams going across to find the Provo hard men who were resting up around Roscommon. In defense of free institutions.

"I'm on the side of the quiet life," I began, "but like most journalists, the less quiet it is, the more stories I write and the more money I make. So there is a built-in bias. You are in the same position—you took a degree in political science. So you are equipped to comprehend things like confrontations, to make a living out of them. I have been a soldier, like your father, fighting for something I'm not too well equipped to judge. Northern Ireland was an easy choice compared to Vietnam. We can all say we hate terrorists, but the labels don't mean much unless you watch who is sticking them onto people. The Catholics called us terrorists, and at times I couldn't blame them."

I couldn't look at her because I was talking a lie. It was easy enough to claim I was a humble reporter and I didn't make the judgments and I could have stopped the conversation with that. But I had been troubled about it all before. There were nights in Somerset when the callousness of what we were learning to do opened up like a huge dark pit of sleeplessness before me and I used to get up and read in the night until it all went away.

"What did you do that made them call you a terrorist?"

"The search missions, mainly. If you had to arrest somebody you did it at night to be sure he was in, and you had to pull the house apart searching for arms while the kids were under your feet and crying everywhere and his wife was screeching at you and the neighbors were banging their garbage can lids on the pavement so that his mates could set up an ambush at the end of the street. It was mainly that, but we could have gone in as nice as pie and they would still have called us terrorists. Just because we were there and we were not Irish. It was the label they stuck on us. There aren't any pure wars, love. Even the one against Hitler involved things like strategic bombing and Hiroshima and letting Stalin get his bloody hands on half of Europe. He was a Hitler, too, but we couldn't do without him. Christ, you Americans ought to know. Look at your own Civil War, and don't say it was fought to stop slavery or I'll puke."

41

"Warfare. Love it or leave it," she said, reaching over me for the wine bottle. "All right, Dave, I know you don't always get the option. But what do you want to see happen in Portugal? Do you want to see a nice Western European democracy come out of all this, or a nice soft European kind of Communism, or what? Where do you stand now we're in the country?"

"I want to see them get the democracy first and then find out for themselves. I'll know it's working if the police take their guns off and start cycling around the countryside like the British bobbies used to. And when I see newspapers that aren't owned by rich men or big political parties, and radio stations that let people talk back to them. I don't know, love. One thing is for sure—they'll need to get rich to do it. That's why Britain used to be so nice and why it's getting nasty. Wealth. It's as simple as that. Even your precious anti-Vietnam peace movement wouldn't have meant much unless America was so rich it could afford to maintain the world's biggest student population. Poverty makes for harsh solutions, Marianne. You know what Germany went through before Hitler clawed his way to the top. Prosperity, jobs, free education, lots of choices—that's what makes a democracy work. That's the long-term answer for Northern Ireland, make them all rich enough so they all have jobs and so unemployed Catholics don't grow up hating the Protestants. It will be the same in Portugal—joining the Common Market is the only solution. The country is too small and too poor to make it alone."

I could hear my voice trailing off in the hot sun, and Marianne had her eyes closed and her head resting on my thigh. She wasn't quite asleep and she said she really had been listening, but it took us another twenty minutes to get the car packed again and to get back on the road.

Near Santarem I turned off the straight road through the Alantejo farmlands and drove north to the plateau where the cavalry school trains its armored cars and light tanks. The plain was empty, and from the road above the barracks I could see the tanks lined up, unused. On the square, soldiers lounged. No squads on parade, no shouted orders. Whatever else the Portuguese Army was doing, it wasn't training. Marianne said they all looked kind of lazy and I told her how they had been defeated by the guerrillas in Africa and how defeat always shamed an army.

Like the Viet Cong, she said. Yes, I said, but the Viet Cong had a regular army to back them up. There were no disciplined battalions like the North Vietnamese on the side of the Africans. They did it on their own, and they still won. Guerrillas always win, she said, so I told her about the British winning in Malaya in the 1950s and how Che Guevara failed in Bolivia.

We drove on to Lisbon and she asked me to tell her more about Wellington's campaign. We were passing through the low jumble of hills that Wellington had fortified to hold off Masséna's invasion. I told her how Wellington retreated slowly, delaying Masséna's army as it ponderously invaded Portugal, and using the time to drive all the cattle and all the people and carry all the food behind the fortified lines he built. The road climbed and there was the wide river Tagus on our left.

"The defense lines went from here to the sea. He used every hill and every fold in the ground and built strong points and trenches, and Masséna took one look and knew he would never break through to Lisbon. The British Navy held command of the sea, so Wellington could be supplied and reinforced, and the Navy also held the river. Masséna spent a hard winter in front of the lines, and even tried to build a bridge of boats across the Tagus, to take the fortifications in the rear. But the navy gunboats and the Portuguese guerrillas and his own soldiers' hunger stopped him and he retreated back into Spain."

She asked intelligent questions—how much ammunition they carried, what the range of their muskets was, how they transported artillery, could an army live off the country? We chatted military history as we drove by the Tagus, and then in the distance we saw the huge bridge that spans the river at Lisbon. One of the longest and most magestic in the world. It was a kilometer wide and the towers rose more than six hundred feet. The sun was starting to fall in the sky behind it, so it seemed to dance about the glinting surface of the river.

We reached Lisbon and drove straight to the Tivoli, where all the journalists stayed. I had a press card, a telex credit card for an Australian newspaper and a British feature agency. I'd have to go to the ministry for a place on the interview list and Portuguese credentials. I had heard enough of the gossip back in London to take an annex room with a balcony, and we showered and drifted into the bar. It was very good for the national ego. Dutchmen, Swedes, Italians—when the world's press gathers it gossips in English. All except the French, and they usually don't gossip.

So. If you wanted to interview this general, take a bottle of Black Label. That general hangs out in his nightclub. This politician likes blonds. The Communists are being challenged by the Maoists in the Chemical Union. Go and see the Lisnave shipyard. Used to run three shifts a day and now they hold political meetings in the dry dock. The commandos are being moved to a new base. Extra artillery loads going to the coastal batteries at Cascais. The new American ambassador was in Chile when they had the coup—know what that means? The Chinese agency Hain-Hua had a man in town. He saw the Tass man come into the same restaurant so he left, spitting as he walked past the Russian. Reuters were in trouble—the bureau chief was on his honeymoon and they had brought a new guy in from Algeria. UPI had been beaten on the new government. That general was a queer.

A boy brought the evening papers, and the pocket dictionaries came out, people poring over the pages, drifting to telephones. Reverse-charge call to Amsterdam, London, Stockholm. What are you doing for dinner tonight?

I was going to Estoril, a day ahead of schedule, to check out the bar where I was to meet Joao. We were finishing our beers when one of the younger journalists drifted over. He had long hair and a denim shirt with Portuguese cigarettes sticking ostentatiously from a pocket. Heavy Spanish boots and tanned hands. Marianne studied him with interest. He smiled at us and sat down.

"Hi," he said. English.

"Hello," I said. "Your father sends his regards. He was very pleased by a bullfight."

"Phil," he stuck out his hand. We shook it and I said this is Marianne and I'm David and asked what he would like to drink.

"Dad called last night. He said you'd owe me a beer. That'll do. You want to know about the Left here. You in journalism too?" he asked Marianne. She smiled, saying nothing. Clever girl, Marianne.

We drank for an hour, listening to Phil talking about the evils of the Portuguese Communists, who were almost as evil as the old Fascists, and the beauties and clarities of the far left groups who would never betray the working class. The fat man had done well enough out of the Madrid job to send him to boarding school in England. That and a year or so at a new university, one conviction for possession of hash, one conviction for obstruction at a Vietnam demo in London. He hadn't come very close to the working class. Maybe he preferred the ones who didn't speak English. He had a Canon around his neck. The file in London said he scraped a living as a press photographer. A left-wing paper in Paris and occasional shift work for the magazines. I said I'd buy him lunch tomorrow and Marianne and I drove to Estoril, taking the *autostrada* out of town and then the coast road. She observed that the water was dirty and I tried to translate the painted slogans that hid the walls.

"Armed Forces and the People—forever"; "Fight the social fascists"; "Death to Spinola and the CIA"; "Kill the reds." All very unimaginative. Social fascists were Communists as seen by the Left—I think. These things change. The heat was out of the sun and the town streets were beginning to fill with strollers. The cafes were full and lights beginning to glow in the taller apartments.

The bar called the Navigator was just beyond the chic little square where the fishermen were selling fresh sardines. There was no street lighting and the road was holed. The front of the bar was painted green, with obscene red squids and blue fish leaping around a huge painted sailing ship. There were beads on the door and the sound of a jukebox. We went in and ordered two beers in touristese.

London had given me the personnel files on the old Angolan

network, the little importers and railroad shipping clerks and dock officials who made up Britain's team to stop illegal supplies from reaching Rhodesia. All the files were very thin, not even bulging with the pink expense slips, but they all contained a photograph. There was nobody here I knew. We nibbled at the little yellow beans the barman brought us on a plate, and looked at the bar.

There was one door to the back, marked with cutout signs for a man and for a woman. The window at the front was high and covered with heaped cans of beer. There were strip windows high at the side of the room and about a dozen tables. Five other people, not counting the barman. The record changed on the jukebox. I used the toilet. A window just big enough to crawl through, too small to escape through if you were in a hurry. I soaked some toilet paper and folded it into a wedge and put it behind the door. Just in case.

There was a new face at the bar when I came out, and I knew him. He had run a shipping office in Luanda and had been paid a bonus for being the first to let us know about the Yanks buying Rhodesian chrome. Chisholm had liked that and sent him a bonus. His name was Joao, but there were two others called Joao on the files. There was something else about this one. I forced my memory back to the library in the basement off Curzon Street. The green and yellow walls, the gray banks of files, the codings on the files with the brown strips to show the network was being shifted. The bonus payment, the address, the name of his bank, the birthmark on his left thigh. Note—thought to be homosexual, possible pederast. Ah yes, that Joao.

I had told Marianne we might be meeting somebody, and she was studying the faces. Joao had a neat little bum, tightly packed into his new jeans. She looked at that. Careful, I told her, he looks like a fag. How can you tell, she asked. Intuition. He might be bi. He might. I ordered two more beers, grinning at the barman and holding up two fingers.

"You English," Joao said. I nodded. "They want two more beers. Cold ones," he told the barman. "On holiday?" he asked

46

me, making conversation. "A lot of English come to Portugal on holiday," he said.

"They used to. Before the revolution." I waved for a third beer and he joined us at the table, hitching up his jeans at the knee.

"Maybe the tourists prefer Spain," said Joao. "They like the bullfights. We have bullfights too. Only thing is we don't kill the bull. That's the difference between us and Spain. The tourists like to see the bull killed."

"What happens to the bulls in Portugal?" said Marianne. Joao told her how they fought them with horses. His hands toyed with a tiny spill of folded blue paper. He opened it halfway so I could see the picture of the Madrid bullring and then folded it again. This was the right Joao. He talked on about the bulls, turning the half-ticket in his hands. He dropped it on the table and went to the bar for more beers. I took the half-ticket and went to the toilet. It matched the half in my hip pocket. The fat man had got it here very fast, and I was a day early. I went back into the bar.

"I lost my business in Angola," Joao was telling Marianne. "Maybe I'll try politics here. Everybody is in politics. We're all Peoples' Democrats now. Maybe I'll call myself a Portuguese Peoples' Democrat. Free bullfights twice a week and no taxes."

Marianne went to the toilet. I told him the car was open and the packet was under the driver's seat. There were 100 grams in the packet and the rest could wait till we met again with the others.

"We'd better meet later tonight," he said. "Can you get rid of the girl?" I nodded. "There'll be some others at the meeting tonight. Some Lisbon people. We had to bring them in because of the . . . you know." He shuffled his finger and thumb. He meant because of the heroin.

"Who are they and what do they want?" I didn't like this.

"One of them is my brother-in-law. It's okay. He was in stolen cars and things. He has friends in the docks. Smuggling. He was starting to go straight before the revolution. Buying property and villas in the Algarve. Honest robbery. He'll be there and his partner. They like dealing in this stuff."

"What do they know about London?"

"They guessed a lot. My brother-in-law knows that I'm getting the stuff from an Englishman. He knows I don't deal so he wonders why. His partner has a cousin who was in our group back in Luanda. These are two bright guys. They can work it out. You'll meet them tonight. You know the maritime station, down by the river? Eleven o'clock." He rose to go, then turned. "Can you get a small truck? Hire one for the night?" I nodded. "Bring it with you. There's something we can do first."

"Where's Joao?" Marianne said. I hadn't heard the toilet flush. She had combed her hair and there were drops of water on her eyebrows.

"I was right about him," I said. "He made a dirty dago pass at me. I told him you'd taken all my energy."

She grinned. "We haven't started yet. Let's go back to the hotel, or are you still waiting for someone?"

"All my life, love," I said. "Waiting."

Back in the car I groped under the seat. The package had gone. Marianne fiddled with the radio and found some music and took off her shoe. She reached to the back seat for a magazine and spread it on her lap and pulled the Rizla papers from my shirt pocket.

"Try it the British way," I said. "Stick two of them together so they're double the width. Now stick another along the two edges. Now roll the grass in the big paper." She made a fat, ugly joint. I told her to tamp down one end with a match, and roll a tiny roach of cardboard as a filter.

"You see how it makes the smoke cooler," I said, as she took the smoke in.

"I prefer the other British way. Last night's way." Her finger traced the inside of my thigh. I put my hand on hers and squeezed it. She passed the joint. With the car windows open, the smoke swept into the evening. Joao's brother-in-law could be very useful. Small-time Lisbon hood going on big time with interests to protect. No wonder he'd like some British insurance.

We'd have to see what kind of operation he had, whether he had got the docks sewn up or whether he just had a couple of sailor friends who smuggled for him.

It's always useful to have some hoodlums in a network. They don't mind the rough stuff and they usually have good friends in the police. Ever since 1943, when the Americans worked with the Mafia to prepare for the invasion of Sicily, crime and intelligence have gone happily together. If the political idea got off the ground we'd need some hard men to guard the rallies. And to break up the other side's meetings. We'd need some tear gas, smoke bombs. It had been easier in Northern Ireland. We just borrowed the stuff from the army. We got one politician the nickname Crying Mike. Every time he spoke, we tear-gassed him. With any luck, Joao's brother-in-law would be bribing some fat bastard in the local police. They'd have all the supplies we'd need.

I parked the car beside the hotel, and we stood on the steps with all the other press people and watched the firemen's trucks driving slowly and hooting down the main avenue. They were on strike for more money. The gray-clad police held up the traffic so the fire trucks could creep past. Half the reporters were holding up their cassette recorders, taping a little authentic background noise for the radio bulletins. There was a touch on my arm. Phil was beside me. His eyes were red and I could smell the grass on him. He was stoned. Not slurring any words and he was in control, but stoned.

"Before that lunch tomorrow, I'll take you to see MSR. We've got an appointment with a major who's on the executive committee. They're about the sharpest of the left groups. I'll meet you here at eleven."

"Phil." He turned back to me. "If you're going to smoke in a car, keep the windows open like I do. Otherwise it soaks into your clothes. You smell like a head shop, and that can be embarrassing." He grinned and jumped down the steps. Marianne and I went to our room. There were no messages. She climbed into the shower and I called the car-hire desk. A light truck. It would be ready in one hour. Thank you, American imperialism,

Hertz and Avis and Coca-Cola. I joined Marianne in the shower.

She was a girl who liked to get her hair wet. It was long enough to hang in streaks on her breasts. I began to soap them and she opened her mouth to catch the water cascading from my nose. I soaped her until I built a huge pile of lather, a third breast between hers. She scooped off a handful and dabbed at my chin and my ears. Her skin slid on me and I braced my feet against the sides of the bath. She turned to the shower faucet, filling her mouth with the hot water. Then she turned and knelt to me, slipping my rising cock between her lips. The hot water and her tongue felt very loving. I caressed the top of her head. There wasn't much else I could reach and still keep my balance.

I reached for a towel and threw it on the floor of the bath and knelt down, my knees cushioned on the towel. I lifted Marianne so she sat on the end of the bath, her thighs around me and the shower water still pouring onto both of us. She pushed the tip of my cock to her clitoris and I reached behind her for the oil. I poured it into her pubic hair and she grinned, running the head of my cock through the electric fur so it glistened with the oil. I poured some oil into my hand and ran it over her buttocks, over my balls and around her slit. She eased me inside her, still tight from the water but the oil easing the way. Knees braced on the wet towel, I began to move from side to side, stirring, not thrusting. Her eyes closed and her hands rose to toy with her nipples. I slipped an oiled finger into her bottom, feeling it squeeze around me. I crooked the finger, feeling my cock inside her just a membrane away.

Her head began to fall back. I pulled another towel from the side of the bath to lay it under her back as I strained up from my knees to stay inside the rising swoop of her hips. My finger slid out and I brought it around to tease the little nub of her clit. The sides of her cunt began to squeeze me like a closing fist and she breathed in gulps, the water still streaming over her face. Her hair was stuck to my chest, our loins slipping over each other with the oil. I put my hands under her buttocks and heaved myself to my feet, still clutching her to me, her feet locked around my waist. She must have felt her entire weight was resting on my cock and her teeth bit deeply at my neck. Her body still trembling, I stepped out of the bath still holding her and staggered into the bedroom. I laid her down, still gently rocking my cock inside her, and rose on my hands. The only part of my body that touched hers was my cock. She opened her eyes and raised her head to look down at where our bodies met.

"Jesus," she said, and one hand went to my buttocks and the other slid between us to knead my balls. She squeezed the base of my cock twice, hard, and then pulled me roughly to her. Half of Lisbon must have heard us as we came, though my voice was muffled by her wet hair. She poked a finger in my mouth to pull the hair out. It tasted of us.

# 5

By the time I picked up Joao at the maritime I had showered again, alone, and left Marianne sleeping with a note taped to the mirror. The grass had gone from my head and the night air was cool. My shoulder was sore from her teeth and my hair was still wet. In spite of the soap I could still smell her scent on my fingers. I imagined it drifting up from my chest and tried to stop grinning.

Joao directed me along the waterfront to the foot of the huge bridge that spanned the mile-wide river. It used to be called the Salazar bridge, after the old dictator. Now they called it the Bridge of the 25 April, after the date of the coup. And they had increased the toll charge to 20 escudos. Progress.

The side of the road was piled high with crates and boxes shipped back from Angola. We drove past them, shipload after shipload, for four hundred yards. They stretched back another two hundred yards, containers, wooden cases, all marked "Port of Lisbon" and all carrying personal names and addresses.

"This is a personal thing," said Joao. "My possessions from Angola. I needed a truck to collect it. I also need 2,000 escudos to bribe the guard. We do it this way or I wait three months for the Customs to clear it."

I nodded. A personal favor was fine by me. Anything was fine by me. Some of the grass was still soothing me, and there was a warm heaviness in my groin. Sure, I told Joao. After a key of heroin, what's 2,000 escudos? We drove to the back of a small office building. Joao went in with the money. After five minutes he came back with a guy in civilian clothes, wearing a military webbing holster with a heavy Browning at his hip. He climbed into the cab beside Joao and pointed to one side. We drove into the streets of crates, the avenue of them stretching left and right to infinity at each junction. The guy with the gun consulted a plan in his hand and turned right. He stopped us beside a fork-lift truck, and Joao climbed out to show him the crates. Three minutes later we were back on the waterfront road, heading for the bridge.

"You have a lot of possessions." I jerked my head toward the back of the truck. "Four big cases. None of them addressed to Joao."

"A man has to live," he said, handing me money for the toll-gate. I drove slowly, feeling the wind rocking the truck. The bridge must have been five hundred feet above the water. There was a big floodlit statue of Jesus, arms outstretched, at the far end. It must have been almost as high as the bridge. They think big, the Portuguese. We took the road to Setubal, the industrial city that the Communists controlled.

"The beaches down there." Joao gestured to the west. "Holiday beaches, holiday camps, but no tourists this year. So they're full of refugees from Angola. I spent a week there till my family managed to bribe me out. Some of the network are still there. One of them's living in a tent."

We turned off before Setubal, going through a darkened village, and as we pulled off the road again I braced myself on the wheel and stamped on the brake. Joao bounced back from the windscreen, dazed. I jammed his face at the screen again and took the gun from his waistband. I pushed him out of the truck, the gun in one hand and the flashlight in the other, and prodded him to the back.

"Open the crates. Just enough for me to see what's inside."

"You know what's inside. We're going to need them."

"Open them anyway." I had known they were guns as soon as the forklift dropped the first crate onto the truck. The springs knew they were guns too. Guns are heavy, even when they are wrapped in light, bright-colored Angolan cloth. The smell of the oil was in the air. NATO-pattern FNs in two crates, GP machine guns and cartridge belts in the third. Grenades and ammunition in the fourth. Joao started to close the crates again.

He sat on the tail of the truck, nursing a bruised finger and a bruised face, squinting his eyes against the light of the flashlight. I didn't know enough to trust him, and I didn't know enough to discard him. He'd have to stay on ice.

"That bar in Estoril. The Navigator. Does it have a phone?" He nodded, knowing what was coming.

"I'll call you there tomorrow night at seven. If you're still conscious. Climb off the truck and turn around."

He knew I wasn't going to kill him so he braced himself for the gun butt on his skull. These days they teach us better than that. I put my thumb under his collarbone and pressed the carotid artery. He went straight out. I took his shoes and trousers and threw them into the back of the truck. Then I left him there and drove back to the main road and drove south, away from Lisbon. I had to work this out.

I had to hang onto the guns, mainly because I didn't know what else to do with them. I couldn't make Joao and his chums a gift of that hardware, but where could I hang onto them? That was why I was driving south. I had been in Portugal once before with a girl. Her father was a golf professional at one of the big hotels on the tourist coast of the Algarve. We'd stayed at his villa while he was playing at some tournament. I remembered the way to the villa, and I remembered it had a big garage. In the gossip at the hotel bar that afternoon one of the British journalists had been talking about his story on Henry Cotton, another of the golf professionals, having his golf club taken over by the workers. As the truck climbed up the plateau of the Alentejo, I hoped the bloody workers had dispossessed my golf pro too.

It was a four-hour drive to the Algarve, and I thought it all through again. If Joao only needed a truck and 2,000 escudos to get the crates, why drag me into it? He could have picked them up any time. Or perhaps only tonight. The guy with the Browning at the crate depot didn't look like an ordinary security guard, even though he knew his way around the crates and could handle a fork-lift truck. Okay, so they had planned tonight to take over the depot and pull out the guns. But why did they need me?

Two possible reasons. The first was I was handy. I just happened to come along and just happened to be able to get hold of a truck and it was useful. Not good enough. I wasn't even expected to make contact until tomorrow night.

The second possibility was that they wanted me to have the guns, and Joao had cooperated in letting me think I'd been very clever. In a revolutionary situation, anybody who finds an Englishman with dubious press credentials driving through the night with a truckload of NATO weaponry has a ready-made diplomatic incident. Who would like that to happen? Just about anybody. The Communists would love it. The far Left would cream their jeans for it. The Yanks would laugh about it and the French would crow. Britannia catches her tits in the mangle.

But if I wasn't expected to show up until tomorrow, Joao and his chums can hardly have had the time to organize the take-over of the depot. It still didn't make sense. The only thing that made sense was to get the guns hidden where only I knew about them, and then make contact with Joao tomorrow. That meant being back in Lisbon tomorrow. Christ, I was supposed to meet Phil in the morning and talk to the far Left. I looked at my watch. One A.M. Three more hours to Lagos. And four hours to drive back. It could be done, but I'd like some sleep. I could unload the guns and take the truck to Faro and catch a morning plane back to Lisbon. No I couldn't. I couldn't unload the bloody crates without a fork-lift truck. The guns and the truck stayed together. Maybe there'd be a car in the garage. Maybe I could steal one.

Maybe I could rustle up some help. Now there was an idea. A reverse-charge person-to-person call to Chisholm's little detached house in Pinner, the phone by the bed, his wife with her hair in curlers going to get some tea while I told him over an open line that I was sitting on enough weaponry to take the Tower of London. He'd spill tea all over his pajamas.

But there was part two of the operation, the part that London hadn't told the fat man. Chisholm's little brainstorm that I hadn't taken too seriously. Chisholm was a good little bureaucrat. He knew it wasn't enough to be negative, you had to have an alternative policy. So if you hated the Yanks you had to love somebody else. Chisholm loved the Europeans. Or rather he loved the idea of extending his own little empire so that he controlled the French and the Germans and the Italians and worked up a grand alliance so we could all be beastly to the Yanks. Chisholm was a good European, which was another reason why he sat behind the desk he did. The Minister was a good European. The last Minister had been a good European. And both of them had boosted Chisholm.

The road was reasonable, and the truck was going well. The signposts were reading Lagos now and there was no other traffic. Petrol still okay. I eased Joao's gun in my waistband and wet my fingertips and rubbed them on my eyelids. It's an old wake-up trick and it still works. I ought to use it whenever I see Chisholm.

He loves sitting behind a desk and droning on. Like this Portuguese road, and they think it's one of their better ones. They have two stretches of *autostrada* outside Lisbon, and after that it's two-lane highway all the way. Endless cork trees in the wash of the headlights, looking naked with the cork cut away. Farther south, the cork trees gave way to the warped and twisted olive trees, and at last I reached the little barrier of mountains that had slowed the land routes between Portugal and the Algarve until Salazar built bridges and forced the roads through in the 1930s. It was just on 3:00 A.M. when I drove the truck quietly past the sleeping town of Lagos on the coast road to Sagres. Across the bay, there was moonlight on the long beach that stretched to Portimao.

I parked the truck at the beginning of the dirt road to the villa and walked quietly to the darkened house. All the shutters were closed, and the rubbish bins were empty and the bottled gas canisters were switched to Off. Nobody was living there. The back door was bolted and the front door was double-locked, so I forced the garage door. It was a simple tumbler lock, and with some pliers from the garage I bent the metal catch back into enough shape to hold the lock's tongue. There was no other car in the garage. I drove the truck inside and closed the spring-loaded door just enough so I could crawl under it. Then I tied rope around the door's springs and the truck's back axle and took out the rotor arm. Now if anyone wanted to open the door he'd also have to lift three tons of truck and guns. I slid out under the gap in the door and heaved it closed. The lock clicked.

As I walked back on the road to Lagos, I wondered what time the fish trucks would start out. They reached Faro in time for the morning markets, but it would be a smelly way to travel. I went under the old gate into the town, looking for one of the buzz-bikes the Portuguese love. They sound like a thousand buzz saws and don't go much faster than a kid's tricycle. I turned a corner and there was a pack of them, and half a dozen cars, parked behind a white-painted house that leaked music. It called itself the Phoenix bar-disco and at 4:00 A.M., in the worst tourist season the Portuguese had ever known, it was doing its best. It looked new—some poor bastard had probably sunk his life savings into this before the revolution. It would have been a gold mine then, and it might still be one, but there were some bad seasons to live through, and bad times. I had heard of some tourist-bar owners sleeping behind their own bars at night with a loaded shotgun, just in case the staff decided to try some freelance nationalization.

The guy behind the bar was English, and he looked worried enough to be the owner. The girl at the discotheque kept glancing at him. Maybe his wife. She also kept glancing at a small group of four young Portuguese lounging in a corner. Two soldiers danced alone on the floor. There was a little balcony and a spinning light show and lights that flashed with the beat of the music. They had taken a lot of trouble to build this place.

I sat at the bar and ordered a rum and Coke. He grinned at the English voice.

"You're open late," I said, rolling a cigarette. "Good season?"

"No. A bad one and I want to close but . . ." He looked at the little group of Portuguese and shrugged.

"So another Englishman is welcome?" He nodded. "I came in here to see if somebody wanted to earn 1,000 escudos driving me to Faro. My girl ditched me and I've got to catch a plane. But I guess it's a bad time." He nodded again.

"I'd like to help," he said. "Sorry, it's difficult here now." His eyes narrowed as the two soldiers left. He signaled to his girl at the disco and the music stopped. The little group of Portuguese all groaned together and laughed. I looked over the bar. The owner had a pickax handle beside the sink. He looked at me and shrugged.

"*Obrogad, senores a bon noit.*" His voice was level and steady. One of them came up to the bar, slammed down his glass. "Whiskey and music," he said. The barman didn't move. "Whiskey," he repeated. The barman shook his head and said again "*Bon noit.*"

The three others got up from the corner and began to move across. The barman picked up the pickax handle and showed it. "Out you bastards," he said. "Now."

The one by the bar leant and swept his arm across the counter. A dozen of the new-washed glasses crashed to the floor. My glass was down by my side and I swung it up hard so the rim of it ground into his balls. He bent in the middle and I helped him along, rabbit-punching his neck so his face knocked into the counter. I spun for my bar stool and threw it at the legs of the three coming toward us. One went down and I jumped the others.

When we had them all down I asked the barman how much they owed him. He said 600 escudos so I took 200 from each one. The last one tried to cover his hip pocket so I stamped his hand into the broken glass. I went to the first one, the bastard who had broken the glasses, and turned to the barman. "This one speak English?"

"Yeah, good English. He used to work for me. He was stealing from the bar so I fired him. Now he's saying he's going to take over the bar. I'm a foreign exploiter."

He was still holding his balls where the glass had caught him. His nose was bleeding from hitting the counter. I turned him over and backhanded him twice. I reached into his back pocket and pulled out 500 escudos and tossed them to the barman.

"That's for the damage—to the glasses." I put the flat of my hand to his crushed nose and splayed it a little farther. "You shit. You didn't know about his cousin, did you?" I jerked my head toward the barman. "Do you know what I'll do to you if you ever come here again?" He nodded and I climbed off him.

As he rolled to get to his feet I kicked him very hard at the base of each kidney. His friends carried him out. He'd piss blood for a week. We locked the door behind them and the owner went to the bar and poured three whiskeys.

"I'm Ron," he said. "This is Valerie. Meet my long-lost cousin." I told them I was David and asked if they expected any more trouble. Ron thought not. His former employee had been the cause of it and he wasn't likely to try again. I asked if the guy was in any of the political parties and Ron said no, just a beach-boy.

"You'll be okay then," I said, finishing the whiskey. "He won't show his face for a while. The story will get around town—and the word that you're ready to fight back." Ron poured me another and said he could drive me to Faro.

We went back to their apartment first, carrying the disco gear and the booze stock. Ron said it had become a habit. Val made us some coffee and breakfast. I asked them who lived in the villa up the hill that used to belong to the golf professional and they said nobody. He'd gone back to England when the workers took over the golf clubs. They didn't know his daughter, so I said she was an old friend and if squatters or anybody tried to move in, to phone a message to me at the hotel in Lisbon. Ron poured a slug of scotch into the last cup of coffee and we left for Faro.

The drive took about an hour, the dawn breaking ahead of us and moving spikes of light into the hills above us. We passed some fish trucks and Ron told me about the buying of the bar the year before the revolution. He'd been a drummer in a rock group that hadn't quite made the big time. He'd got out with $10,000, Val, and stomach ulcers from the highway cafes. It was the night-driving and the greasy food that finished the business for him. Playing in Newcastle one night, Liverpool the next, Birmingham the next and sleeping four to a room in cheap hotels. Sometimes sleeping in the truck with the amps and guitars. He'd even sold the drums. He said he would hang on in the Algarve for a couple of years and see what happened to the tourist trade. He'd sell if he could get his money back. At Faro he tried to refuse the 1,000 escudos. I pushed it into his shirt pocket anyway and told him to buy some new records. He said he didn't even like the old ones anymore, and we parted. There was a plane for Lisbon in two hours. I slept in the tiny lounge.

In the plane I thought about the dozens of others like Ron and Val, sinking everything into a place and then some thug reckons he can grab it just by calling them foreign exploiters. Whatever else the revolution was for, it wasn't to ruin kids like that. Ron had been lucky enough or determined enough to make enough money to keep him off the factory floor. Good luck to him. There had been kids like him in the army with me, standing facing the bricks on the Falls Road and still dreaming of buying themselves

60

a guitar with the gratuity and being a rock 'n roll star. None of them ever did. Most of them stayed in the army. Sometimes I thought I should have, but I didn't fancy a lifetime in the sergeants' mess.

It was almost ten when I got to the hotel in Lisbon, too early for the journalists to be up, but the lobby was crowded with them. I didn't see Marianne so I went up to the room. She was in the shower, some orange juice still on the breakfast tray. She didn't ask where I'd been and said she'd seen my note when she woke. I fell into the shower. Hot—cold—hot—cold and a shave and I was human. We went down to the lobby. Half the guys had gone and the other half were fighting for taxis.

I tapped a Yank I knew on the shoulder and asked what was happening. He said did I have a car and I nodded. He'd tell me on the way. We drove to the base of the bridge, and armored cars blocked the road. Men in camouflaged uniform, wearing the shoulder flash of COPCON, the internal security force, kept us away from the huge field of wooden crates I had first seen last night. They were looking for guns, the Yank said. They'd had a tip-off that the guns were coming from the old army arsenals in Angola, disguised as refugees' possessions. We could see them prizing open crate after crate and running metal detectors along their sides.

"The tip-off was anonymous," the Yank said. "I know a guy in COPCON. He said he thought the guns were for the Communists. They'd need cooperation in Angola, and the military governor there had been friendly to the Reds.

"They arrested four guys. Communist members. The troops found them in the office, with the two guards tied up and a bit bruised."

"Do we know what the guards are saying?" I asked him. He shook his head. But the guards must have been tied up before Joao and I got here last night. Maybe the Communists had come later. I asked him if the troops had impounded any vehicles, and he said they had found a pick-up truck parked outside the office. It was registered to one of the Communists.

There was a guy standing on my car roof, trying to photograph the scene with a long lens. It was Phil. "We've got an appointment," I called to him. He nodded and held up five fingers. Five minutes.

The pressmen were standing around a little Portuguese officer who was answering questions. Are the four men still being held? —Yes. Have you found any arms in the crates?—No. Are the four men Communists?—We don't know. Are you sure about that?—He shrugged. Are there any reports of arms missing from Angola? The little guy got angry. We lost 20,000 men there and you want to know about arms. Probably we lost some. Nobody knows. Will the four men be charged? We don't know. What about the two guards who were tied up? What do they say? They say they were jumped before midnight.

Before midnight. The questions came faster. What time did the troops get here?—About 5:00 A.M. The four Communists had been there at 5:00 A.M.? Did the guards say the Communists jumped them?—They don't know who jumped them. Did the guards say when the Communists arrived?—Just before the troops. Are any crates missing? Could some crates have been removed before the Communists arrived?—It's possible. We're checking the crates now.

Phil tapped my shoulder. "Ready," he said. I'd heard enough from the officer. The journalists were repeating their questions. Over by the crates, one of the metal detectors squealed and the two soldiers crowbarred the crate open. An oven, a refrigerator, and a kid's buggy. Phil photographed it and we drove off to see the man from MSR.

# 6

Marianne wanted to be dropped in town. She said something about shopping. I left her in the Rossio Square and drove up Liberdad. In the rear-view mirror I saw her standing, watching me and the car pull away. When I'd got back to the hotel this morning I'd put my hand in her bed. It was cold and the sheets were unruffled. In the corner were two pairs of discarded panty hose. When I left the night before there had been one pair. I picked up the top pair and sniffed the crotch. Whatever else she had been doing when she went out it wasn't screwing. I cast my mind back to her passport. Marianne Thayer.

I drove around Pombal's statue and went back to the Tivoli. Phil objected we'd be late. I said I forgot something and went into the hotel. Behind the reception desk there was a telex machine the journalists used. Above it was a shelf with reference books. I pulled out the diplomatic list and checked the entry for the USA. There was a Major George F. Thayer, on the staff of the military attaché. I went back to the car and we drove to the MSR building.

It was very imposing. Phil said one of the bosses of PIDE, the old secret police, had lived there until MSR evicted him. Between the four main windows on the first floor were three huge posters. Lenin, Mao, and Che. That covered most of the options. On either side of the entry doors were stunning paintings. A large red orb with a yellow star in the corner, supported on the shoulders of a marching bank of people etched in black and white. The stylized fists and clenched guns of the marchers bit into the red sun. Above it all was written MSR. It looked very good.

We pushed at the door and stepped into the dark. A guard leaned against the door, a machine pistol crooked in his arm. He motioned us against the wall and another guard frisked us. Joao's gun was back in the hotel, taped to the lid of the toilet cistern. The guard tapped something in Phil's pocket and pulled out two small cans of film. Phil said "Major Antonio . . ." but the guard just nodded. We were expected.

MSR stood for Social Left Movement, and the file back in London had said it was small but important. The political appreciation files are good on that kind of thing, even though they're usually drafted by the Foreign Office. The files put MSR third in influence in the Armed Forces Movement, after the Socialists and the Communists. Most of its members were officers, and it was strongest in the paratroops and the commandos, the units who had fought the bulk of the war against the guerrillas in Angola. Therefore the units that had most cause to respect the ideology that fired the Africans. Once a soldier realizes he can win all the military battles but still lose the political war he becomes a different kind of soldier. It had happened to me in Northern Ireland. It had happened to the Portuguese in Africa, and they came home and started a revolution. Maybe we should have thought of that in Belfast.

I forget how many other parties there were in the alphabet soup that made up Portuguese politics. PS, PCP, UDP, PRP, MDP, MRPP—the list went on. Two Portuguese made a political party. Three made a schism and two parties. That's what you get after forty years of dictatorship that forbids political action. Everybody wants to be president.

Major Antonio looked like he deserved to be president, as though he practiced it each night before the mirror. Impeccably dressed in a gray-blue suit, cream shirt, and red tie. His hair was short and neat, his nails buffed and shining. His glasses were heavy hornrims and there was enough weight at his neck to make him look mature, but his belly was flat and there was a slight bulge at his left shoulder. He sat behind a cheap desk, on a cheap black vinyl chair. His left hand was on one of the two telephones and his right held a pen over some papers. He might have been posing for an election poster. In the corner behind him a TV set and a military multiwave radio stood on a low filing cabinet. On the wall was a poster of Che. The revolution you can trust.

"Thank you for seeing me, Major." He nodded graciously. "Where's your uniform?"

He didn't move a muscle. Then he smiled. A nice smile.

"In Portugal today, the loyal soldier fights for the people. The people do not need a uniform. But it's in the cupboard behind you." He gestured.

I went to the cupboard and opened it. There were parachutist wings on the left chest and a red dagger flash on the sleeve. I sat down again.

"Which are you, Major—Paras or commando?"

"I am attached to the paratroop base at Tancos. I did a NATO commando course. Hence the red dagger. But you wanted to know about MSR. Might I see your press card?"

I handed him the British union card and told him my Portuguese credentials were still being processed.

"Maddox," he said. "David Maddox. Your face in this photograph seems familiar, Mr. Maddox. Perhaps it is the shorter hair. Very military." He looked at me again.

I remembered him too. I remembered as soon as he mentioned the NATO commando course. They always used us for the last part of the course. They would take a platoon of the trainee commandos and give them all light battle kit, about thirty pounds. They took two SAS men and gave us sixty pounds each and a thirty-minute start. They were supposed to catch us over a marked course through the Cairngorms. They knew the checkpoints we'd have to make, and in theory they could detach some of their men carrying only rifles who could sprint ahead and ambush us. In theory. It never happened.

"The policy of MSR is very simple," he said, leaning back in his chair. "We want a Portuguese solution for Portugal. Socialist but Portuguese. We do not want Moscow's Communism because we are Portuguese. We have got rid of one dictatorship and we do not want another. We are very suspicious of the USA and of the European countries. All they have done for us so far was to support the old dictatorship and exploit our countrymen who worked in Europe and exploit the ones who stayed in Portugal with their multinational companies and our low wage-rates. That era is ended now."

"There's no chance of the Right recovering power?" I asked. He shook his head. The army would not let it.

"What about a moderate Right, backed by the USA and the Europeans?"

"We expect that to happen, but it will be a short phase. Portugal is a poor country, and without the oil and raw materials of the African colonies she will be poorer. We have to import a third of our food. Normally we can pay for that with earnings from tourism and the money sent home by Portuguese workers in Europe. Tourism has collapsed and there is a recession in Europe. We are running through our foreign exchange reserves —the next step by a moderate Right government would be to cut the workers' wages and their living standards to cover the deficit. The moderate Right would have no other solution, but after forty years of dictatorship and two years of freedom and high wages, the working class would not let their wages be cut."

"When you say the working class, do you mean the Communist Party or what?"

"The Communists control the trade union movement, the Intersindical. It is their key weapon. But it wouldn't need Communists to mobilize the workers if their wages were threatened. They have learned how to strike now. They can do it by themselves."

"So why do they need MSR?"

"They need MSR for two reasons. First, to convince them now that the Communists are not the only ones who claim to fight on their behalf. Second, because after the elections and after the moderate Right or centrist government fails, the workers will realize that they will have to run Portugal themselves. We think we can help them to do that. In the short term, MSR is anti-Communist. In the long term, we are pro-Portuguese and pro the working class."

"What does the working class have in common with officers in the Paras?"

"You don't know much about the Portuguese Army," he smiled. "The officer corps, like the one in Britain, is an old and honorable profession. But the gentlemen are too honorable to join the Paras or the commandos. They join the cavalry, or the guards units. My father was a poor farmer from Tras Os Montes, up in the north of Portugal. His sons had two ways of getting an education. You either went into the seminary and became a priest or you went to military college and became a soldier."

"Are you sure you don't fear a coup by the Right? The old police chiefs are still in place. What about the gentleman officers?"

"We watch them. There is talk of a secret 'liberation army' mobilizing in Spain." He shrugged. "It probably isn't important. At the military bases we have our supporters and the Communists will work with us to stop any games by the Right. The units loyal to the revolution are in the right places. Did you drive in from the airport?" I nodded.

"Then you'll have passed the RA-LIS base. They are light artillery, very left wing. They're even electing their own officers now. Their guns control the airport and the road from Santarem. Lisbon won't fall without them. At the other entry to Lisbon, at Amadora, we have the commando barracks. Some of the officers are dubious but the men are sound. MSR is very strong there. The army as a whole is committed to the revolution. It made it. It might be persuaded to support a rightist government that won an election. But not a coup."

There was a click from my cassette recorder. I turned the tape over. "Sorry about this, Major. I can't take notes fast enough. You're being very helpful. What about popular discontent? You're going to have a million angry refugees from Angola and Mozambique and unemployed workers coming back from Germany. There's no work for them. What will they do?"

"We don't know. The refugees worry me most. We call them Retornados—the ones who returned. They're energetic, ambitious people. They had to be to go out to the colonies. They have lost their possessions or most of them. A lot of them come from the north, which is still very conservative. The Church is very influential. They might join the right-wing or centrist parties. We'll have to convince them otherwise. But this year they are useful. They are part of the weight in the balance against the Communists. We need them for that."

"So an alliance against the Communist Party is your first priority? The extreme Left and the Right against the Communists?"

"Yes, but remember we need the Communists to stop the threat of a surprise coup from the Right. It's a distant possibility but it's still there.

"We will fight them in the Intersindical, the trade union movement, because we must. That is the center of their strength, because during the years of the dictatorship they built up a secret movement that was ready to take over when the dictatorship collapsed. They control the structure, the offices, they have the key jobs and the expertise. The workers know them and a lot of them are trusted. They have some weaknesses there that we can expose. Workers don't like being manipulated. The Communists are getting too confident.

"But the struggle in the Intersindical will be a long-term one, Mr. Maddox. There will always be Communists there. In the meantime we can strike at the Communists in the north where they are weak. They have to stay there, they dare not run from the north but they know they are hated. The priests hate them, the *caciques* hate them . . ."

"The who?" I interrupted.

"The *caciques*," he smiled. "It's a very Portuguese institution. They are the respected men of property in the north who run the villages. They are unofficial mayors. Not necessarily the richest men, but the ones people trust. The *cacique* structure works in northern Portugal, but the Communists cannot understand it. So the *caciques* hate the Communists.

"Do you know the north, Mr. Maddox? No? You should go there. I think you may be going there very soon. You and all the other journalists." He looked at his watch. We were about to be dismissed.

"One last question, Major. Do you have any idea what happened to those guns that disappeared last night?"

"No, but we'll find out." He smiled at me. "I have a question for you. The girl you are staying with at the hotel. Do you know who she saw last night?"

"She has family here," I said. Major Antonio was very good. "She saw her father. He's one of the attachés at the embassy."

"Military attachés, Mr. Maddox. That's more than simple diplomacy." He rose. "If I have been frank with you, Mr. Maddox, it is because we have certain interests in common. Up to a point. But I am still very curious why a man from the British SAS arrives in Lisbon with the daughter of an American military attaché."

Phil was staring at both of us. But he knew what was going on.

"If you're looking for coincidences you haven't mentioned Phil's father," I said.

69

"We know about your man in Madrid. Good-day, Mr. Maddox. Interests in common but only up to a point." He opened the door for us and shook hands.

Phil went through the door. Major Antonio held me back.

"How did you do it, in the Cairngorms. How did you outpace us?"

"Easy," I said. "As soon as we left camp we marched straight to the finishing line. For the first two days we walked toward you, signing in at the checkpoints, then we walked around you to the first checkpoint and followed your route. When we had checked in at all of them we marched straight home. The rules were to stop at the checkpoints, not to stop at them in any particular order. It worked every time. It meant we walked about forty miles farther than you, but you were never going to catch us."

His brow furrowed. "You must have walked four hundred kilometers in five days—in that country."

"Training, Major, training." I grinned at him. "Up to a point."

# 7

As Phil and I went down the stairs and past the lounging guards, I tried to think of an innocent reason for Marianne not telling me her father was in Lisbon. She said they didn't get on well, but she had been to see somebody the previous night, and her father had served in Chile. The Chile program we had run through the computer in Somerset had made it clear that the CIA had done the softening up of the Allende government, but the coup itself had been coordinated with U.S. Army Intelligence. And then there were my doubts about the way we had met and her willingness to come to Portugal with me. As we got out into the street sunlight I let the suspicion grow, the thought that I was falling for the oldest trick of all. A man's vanity is a vulnerable thing. I had a sudden memory of the way we found the three dead Scottish fusiliers, none of them yet twenty, with the backs of the heads still seeping blood onto the Belfast pavements. They had been picked up by three pretty Irish girls and taken back to the ambush.

I looked across at Phil as we walked to the car in silence. His face was stern and set. I could almost see him thinking about Marianne and her father and about me and the SAS. I wondered how much he knew about his father. He was a good-looking boy, almost pretty with his long hair and his shirt unbuttoned to flash a hairless chest. Maybe he was handsome enough to be certain that women wanted him for his own sweet self, but I wasn't. The more I thought of me and Marianne the less likely it seemed.

As we waited for the usual madness of Lisbon traffic to slow enough for us to cross the street, I told myself to remember how little I knew of women. I had never lived with one. There had been a lot of pick-ups, a lot of quick fornications, and a few of the married ones at the barracks and a lot of professional ladies the army laid on for us in Ireland, to keep us out of temptation. There had never been a Marianne before, and again I reached the conclusion that I had to stay with her till I knew who was screwing whom.

But I didn't have time just to wait and see. I had to bring it to a head, to lay some kind of trap and see if she fell into it. Phil suddenly nudged me. There was a break in the traffic and we crossed to my car. I tossed him the keys and said he could use it to take his films to the airport, but he shook his head. He said he wanted to know about the SAS. I told him his films would miss the plane if he hung around. We could meet back at the hotel for lunch and we could talk about it then. He shrugged and climbed into the car, his face set into a pout. Maybe I should tell him who paid for his expensive school bills. Maybe after Major Antonio's little phrase about "your man in Madrid," he already knew.

I walked down the street to the crossroads that would take me back to the Liberdad and the Mercedes Benz showrooms. Otto's offices were on the second floor. Germans sticking together. I thought about traps and Marianne. The classic ploy would be some disinformation, something false I could feed her that she would pass on to the Americans. It would have to be urgent enough for the Americans to act on it—if she was telling them. But I had to remember that she was no fool. If she had picked me up because she was told to, then she knew my job in Portugal. And she had told me enough about her father to make me suspicious, so maybe she was waiting for me to set a disinformation trap for her. Then she could evade it, win my trust, and she would be ten times as useful. The logic of you know that she knows that you know that she knows spun around and around my head in the midday sun.

If I wanted to play the disinformation game it would have to be with a bait too important for her to ignore. The only trump card in my hand that was that important was the guns, but I hadn't even told London about the guns. Nor did I intend to. They were my insurance for Joao and his network. Maybe her father was a weak point—if I brutally accused her of being to see him last night, of her talk about Vietnam being so much balls. But if she was any good she wouldn't react. I reached the Mercedes Benz building and went up the stairs. Elevators are watched.

"I've been expecting you, Maddox." Otto rose from the desk, where he'd been signing letters, and pumped my hand. "I've got all the stuff ready. We bought a small print shop, very cheap, and the offset equipment arrived yesterday. Silkscreen set for posters. Some video. All German, but you understand."

German Residents always worked the same way. They built their cover jobs so cleverly they actually made money. Otto had been running his import-export agency for twenty years. We had met in London for the briefing last month. He provided the gear we needed to build the political party. The Germans paid for it and pushed the subsidies, just as they were siphoning money into the social democrat groups. This was Chisholm's brain wave. German money and a British plan. The politicians loved it. Britain's social democrats and Germany's social democrats saving Portugal from the naughty Reds. Otto thought it was a joke too. We'd talked it through in London.

Otto liked the game because he hated Communists. Or rather, he hated the Russians. They had taken him prisoner somewhere in Poland in 1944 and released him ten years later. His wife was dead, his kids disappeared. He crossed into Berlin as soon as he had a chance and was recruited by Gehlen's boys. They liked men who spoke Russian and hated them. Otto had told me of two or three jobs he had done in East Germany, building new networks. On the last one he got four bullets in his leg and still managed to walk onto the S-bahn into West Berlin. When he recovered, Gehlen was gone, but Otto was well enough thought of to be given the number two job in Lisbon. It was supposed to be a pension, but Otto had done well. A lot of Germany's best troops had done their combat training in Angola and Mozambique, thanks to Otto. The Portuguese liked him. So did I.

"Otto, two things. How much notice will you need to lay on cargo aircraft, short take-off, four-ton load? Two, what's brewing in the north? You've got connections there. Something about the Communists."

"The plane is no problem. I can hire you one with a discreet pilot. I have an interest in an air-taxi firm. In the north? The Communists are strung out in party offices all over the country. The people don't like them. There's been some stone-throwing, fights in cafes. Nothing much yet, but it could get nasty. Depends on the police."

"Why the police?"

"So far the police have shown themselves. A cop stationed outside the party office door. So nothing serious happens. But if the police get orders to stay out of sight, you could get petrol bombings. It depends on the local bosses."

"You mean the *caciques*?"

"You've done some homework. Yes, the *caciques*. If they want to run the Reds out of town they'll check with the police and then they'll run the Reds out. Burn them out. Just what this country needs. The Reds are all in the open now. The revolution brought them out from underground. If we do the job right there'll be no more Reds in Portugal."

"You're a bloodthirsty old Kraut."

He laughed. "I'm a man of property with a business to protect. I'm a foreign exploiter. They'd like to take over my business. I'll find out what the police are doing. I know them up there. You're going to have to move fast with your Angolans. Things are moving fast now."

"The elections aren't till next spring. We've got till then."

Otto shook his head.

"The Reds know that too. They've got the trade unions, they've taken over the rest of the newspapers, and they've got as much of the army as they'll ever have. They must make a move soon."

"What sort of a move?"

"A legal one. Subtle change in the constitution. A couple more ministries, a purge of the police forces. Long-term deals with the Russians. Oil for wine; shoes for steel. Link the economy in Eastern Europe. It's the obvious way. Then a courtesy call by the Russian fleet. Christ, you English have done it often enough. They're negotiating one trade deal now. The wine deal —Portugal has always over-produced and their wine doesn't travel well enough for the export markets. Russian palates know no better."

"When do you launch the new newspaper?"

"Next week. The editor's an old friend. I didn't even have to put up any money. A lot of people I do business with, they want a new paper again. They put the money up. All I did was provide the printing. No Red printers, no strikes, no workers' take-over."

"I'd better meet the editor. How much does he know?"

"As far as he is concerned, we are merely good friends. That's official: well-intentioned Europeans, social democrats, our duty to support free institutions. But he's no fool. He knows my job and

75

he'll work out yours. But don't worry. We all want the same thing. His name's Raul. He lost his old paper to the Communists."

"One more thing. Can your friends in the police get some tear gas and smoke bombs? There's a Communist rally at the weekend. It needs livening up."

"I'll get them. How many men do you need for them? Will twenty do?" I nodded. "I'll see to it." He scribbled a note on his desk pad.

"One more idea, Otto. That air-taxi firm—has it got any helicopters?"

"We've got two," he said proudly. "One is a Bell, very modern with . . ."

"That's fine, Otto. Why not print a few thousand handbills— 'Communists out of Portugal. Freedom Now'—nothing sophisticated. Toss them from the copter. All the press will be there —it'll get good coverage."

Otto smiled. "They run the radio and TV here; handbills will have to do."

"Those four Communists they arrested this morning by the bridge. The ones after the guns—get photos and names and particulars of all four of them from the police and print up a few more handbills. Make them read: 'These criminals want to bring guns to Portugal.' Get the idea? Then start getting the criminal records on the other CP boys here. Print those up too. It'll help. Otto, are you a Catholic?"

He nodded, still smiling.

"What about distributing some more of these leaflets at the churches? Would the priests go along?"

"Some of them. In the north, yes. Around Lisbon and the red belt—I'm not sure. A lot of Marxist priests now."

"Do what you can. I'll see you tomorrow. Oh, and Otto. At 10:00 P.M. tonight I've got to meet somebody in the space by the National Stadium. I might need some insurance. Have you got a man who's good with a rifle? He'll need a night-sight."

"He'll be there."

"Otto, I'm tired. I'm forgetting things. There's an American

76

military attaché called Thayer. Can you run some checks on him? His family, where they are. What jobs he's done. Just the basics."

I walked back to the hotel. Marianne was in the bar, reading a *Herald Tribune*. I walked past the bar and checked the car park. Phil was just driving in. I waved and he parked and came over.

"Phil, I need a favor tonight. I just want to know where somebody lives and where he goes. It'll get you 1,000 escudos."

"Tell me about the SAS first. That was a very unusual interview we had this morning. I know those guys and they don't talk like that."

"Phil, you know what your father does. You know why he does it. Don't tar me with that brush. You know what the SAS was when I joined it?"

"Yeah. Britain's Green Berets. Death and glory. Our heroes."

"Okay. Be like that. You know why I left them? You know what they're doing in Ireland? How they're being used now?"

"I read the papers."

"So you know about one-tenth of it. Why do you think I changed jobs? You know I was good at it. I left because I didn't want that. I don't play your father's game, but I know who they are and what they do and I'm a better reporter because of it."

They should give us Oscars at the training school. Interrogation procedures. How to defend a crumbling cover story. How to keep a straight face. We stood at the side of the car park, both of us looking down, scuffing our shoes in the gravel. I must have looked very earnest.

"I've got a line on some Angolans. It could be important, Phil."

"What do you want me to do?"

"There's a bar in Estoril. A guy will be in there. Wait outside and follow him when he comes out. If he goes home, I want to know. If he goes someplace else, I want to know. If he meets anybody, I want a photograph. That's all, Phil."

"I want an equal part of the story, if it makes." I nodded. He could have every by-line in Fleet Street for all I cared. "And I want to know about Marianne. What's this about her father?"

"The first I knew of it was when I came back to the hotel this morning with you. It was just a hunch and I checked the diplomatic list. There was a military attaché with her name. She's a military baby, Phil. I was one myself. I sensed it, that's all. How your MSR friends checked it out I don't know. They must have somebody in the hotel, somebody who followed her to where she met her father. That's all I know but I'll find out. Okay?"

He nodded and I gave him Joao's description. I was about to say he'd probably wear jeans, but I remembered they were still in the back of the truck, parked in the villa garage. We strolled into the bar and joined Marianne. A tall, middle-aged man was with her. Civilian clothes but worn as though they were uniform. He had to be her father. She introduced us all, and I told him about Major Antonio.

"You almost had us fingered as CIA spies," Phil grinned.

It's something I never enjoy, meeting the father of the girl you're screwing. You can see something in his eyes, some paternal imagining of a strange male locked into his little girl. An Oedipus complex in reverse. Fathers and daughters, daughters and lovers. His eyes were measuring me. I concentrated on rolling a cigarette and wondered if he knew about the little package of marijuana his daughter kept in her shoe.

"How long you been in the press game, Dave?" he asked. I told him three years. In fact, the army first started giving us press cards in Northern Ireland a year before that, but they were fake ones. Three years ago, they made it all look legal. He could check that and he probably would. I asked him how he liked being a soldier-diplomat.

"Better than training raw recruits at Fort Bragg," he said. That registered. They don't train raw recruits at Fort Bragg. They train good ones. They train them the way the SAS trained me. He asked me where I'd been reporting. I told him mainly Northern Ireland and the Persian Gulf. Oman was the Persian Gulf, but the press cover wore pretty thin out there.

"Learn any Arabic?"

"Enough to get by. It's like my Portuguese and my Spanish. I use a lot of English words with O on the end."

"You look pretty fit. How d'you stay in shape in this business?"

I screw your daughter, I thought. She's like ten rounds with Muhammad Ali. "I play a lot of squash when I can," I said. "It helps get rid of the alcohol us reporters need."

"We've got a court down at the Military Club. I'm not too fast anymore but I'd be glad to give you a game. We've got some spare sneakers and rackets."

I said that would be nice, looking at his build. Lean arms, no gut, and he moved well. He'd be a cunning old bastard and fit. Career soldiers who trained at Fort Bragg always are. Part of their course was three weeks in the Arizona desert living on the snakes you caught. We fixed a game for the next morning and he kissed Marianne and strolled off to lunch at his club. The three of us walked down the street to a basement place Phil knew. He ordered a bottle of the green wine, the *vinho verde*, that my dumb throat prefers to champagne. The waiters brought us little bowls of fish paste to nibble and took our orders. Phil insisted we eat the giant prawns with the piri-piri sauce.

It was a nice lunch. We'd all cleared up the business of Marianne's father and Phil thought I was on the side of the good guys and the lunch was exotic enough to be interesting, familiar enough to reassure. We had another bottle of the green wine and I told Phil I'd heard there was going to be a new newspaper. They might need some more photographers.

"Lot of work, all of a sudden," he said.

"There'll be more, if our MSR friends are right," I said. "If the north blows up every paper on earth will be screaming for pictures. It's the perfect story for the summer. All the parliaments and congresses and assemblies are on leave. People are on holiday so there're no news stories. Papers call it the silly season. Nothing like a nice revolution to cram the front pages."

I asked Marianne where her father had been stationed before Lisbon. She said he had been in Chile for three years. Phil and I exchanged glances. He'd been there during the coup. What Phil didn't know was that the U.S. military had done a lot more to help prepare the coup than the CIA ever did. The Chilean officers had been trained in the USA, some of them at Fort Bragg. The CIA just provided the bankroll and planned a transport strike. The coup was an army job all the way.

The new American ambassador had been in Chile, too. It looked like the Yanks were bringing in the first team. Chisholm would like that. Us, the Yanks, the Germans. The Russians with their wine deal and Christ knows what else. It's going to be quite a party. The French would be sniffling around, and the fat man had already warned me about the Spanish.

I needed some sleep. I told Phil to be at the bar by six thirty. I was calling Joao at seven so he'd be there. Phil left, Marianne went to the ladies'. I went to the phone and dialed a number. It rang twice. I put the phone down and dialed another number. It answered at the first ring.

"Seven thirty," I said clearly. "The usual." The phone went down. I went back to the table and paid the bill. Marianne came out and we walked back to the hotel. I told her I was sleepy and she grinned.

The balconies in the hotel annex are dreamy, twilight little places, with ivy hanging down to shade the worst of the sun and those long sun-chairs. Marianne said she'd oil my back. Suntan oil, she added. I grinned and stripped and lay on my face on the lounging chair. I closed my eyes and felt her pour the oil on my back. Her palms slid up to my shoulders and around my arms. She poured some more in the small of my back and her fingers trailed it over my buttocks and down my thighs. I felt her roll onto me, squirming her own body to oil herself on me. I rolled my shoulders and purred. She raised her back off my chest and I felt the twin points of her nipples drift down my back. Her teeth nipped at my side, so I turned over, the oil covering us both.

"You're sleepy," she said softly. "I'll do it to you."

My reputation suffered. I was sleepy. Sleepy and randy too. Her body glistened with the oil above me, the sun in my eyes so she was a dark silhouette, shapely and remote, a glare around her head. She lowered herself onto me and lay on my chest, rose up again, and my breath caught in my throat. I was starting to come. I reached for her breasts and called her and fell, fell away.

The sun was low in the sky and she was licking my eyelashes to wake me. She smelled of toothpaste and the shower. The oil had gone. I felt myself, still slimy. I remembered coming, her face distant above me.

"I owe you one," I said, and brought her hand to my face. I licked the palm. "I owe you lots."

"Premature ejaculation. A common complaint." She smiled and kissed my chest. "It often happens with older men. If you masturbate first and then screw you'll go on longer."

I half-opened an eye to see if she were serious. She put her watch in front of it. Six thirty. I sat up and looked at her. She didn't look frustrated. I went into the bathroom and took a long pee. I brushed my teeth, scrubbed off the oil with a towel, and was back by six thirty-two. She was standing at the door to the balcony, the sun still behind her, strong enough to show her body through the loose white robe.

I walked and stood behind her, kissing the side of her neck, my hands around her waist. She laid her head back against my chest and her buttocks swayed a little at my groin. My hands moved inside the robe, opening it at the waist, and I trickled my fingers down to her dark hair. Her hand slipped behind her, between us, her fingers teasing at the hairs on my belly. She gripped me, her hand tight around it, and began to squeeze. She turned around and went to her knees, kissing my thighs, her eyes open.

"You know what's nice?" she said. "This is nice." She licked from root to lip, her tongue circling, one hand weighing my balls. "It's still all there." She tried to pull the foreskin down with her tongue, and sank her mouth to it, working the loose skin down so the head stood purple and free. Her fingers pulled the foreskin back up. My knees began to tremble.

"I've never had one of these before. Circumcised ones all look the same."

"You shouldn't . . ." I was trying to speak clearly but my throat was dry. "You shouldn't speak with your mouth full."

She laughed, and then she gagged. It felt like she was trying to swallow it. She pulled free, her face glistening with her own

81

saliva, and laughed as she rose and shed the robe. She took my hand and led me to bed.

Still laughing, I entered her, our eyes wide and dancing at each other. She pulled my head down and licked my face as we began to move. She threw her legs up, crossing them behind me, her heels pulling me to her, kicking to boost my pace. Her hands slid down my back to grab her own ankles, jerking her feet faster into me. We were pounding at each other, our breath in sprints and grunts as we drove the air from each other's lungs. I felt huge, the tallest, highest, thickest . . . and my balls were hard and tight, bouncing on her bum.

"Bouncing on your bum," I gasped and giggled and she giggled and we laughed ourselves silly as we came. When she laughed, her belly muscles clamped on me and I gasped again and she giggled again until at last we calmed, her hands very smooth and dry on my back. She brought them up to my head and held it tight and kissed me very firmly. Then she wriggled away from me and bent down to look at my shrunken cock. The foreskin was still pulled back.

She bent to it and put her mouth around the end and sucked the foreskin down. It felt like warm velvet on me.

I looked at my watch on the bedside table. Six fifty-five. She saw me looking. "You older men," she said. "After one thing. And when you've got it—pow." She sniffed. "That's when you can get it up at all." She kissed the top of my head as she went into the bathroom. I heard her start to pee. She must have needed one too.

# 8

Joao had answered the phone. I asked if he had found some more trousers. He didn't laugh. He didn't sound pleased at all. I said he should meet me at the National Stadium, out on the road to Cascais. He knew it. I told him to bring his brother-in-law and another Angolan called Luis. The files in London said that Luis was very cautious. He had been a customs man in Luanda. He was still a customs man. That made him cautious.

I told Joao not to worry about his merchandise. I was looking after it for him. He said it wasn't his. I said he was right. It wasn't.

Then I called Otto and asked if he had any of the little flashlights with timers. They use them on boats. You can set the flash for different times. Otto said he could get them by nine thirty. He'd deliver them to the hotel. I told him to put it on the bill. He'd run a check on Thayer. Forty-two years old. Drafted into the army for Korea. A Purple Heart and left the army as a lieutenant. After the army he did a bachelor's degree in political science at Notre Dame. That made him a Catholic. He had been their mile champion. Stayed on for a master's degree and then joined the Department of Defense as a civilian. He reentered the army in 1966, accelerated promotion to captain. Made a major in 1968, served at staff HQ in Saigon. From 1969 to 1971 he was in Washington, then in Santiago, and now Lisbon. No promotions listed. Three kids, two daughters, one of twenty-four, graduated from Berkeley. One of nine at school in the States. A son of eleven, also in the States. Wife killed in auto accident in Chile.

"That's a very unusual career, Otto. Is there a date on that car crash?"

"This is just a military record, Maddox. He applied for a grant to repatriate the body from Chile in September 1973. You know what month that was?"

"Yeah. That was the month they pulled the rug from under Allende." We hung up and I started climbing into some clothes as Marianne came naked out of the bathroom in a cloud of steam.

"You're going out again." She said it as a statement, not a question. I told her I had to meet a contact, but I would be back inside an hour and maybe we could have dinner before I had to go out again.

"Every other journalist I've met here spends his evenings eating pretty well and trying to get laid. How come you're the only one with the midnight sources, Dave?" There was no suspicion in her voice, and as if to prove it she came and knelt on the bed and kissed the back of my neck while I buttoned my shirt. I grabbed for my shoes and said something about the story depending on contacts with the army and with the Communists and the time to meet them was at night. It didn't even sound convincing to me.

"You're worried about my father, aren't you?" This time it was a question and I turned around to answer it. She had shifted on the bed so she was sitting cross-legged, almost in a Yoga position. Her thighs yawned and my eyes fell to her tuft, the lips still more red than pink peeking through. I grinned at her and put my hand lightly on it.

"Not as much as I am about his daughter," I said, and leaned forward to kiss her. Her thighs suddenly straightened and squeezed, trapping my hand. "I'm serious, Dave. What is it about my father?"

"I think he's more than just a soldier, love, and that could be significant. This country is a political jam-pot, and he's one of the funny bees that have started buzzing around. But I'm with you and that means a conflict in interest. What happens if I start writing about him and what he learned in Chile? Where does that leave you?"

"It leaves me in bed with you. He's my father, Dave, but hardly so you would notice. I didn't even want to see him when I was in Europe, but you were coming to Lisbon so . . . I'm as much an orphan as you in a way. Another military baby. Another orphan."

I looked at the watch. Jesus. Seven ten. I had to leave but I wanted to talk this out. I wanted to pack her up and send her away somewhere safe and pleasing, where she could stay until I had finished this job and finished with Chisholm, and go back to her and carry on like this, my hand trapped in that sweet fork of her thighs. We locked eyes for a long moment, everything in me believing in her, her face as open and fond as a baby's. There was even a scent of soap on her skin.

I put one finger to my lips, kissed it, and placed the finger on her nipple. Her eyes smiled at me. Through a blocked, dry throat I said I had to keep an appointment and I would be back as soon as I could, and if she wouldn't catch cold it would save time if she were still undressed when I got back. It was a stupid thing to say. Her legs jerked and rejected my hand, and then she gripped my shirt and angrily thrust her head forward.

"I'm not a fucking machine, Dave. I'm not here for the balling, I'm fucking worried about you, man." She let go and sank back on the bed. A smile twitched at her mouth. "Maybe the balling is one of the reasons, but take good care. I'll be here when you get back, but for Chrissake be careful. I'm hanging onto you, Dave."

"I'm hanging onto you, love. I really am." I caught her to me and held her very tight, feeling her arms lock around my back and hearing her murmur Dave, Dave, Dave into my neck. I kissed her shoulder and eased her arms apart. She moved them and slid them outside my arms so she could take my head and pull it down to hers. She kissed me chastely, almost dryly, on the lips and told me to hurry back. I got slowly off the bed and grabbed my jacket and moved for the door.

"Dave," she called. "I'm falling and falling hard. You know that, don't you?" I gave her the clenched-fist salute. "I've fallen, love," I said.

I took a cab to Spanish Gate, the center of the Lisbon road system. I dropped the cab by the huge traffic circle in the middle, and walked across the grass. Anybody following by car would be locked in the rush hour traffic. I crossed the streets when the lights changed and was strolling in front of the Gulbenkian building at seven thirty. A green Bedford truck cruised to the curb. MF number plates. The sliding door at the side was open. It slowed and I jumped in.

"This is most inconvenient," the Lisbon Resident said. He was the most elegant old man I had ever seen.

"I'm sorry, sir." The "sir" surprised both of us. You could see he hated sitting in a truck like the Bedford, and he hated talking to people like me. The profession wasn't what it used to be. He'd been the Resident here since 1938, and in the seven years after that, Lisbon was the spy center of the world. When the war ended the Portuguese stoned his house. They thought he was pro-

German. So did the Germans. He was a very good Resident. Everybody knew he hated the British. Everybody was wrong.

"I'm going to need your help with people in the north," I said. "That's where it's going to start and we have to know when. I have my own contacts up there but I'll need you to tell me when to expect it. My own operations here are starting this weekend. Mainly sound and fury. We are launching a new newspaper next week. It will need advertising."

He nodded. "The advertising will be simple, but I'm not sure you comprehend the likely course of events in the north. It will not be a D-Day, young man, not the opening of a campaign. It will be a series of increasingly urgent warnings."

"I understand, sir. Wellington's hit-and-run strategy of 1809 and 1810. Not the thrust through to Vittoria."

"I believe you do understand. I will ensure that you are informed." He put a handkerchief to his mouth and put it back in his sleeve.

"How much do we know about the Americans, sir? Do you know what they're doing?"

"Yes, and it does not concern you."

"It might. Would the American strategy be consistent with their having reached an agreement with the Russians?"

His hands rested on the knob of the black cane. He leaned forward, his chin on his linked hands.

"You mean the Russians have assured the Americans that they will not be promoting the Communist cause here?"

"Yes, sir. Exactly that. You would know better than I, but there is no sign of the Russians pulling out any stops to help the comrades. So far, I've heard of one little trade deal. It doesn't make sense, unless the Russians aren't trying. And if they aren't trying, why not? There must be a deal with the Yanks."

"You are forgetting the little matter of the guns from Angola, young man. They seem to have been destined for the Communists. Would not that indicate a degree of comradely concern?"

"It would if the guns had been Russian. But they were NATO

guns, Portuguese guns, and they came from Portuguese arsenals in Angola. The Russians may not have been involved."

"You may be right, young man. Maddox, is it not? I will make inquiries. The question is, Maddox, if the Russians are giving up Portugal, what are they asking instead? And why have the Americans not told us? You may telephone me in two days. It will be a pleasure to meet you again."

The audience was over. He sat back, his grip still firm on his cane, and we remained silent until his driver pulled in toward the curb by the crowds at Campo Pequena. I coughed. His eyes opened in inquiry.

"Might I ask a personal question, sir?" He said nothing.

"The only people in the world who have ever kept their pocket handkerchiefs in their sleeves were officers in some British regiments. Why didn't the Germans spot that?"

"Officers in those regiments were gentlemen, Maddox. The Germans could hardly be expected to understand." The eyes closed, the side door slid open. I climbed out.

His father had been chamberlain to the last king of Portugal. His mother had been English, his father half-English. He needed the cane because he had taken a German bullet in the knee when Haig crashed through the Hindenburg Line in August 1918. He was seventy-five years old and the best Resident we had ever had anywhere. Even the revolution had come as no surprise. Two of his great-nephews had been among the army captains who planned it. I bet they asked his advice.

I took the Metro back to the hotel. It smelled of garlic and sweet things, a kind of cosy humanity. Metro smells tell you something about a country. In France they smell of rubber. In Moscow they smell of wet clothes. In New York they smell of piss. London's tubes used to smell of nothing at all, bland and anonymous. Now there were hints of New York. We should import some Portuguese. Pay them to ride backward and forward all day, just to sweeten the air.

Back in the hotel room, Marianne was almost under the sheet, one sweet breast uncovered rising with her breath as she slept. I took off my jacket and crept forward to kiss it. Instantly the sheet came around my head and her arms around me.

"I wasn't really asleep," she said between kisses. I said I had realized that and started to undress. She stopped me and laid me back on the bed, kneeling above me and slowly undoing buttons and belts as I lay back and enjoyed the slim length of her and enjoyed the thickening in my groin. When she tugged off my shoes my jeans went with them, and she squirmed forward to straddle me at the waist, my erection throbbing frustrated at her back. She leaned forward and kissed me again, her tongue exploring deep in my mouth and her breath gently seeping into my lungs. I held her to me and rolled so we both lay on our sides, her hand flirting down my stomach and both of us smiling inanely at the other's face, too close to see, too dear not to keep close. Her hand drifted off me and she murmured that she was very wet and very randy and what was I going to do about it. She took my hand and put it onto her. See, she said. Very wet, I agreed, and she pulled my hand up to our faces and I shook with laughter as she stuck my own wet fingers into my mouth and then sank her mouth onto mine, her tongue squeezing in beside her fingers and her shoulders shaking as she laughed. The tongue withdrew. . . . "I love you, Dave." I pulled my fingers out of my mouth to tell her I loved her too and then, still lying side by side, she eased me into her, raising one long leg to lock it behind my back.

It was the gentlest loving I'd ever known, slow and close, like a baby in a cradle, her voice crooning my name between kisses and my hand squeezing between our bodies to circle her breast. Time passed or stopped or reversed itself, an element too far away to trouble us, the rhythm of our hips as slow and mighty as a tide washing over the rocks of the names and promises we gave each other.

The tide reached its full, and our voices whispered faster and our arms held tighter as our loins felt their power. Almost lazy in our quickening movements, Marianne rolled me onto my back and lay flat above me, my head locked between her breasts with her hands at my neck and the bed shifting on the floor. Her shoulders shuddered and her thighs bit and all of me from my smothered head to my thrusting legs was gathered and poured into her, exploding like a flower to flood us both as we came.

Later, slowly aware of her dear weight on me, I felt the juices that had dripped down from her cooling on my stomach. I whispered that I loved her as I gently moved her onto the bed and under the sheet. My watch said nine twenty. She was heavily asleep, curling onto her side as I tucked the sheet around her. I kissed the top of her head and staggered to the shower. As I lathered, my groin ached with sweetness. In the mirror above the sink I looked lazy and sleek, happy from my eyes and all through me. I dried and crept back into the room to dress.

I caught the phone as it purred before ringing. It was the hotel desk to say a package had arrived for me. Good old Otto. They brought it up to the room. Two neat little lights and timers. The scales showed I could set them to flash at anything from ten seconds to forty minutes. There was another package, well wrapped in tape. I took it gingerly to the bathroom and put it in the bath and called Otto. He said not to worry, he had sent that package too. I might need it.

The gun was still taped to the toilet cistern. I checked the action. The firing pin looked blunt and worn. It was a short-barreled .38. It would stop anything I hit, but I'd have to be close. I hoped Otto's man was good with a rifle. I turned to the bath and unwrapped the package, to find a phosphorous grenade. Jesus, he must have thought I was taking on a tank.

If you can throw them far enough, they are useful things. If you are too close, your own grenade will blind you, burn you, and keep burning until every last morsel of phosphorus is immersed in water. Then the doctors try and cut the pieces out of your flesh. The Chinese had used them a lot in Korea. Since then, they had become popular as anti-personnel grenades and as instant fire-bombs. I had used one once in Oman, to take out an Arab dhow we thought was running guns to the rebels. I swam to it and put the grenade over the side. Then I dived as deep as you can go in eight seconds and swam frantically away. The whole sea turned white.

I put the gun in my belt, the grenade in one pocket, and the timers in another. I felt like a Christmas tree. Before I left I looked at her sleeping. I had never told a woman that I loved her before and meant it. I didn't know how long I'd be so I draped a blanket over the sheet in case the night got colder. Then I kissed her hair again and turned off the light and let myself out, grinning at the prancing feeling in my feet. It was supposed to be like walking on air. I'd probably be hearing music too. The things in my pockets brought me back to the job for tonight. I half-expected Joao to turn difficult, which explained why I was glad about Otto and the rifleman.

Phil had taken the car I had brought from Spain to do his surveillance job on Joao. I had hired another for the evening. The keys were at the hotel desk. I drove up and around Pombal's statue and onto the *autostrada*. I got to the National Stadium at about nine forty. Otto's man should be in place by now. I drove down the drive toward the little suburb of Cruz Quebrada, the burning cross. I climbed up the slopes and put one of the light-timers in the trees, with a clear line of sight to the stadium steps. I checked the watch. Joao and his chums were due at ten thirty. I set the time switch for the full forty minutes, trusting to German workmanship. I took four minutes circling around the stadium to place the second one. I set it for thirty-six minutes and went back to the car to wait.

Ten twenty-nine. Four cars had passed, none of them slowly. More lights coming down from the *autostrada*. That meant they were coming from Lisbon. Would Joao not come from Estoril? Phil should know where Joao had gone. I should have arranged for Phil to call me at the hotel before I left. I slid out of the car, close to the hedge, slinking to the shadows near the steps.

It was a Mercedes taxi. I could just see the green of the roof. It slowed as it passed through the drive. The lights flashed off twice. It turned at the far end and came back. The lights flashed off again. It parked, as I had ordered, with its front toward the high curb. No matter what happened, their car would not have a quick getaway.

Three men climbed out, one from the front and two from the

91

back. I didn't think there was a fourth man. I hoped Otto's man had the car in the night-sight. I flashed the flashlight twice from the hedge.

"Come up here to the steps. One at a time." They obeyed. I checked the watch. Ten thirty-one.

"I've got men all around you. Sit on the steps and you'll see them." They sat down. One of Otto's little lights flashed. Perfect. We all stayed very still. Then the other flashed. They got the point. I came out behind them on the steps.

"I like the new trousers, Joao."

"We want the guns back. We were going to tell you about that . . ."

"But you didn't have time. Save it, Joao. You'll get those guns when I say so. The time for guns is not yet. It's coming but it's not yet. We're still trading in other things now, Joao. White powders. Introduce me to your friends, Joao."

Luis introduced himself. He looked like a customs man. Very stolid. Very cautious. A lot of fat at the back of his neck.

"This is my brother-in-law, Carlo." Joao's voice.

"Turn around, Carlo," I said. He saw the gun and turned very slowly. He was tall for a Portuguese, almost six feet, big in the shoulders and big in the gut. A flashy dresser, with two-tone shoes and a thin moustache and a little handbag. I told him to throw me the handbag and turn around and sit down again. Cigarettes, a key chain, a wallet, a comb, and nail file. I took a card from the pouch in the wallet and tossed it back.

"Whose idea was it to use me to get the guns?"

Luis put his hand up. Cautious Luis. He explained slowly in bad English that if the truck were traced to me I could say it was stolen. It was too dangerous to use one of their own trucks.

"So why didn't you tell me? You are forgetting the first thing. I am your control. You know only as much as I tell you. I know the large picture. You listen to me."

"We thought . . . " this was Joao, hesitantly.

"You do not think. You are not people to think. You are not people. You are names in a file in London. I know everything about you. I know where you were born, what you did when you

92

were young. I know the secret marks on your bodies. I know when you sleep with your wives. I know how you take your pleasures in bed. There are pictures of you in London. We know all this. We do not need you to think. What have you done with the heroin?"

"We sold it," Carlo said. "We got 200,000 escudos. We can get more. There are friends of mine." He waved a hand.

"Who runs the bar, the Navigator?" I asked.

"I own it. My cousin runs the bar," Carlo said.

"On Saturday morning, some leaflets will be brought to the bar. You will have twenty men to take the leaflets to the demonstration the Communists are holding by the Pombal statue. Some of my friends will be there with gas and smoke. When that happens your men will scatter the leaflets in the crowd. If anyone learns of this before Saturday I will kill all of you."

"We were told to form an association of Retornados, of the people from Africa," Joao said. "We held a meeting of heads of families last week."

"That is good," I said. "Next week, there will be a new newspaper. You will use some of the money from the heroin to buy advertisments every day. You will announce a meeting for the Saturday of next week, at the Pombal statue. For all the Retornados, to win your rights. It will be a meeting for jobs, for schools, for houses for the loyal Portuguese who have come home. I will arrange permission with the police."

"I have a cousin, a journalist in Angola," Luis said. "He wants to start a weekly magazine for the Retornados. We can use it."

"When the new newspaper comes next week, go to the editor. I will tell him to expect you. You can print on the machine there. You will let him see the magazine before it is printed. Use the money from the heroin. I will give some more heroin to Carlo tomorrow. There is a Totobola stall at the south end of the Rossio. Meet me there at noon. You and I will talk."

"There is the matter of the guns," Joao said. "There are people in the north who expect them."

"I know about the north. They are not needed yet. I do the thinking."

The three men sat immobile in front of me. Their car still looked empty. I stopped my own breathing. There had been a sound. I spun for the hedge.

"Scatter—" The spit of the machine pistol drowned my voice. Someone was gurgling on the steps. There was another burst and then the crack of a rifle and the machine pistol fired on, the sound cushioned so I thought the muzzle was pointing into the ground. A possible hit. It had come from my left. I scurried across the steps to the right. They would cover both sides.

Joao and Carlo were moving to their car. Joao was firing a heavy automatic from the shelter of the cornice while Carlo sprinted and dived under the car. The rifle cracked again, far up above me. That would be Otto's man. A shape rose to my left and sprayed Joao's car. It was a quick burst, and he dropped to the ground fast. I heard him crawling toward me, heading farther left. I waited for him to rise again. He took a breath and cocked the gun and I put three bullets in him as he rose. Five yards. I sprinted to him and picked up the gun. An old Astral, Spanish issue. I moved farther to the left, hoping to God Otto's man knew my shape in the dark. There had to be a car. They wouldn't bring the weapons without a car.

Farther below me to the left the drive went down between tall hedges, curving away. There was a fork there. I should have covered it. I checked back. Carlo had the car started and was reversing it toward Joao, who was still firing from the cornice. He must have seen something. He was firing now at the hedges, and I heard another engine just around the corner of the fork in the road. There was a gleam of light—the car door had opened and the courtesy light glinted on the barrel of a gun.

The phosphorous grenade was in my hand, but it was too close. I put a quick burst into the windshield at twenty yards. The Astral kicked up and to the right. I rolled to my left, rose and put the rest of the magazine into the car, starting at the bottom left of the rear door. The recoil did the rest, the bullets drifting higher through the car. The breech clicked empty, and then I heard the car motor cough and die. Away behind me, Carlo's car was moving to the *autostrada*. Joao had made it. The tail lights faded.

The Astral in my hand was familiar. I sprinted back to the man I had shot. There was a spare magazine in his inside breast pocket. I knew the face. I moved down to where I had heard Luis breathing through a hole in his lungs. There were three holes and he was almost dead. I had the wallet from the man I killed and I would need more, but I had to get the car away. I walked to my car, driving slowly past the big Peugeot I had shot up. The door was still open, the courtesy light on. One of them lay half-sprawled through the door. The other slumped over the steering wheel.

I accelerated down the hill and took the forest track, which would bring me to the top of the hill where Otto's man had been. I drove on side lights, not daring to put the glow of my lights into the sky. The police would not be long. I swerved to avoid a bump in the road and braked.

The bump in the road was dead. Two shots, one in the shoulder, one in the back of the neck. I sniffed at the man's hand. He had been firing a gun. I pulled out his wallet and got back in the car, driving over the hill and down to the modern estate that loomed above Cruz Quebrada. I skimmed the wallet of the man I had shot, the man I knew. He had been the guard at the MSR building, the one with the machine pistol that now lay on the floor of the car beside me. I opened the other wallet, from the dead man on the track. There was a yellow card with a red diagonal stripe and a number in the top corner. A Communist Party card. His ID card said he was Jorge Maria Silva y Castro and he was married. The address was in Ceiras, three miles up the coast. I drove slowly through the town, looking for a way onto the coast road. Two police cars came by, sirens on. The rest of the coast traffic slowed to let them pass and I crept into the line.

At Ceiras I turned off and drove around the streets, looking for the one where Silva y Castro had lived. He was ground floor right apartment of a large building. I checked his ID again. The photo looked like the dead man, even though the bullet had taken half his jaw. I picked up the gun and got out of the car.

I wrapped a handkerchief around my face and knocked at the door. Nothing happened. I knocked again. Jesus, I hoped the neighbors were asleep. The door opened a crack and I kicked it in, flattening the woman against the wall. She slumped, looking at the gun. In a back room, a child wailed. The first room was a kitchen, the second a living room. I snapped on the light and went to the mantelpiece, looking for the wedding picture. It was him. Silva y Castro, just like the name on the door. There was a leather shape, black and almost familiar, beside it. It teased at my memory, but I had to leave. The kid was screaming, but the mother was still slumped and silent as I left.

I took the coast road to the great bridge, paid my 20 escudos to cross, and slung the Astral into the river Tagus. At the other end of the bridge I drove on past the tollbooths to the all-night cafe and drank coffee. Mud on my clothes, and my hands were yellow with the cordite from the Astral. I washed and then flushed the two wallets away, putting the two ID cards and the yellow card with the red stripe into my shoe. This time, when I paid my 20 escudos and drove back over the bridge, I remembered to throw away the phosphorous grenade.

# 9

I woke to the smell of hot coffee. Marianne had called room service. I drank orange juice and skimmed the front page of *Diario de Noticias*. There were two ministerial changes. Commerce and Transport. Another tick for Otto. They had to be Communists. I started on the coffee and turned inside for the regional news. Police had cleared an angry mob from the Communist offices in Braga. The local police chief had issued a statement saying freedom of political thought was the birthright of all Portuguese.

The sound of the shower stopped. I shouted hello through the door. It opened and steam came out. I asked what time I was playing squash with her father. Ten, she said. It was nine fifteen and I had a cover story to keep.

"Will you do me a favor? You know the Reuter's office? It's in that street off the Liberdad opposite the restaurant where we had lunch yesterday. Can you go and read their tapes on Portugal and make some notes? I'll see you back here for lunch at two."

She emerged through the steam. All talcum powder and moist girlhood. I really wasn't up to it and crawled off the bed to prove it. I fought my way through the steam into the bathroom, stubbing my toe on the sink and standing on her hairbrush. I climbed into the shower and tangled my head in some drying panties. Hot water would help.

I turned it on. It was cold. Jesus. I turned on the other tap and sat down in the bath and put my heel in the plughole, letting water build up around me. I was sitting on the soap. I bet myself I couldn't do it and reached up and turned off the hot tap. A burst of cold water. Waking up. I turned the hot tap on and reached for my razor and the shaving foam. The mint smell of the lather helped, and I held the razor under the hot tap to warm it. The first stroke up the neck, get the tough bastards out of the way early. Leave the smooth cheeks till the end. The razor pulled at my skin. I looked at it. Clogged with little hairs, half an inch long. No. Not her armpits. Don't let it be her armpits.

When I came out, still trying to stop the flow of blood from my neck, she was demure and beautiful on the balcony. She had laid out the breakfast. The papers were folded at my place. She had hung up my clothes. She smiled.

"You've got time to drink your coffee. I'll have the Reuter tapes by two, and Phil called. He said there was a press conference at the ministry at noon and he'd see you there." She ate a croissant. I wished I were a croissant. I drank my coffee. She asked why I had toilet paper on my neck.

"My aim is bad in the mornings." I sneezed. Her talcum powder. I couldn't see Phil at noon. I had to meet Carlo at the Totobola. I hope he made it. I'd have to see Otto sometime. There was something about last night I had to remember. I got up and found my shoes. The cards were still there. I put them behind the bathroom mirror. It wasn't that. There was something else. I called the desk to get me a cab for the Military Club. She kissed me good-bye. I held my breath. The talcum powder.

Her father was already changed into neat white shorts and shirt. He pointed to a heap of gray clothing in the corner and said to help myself. There would be something my size. They smelt like I felt. One sneaker was too small, the other too large, but he had got me a good racket. A Red Devil. He wore a headband, in spite of his short hair.

"I'm surprised you're still a major," I said. "After Vietnam, there are three or four generals your age." He didn't react. We went to the court.

We knocked the ball about for a few minutes, to warm it. He hit long and deep, the ball moving easily into the corners where the walls made it hard for me to take a good backswing. I held the racket by its base, belting the strokes so they bounced high and he could take the rebound from the back wall. We changed sides and his backhand was just as precise, the ball bouncing just behind the service court. I moved up and volleyed some returns. He moved with minimum effort, never too far from the central T. He knew how to play.

He won the toss for service and served hard and low, the ball coming off the side wall at waist height, deep enough to cramp my swing. I had shifted my grip, holding the racket high on the grip, and took a flat backswing and dropped the return into my front corner. He was already moving forward and scooped it up, giving me an easy winner to the back of the court.

I took the service and played my usual lob, an underarm shot, which dropped skidding off the side wall and died in the corner. He tried to boast it out from the side wall, but his shot fell short. We changed sides and I played the same shot. This time his boast made the front wall, but I was close enough to smash it into the side and it kissed the front wall before dying in the far corner. He had barely moved past the T.

Serving again, he moved forward to smash the high ball before it hit the side wall. I made to take the same shot, the underarm serve, but flattened the racket and drove a hard one straight at him. He got it back and I drove back down the side wall and danced back to the central T. He drove it back down the side and jostled me for the T as I moved sideways to play the same shot again. He moved back to take it but missed the angle. I had enough room to play a cross-court shot. He moved behind me, expecting a shot into the back court, but I was lucky. The ball hit the side wall first and died in the front court. He was getting mad. We had two spectators, leaning over the back balcony. Fuck him. I turned to him again, a nice one that died in the corner. He tried to smash it to the back wall, trying to give it enough lift to float back to the front, but it bounced in the court. I lobbed him again, a little too strong, and he turned inside the wall, a nice stroke into the side wall, dying in the front court, but I was close enough to play it straight back up the wall and make the T. He scrabbled his shot, giving me an easy volley.

A flat service that he put into the ceiling. A corner lob. Seven-love.

My next lob serve fell short and he smashed it before it reached the side wall. He took the service.

"Is your wife here with you?" I asked as he bounced the ball. "She died," he said. "It must be very difficult bringing up a daughter alone—especially on a major's salary," I observed, tugging at the thin strings at the base of my racket. He served and the ball went past me. "Sorry. Wasn't ready." I smiled at him. He walked slowly to the front court and picked up the ball, visibly counting up to ten to cool his temper.

It was a nice serve, flat and low. I had to return it straight down the side wall, and he was already moving, lifting his racket high for a backhand drive across the court. I was moving to receive it and he flattened the swing and stroked it back to where I had been. One-seven.

100

"You like the tricky ones, Major. Like father like daughter."
He knew I was needling him but the stroke had given him confidence. The next serve twisted off the wall, heading across me. I turned, hoping it had enough speed to come off the back wall, and backhanded it into the nick at the corner. My service again, too short, and he played a drop shot into his front court. I skidded it across court and sprinted back for the T, my backhand ready for his cross-court drive. I played it straight down the wall and won the T position. I put his return down the opposite wall, keeping him running across behind me, and his shot ballooned, giving me an easy corner shot. I served flat and low to his knees —he was standing too far forward again and his return hit the tin. Game to me. The spectators had gone.

I took the next two games nine-five and nine-three. His headband was soaked, and his neat white shirt stuck grayly to his skin. My lob serves were dropping beautifully, and every time he stood forward to try and smash them I served hard and low for his body. My lovely racket, the weighty Red Devil, volleyed all by itself when his serves went loose, and now he was tired. I drop-shotted him or lobbed deep. I took the second set three games to one.

"Do you like a short rally, Major? I like a bit of a run myself."
I was breathing deeply, like a dog, when I moved forward to pick up the dead ball. So I breathed easily as I moved back to the service court and chatted to him. He kept his temper well. It was his serve, a loose one that came easily from the wall to my forehand. My right foot moved back and I aimed the ball hard at his back. It hit low in his ribs and his head jerked up.

"It was heading for the front wall, Major. My point."
I served at him again, but he drifted to one side and played a beautiful backhand drop shot. I told him it was a fine shot and he grunted. His next serve was loose, and as he moved to the T I played it straight back at him. He knew it was coming and his foot went back. He was winding up for a strong drive to the far corner, but his racket hit the wall and the head snapped. We watched it roll to the tin.

"I think that's the end of the game, Major. Thank you." I

picked up the splintered racket-head and handed him the ball. He took them and nobly tried to smile. He was still panting. He looked like a mean old wolf.

"That'll teach me not to play with kids, huh?" He stayed by the side of the court. "From what I hear, you do so little journalism you get a lot of time to practice." He took off his headband and wrung it in one hand. A stream of sweat drops pattered to the floor. His face was still red, but his breath was under control. So was he, but there was still a fine spike of anger in him.

"These have been killing me." I took off the unmatched sneakers and wriggled my toes. "How long do you think you'll be stationed in Lisbon?"

"That's for Uncle Sam to say, not me. Be another year or so, I guess." He made no move to the door, his eyes cool. "How long do you think the story will keep you here?"

"Depends on what happens. The elections are almost a year away. Something's got to happen before then. The Communists either make their move or they don't. Either way it's a story."

"If they don't make a move, there's no story." He was watchful.

"Why shouldn't they? They have the media sewn up, part of the army. They just got two more ministries. There are trade deals in the air. It's all going their way. They seem to have lost some guns, however." Everybody knew about the guns. There had even been a photo of the crate yard on the front page of the morning papers. The *Herald Tribune* was probably running the story.

"What sort of move do you think they'll make?"

"I don't know. If they go this way they won't need a coup. All the strings will be in their hands. It depends which generals get to govern the north, what happens to the chiefs of police, the Ministry of the Interior. There's more than one way to take over a government. And as long as they run the Intersindical, nobody else can govern the country without them. They're sitting pretty."

"They got 12 percent of the vote at the preliminary elections."

"So? What did the Bolsheviks ever have in 1917? How many

votes did Castro get before he took Havana? Come to that, Major, it didn't seem to bother you that Allende was voted into power in Chile. What do votes matter?"

"Chile was different. It was a minority Marxist government."

"So is this one. It's a government. It's Marxist. Even the Socialists say so."

We were both cooling and he walked to the door. The showers were faced with the old blue and yellow tiles, the water piping hot, and clean towels and bars of fresh soap on the racks. His eyes appraised me, partly as another athlete, partly as a man looking at the body that slept with his daughter. I turned my water to cold and concentrated on my shower. He handed me a towel.

"I didn't think you were the kind of reporter who went looking for nasty stories about the CIA, Dave."

"You're not CIA, Major. You've got more sense."

"SAS and Military Intelligence in Northern Ireland isn't what I'd call sensible training for a journalist, Dave."

"You've had long enough to check. We're allies, remember. All in NATO together. The special relationship."

"Portugal's in NATO too, Dave. That's what worries us. We're sitting here in Lisbon wondering what to do about Europe going left and all of a sudden we get our allies riding into town and not telling us anything about it. You even ride into town with my own daughter. Tell me that's a coincidence."

"It's a coincidence, unless you fixed for her to pick me up." I looked at him levelly. "I wouldn't put it past you." He was toweling his hair. His "Fuck you" was muffled.

"Like you said, Major, this isn't Chile. That was on your doorstep. Portugal's on ours. So why not tell your old British friends what you're doing here? Is it the transport unions again, or do you have some new subtle plans for collapsing the economy, like you forced down the cost of copper in Chile?"

"The economy is collapsing anyway. We couldn't even help it along. You're the ones who can do something. Bring Portugal into the Common Market."

"And have a little Communist viper in our bosom? Brussels

would love that, Major. The last time you tried to persuade Brussels to take another country it was the Greek Colonels. Just before they collapsed."

"The time before that it was Britain, Dave. Remember that." His point.

"This grand strategy is a bit much for a major. Why not tell me what your real rank is?" I walked to the hook for my shirt and started to dress. "You didn't invite me here just to lose a game of squash." He dressed in silence and moved to the mirror to comb his hair. I threw my dirty shorts and shirt back onto the heap and slung the sneakers after them.

"We may be in touch, Dave. I can't say any more than that." He put his gear into a locker and moved to the door. "I've got to rush. Thanks for the game and give my love to Marianne."

I sat in thought on the bench until two more players came in, then I walked downstairs to the pay phone and called the MSR offices. Major Antonio came on the line after I gave my name. Life was one bloody major after another.

"I thought you said our interests coincided? Last night I coincided with one of your thugs."

"What do you mean, Mr. Maddox?"

"Did you count your door guards this morning? The ones who frisk your guests. You'll be one short. At least one."

"I'm sorry. I really don't understand. Are you saying there has been a fight with the comrades who guard our building?"

"One of them tried to kill me last night, and he had some friends. I don't know who they were but you'd better make some inquiries. I'll call you back." I put the phone down and dialed Otto. He was out. I called the hotel and asked them to page Phil for me. I rolled a cigarette while he came to the phone.

"Phil, I'm going to have to skip the press conference. I've got an interview. How did it go last night?"

"The conference has been canceled anyway. The Ministry won't say why, but there are rumors something's up. Reuter's is running a story on a possible change of government. They're quoting 'sources close to the President,' but nobody really knows what's up. I've got the address for that guy I followed. He went

104

straight there when he left the bar and came out in different clothes and with his hair wet. Looked like he went home for a bath. Then I followed him into Lisbon. He had a drink at the Beira, a bar on the waterfront, and came out with a big guy with a small moustache. They got into a cab and went up to the Alfama and I lost them in the narrow streets. I got a photograph of the big guy."

"Phil, that's great." He gave me Joao's address and said he was going with some other pressmen to wait outside the presidential palace. If there was a government change coming, that's where the activity would be. I said I might see him there later.

I checked my watch. An hour until I was meant to meet Carlo. If he showed up. Not long enough to check on Joao's house. I called Otto again. Still not at the office. Through the glass of the phone booth I saw Major Thayer walking out of the club with a Portuguese officer whose face I knew from the papers. He had been the deputy commander in Mozambique, not known to the political, but a professional soldier. There were parachutists' wings on his blouse. He had just been named as the new governor of the Azores Islands, part of the collapsed empire the Portuguese were determined to keep.

They were joined by a third man, a colonel whose face I did not know. There was a red dagger on his sleeve. Gray hair, gray eyes. The three walked out of the club together and climbed into a large black Mercedes. I called MSR again and spoke to Major Antonio.

"A commando colonel, forty years old, five-eight. About a hundred and fifty pounds, very fit. He wears a black beret and a wristwatch on each wrist. Who is he?"

"That's Jaime Lores. He's the acting commander at the Amadora barracks. None of the guards arrived this morning, Maddox. One of them telephoned the duty comrade early this morning and said they had to go back to Spain. I've sent two men to the house where they lived."

"Why Spain?"

"They're Spanish. We had better meet. I don't like phones."

"I'll meet you at the Roma Cafe in ten minutes. I can't stay long. And Major, bring me everything you know about the Spanish comrades."

In the cab I was trying to work out why MSR had Spanish guards. And why they had a Portuguese Communist Party member with them when they ambushed me at the stadium. I still didn't know how they knew where I would be. Otto knew, Joao knew, Joao could have been followed. I could have been followed from the hotel, but that didn't give them much time to organize an ambush party. And why try me at this early stage?

I was pouring my beer when the major arrived. We sat in the open air. The tables around us were empty. The major was smiling.

"The fourth man was still at the house when my man got there. He's at our office now. Under guard. So far he's saying nothing, but he probably will. He was one of four from Spain. They were sent by trusted friends."

"How long had they been with MSR?" I asked.

"Since November, the first two. The second pair, including the one we have now, came in February. The first two were Portuguese who had left to evade the draft. They were known to some of our militants. They had no orders to fight with you, Maddox. They had no orders about you at all."

I told him briefly that I had been meeting some people at the stadium and had been ambushed. I told him about the Portuguese Communist, Silva y Castro. And I told him that the police would probably have the missing car and the two other comrades.

"So they are Communists. Infiltrating us." He shrugged. "It is to be expected. We will find out all about them from the one we have."

"You'd better double check everybody who introduced them to you. And check back over every difficulty you've had since they arrived. Any men you've lost, papers that have gone missing, things that have gone wrong. And then double check your security people. They're either cheating you or they're incompetent."

"All this is already being done. We're not playing at this,

106

Maddox. This is serious. As soon as you called this morning I thought of two things, two car accidents. One was our best man in the bank union. The other was the deputy secretary of the teachers union. He was a secret sympathizer. Both those unions are controlled by the Communists now."

"They need not be Communists, Major. They could be anything from Spanish Intelligence to the Maoists. You know that. But we have to know soon."

He nodded. "MSR is a small party, Maddox. An elite. Kill a handful of us and there's not much left. But there are too many Communists. We can't just kill them back."

"There are other ways, Major. You know that. There are places where they will hurt. Their printing presses for one. Their files. Their allies—hit the Russian Embassy, or the Polish, and the comrades will be very embarrassed. If you wanted to hurt them like they did you, which union would you pick?"

"Two. The shipbuilders, where the UDP and the Socialists challenge them for control, and the chemical workers, where the Maoists are strong."

"What about the dock workers?"

"It's not a big union, but it's been well-organized by the Communists. They used it as a training ground for other union officials. They are too strong there. It's a rich union—there's always been a black market in the docks. A lot of that money stays in the union."

"If the Communists suddenly weakened in the docks, could you be in a position to take over? Are there any unions you could take like that?"

"We couldn't take over the docks. We could take over the teachers, the bankers, the electricity workers. Maybe the sewage workers. We could run them, keep the administration going, but we couldn't control. We are too small. We haven't the representatives in each factory, in each office. The Communists have their men everywhere. If we ran the union secretariat and ordered a strike, nothing would happen. The local branches would ignore us."

107

"What if you concentrated all your people into one key union?"

"You don't understand, Maddox. Unions don't work like that. At local level they are run by local workers, men who have been there for years, local officials known to everybody. You can't just bring in strangers and expect it to work. It's not like an army, Maddox."

"So how did you ever hope to challenge them in the first place?"

"I told you yesterday, it's a long-term thing. We are strongest in the new unions, the office workers, the banks, the computer people. The Communists are still stuck in the old industries. We are organizing the parts of the economy that will grow. It's not our job to challenge for the steelworks and the shipyards. The Socialists can do that."

"I'm not arguing with you, Major. I accept what you say. But I was not suggesting you try and supplant the Communists overnight. I was suggesting that you scare them. Even a weak threat against one of their strongholds will frighten them. They won't be expecting it. And you needn't make it look as if you did it—blame it on somebody else. Leave some right-wing leaflets around if you rough up an office. Phone bomb threats and say you are from the secret army of liberation. Make them panic."

"Have you done this before, Maddox?"

"Not quite on this scale, Major. But the principle's the same." I rose and put a 50-escudo note on the table. "I'll call you this afternoon. I want to hear what your Spaniard has to say." My watch said eleven forty-five. I wanted to get to the Totobola shop well before Carlo, to check the place over. I didn't know what it looked like inside. I had left it late. I called a cab and looked back at the major. I gave him the clenched-fist salute. He stuck two fingers up and grinned. He'd learned that from the SAS.

# 10

They jumped me as soon as I got in the door. It was very professional. The sack came over my head at the same time I felt the gun in my side. I heard the door slam behind me. The last thing I had seen was a counter, crowded with men making their bets on the Totobola. They didn't mind being rough in public. Either Carlo was too angry to care or he ran this part of town.

They pushed me along, through a side door, down some steps

and along a corridor. It smelled damp, and the men with me stumbled. We came into the open air but it was too quiet to be a street. I was half-pushed, half-thrown into the back of a truck. Somebody knelt on me and fixed handcuffs. The truck drove off. Usual traffic noises, nothing I could pinpoint, but the truck was climbing steadily. They were taking me to the Alfama, the maze of streets in the old city that nestled under the walls of the fortress. Bars, cafes, restaurants, whores, and trendy apartments. This was more Carlo's kind of country. The truck stopped. I was pushed over the tail, landing heavily on my side. Somebody pulled me up and we went down some more stairs. A smell of cheap perfume and stale wine. They sat me in a chair and took the sack off my head. Carlo sat across the table. There was an ashtray on the table. It said Bar Montegordo. The fat mountain. At least I knew where I was.

"Congratulations," I said. "I liked the way you got away. You forgot Luis but he won't mind. He's dead."

"You owe me 900 grams of heroin and a truckful of guns," Carlo said. There was a long scrape down the side of his face, very fresh. From last night.

"I owe Joao one pair of trousers and some shoes. That's all," I said. "You owe me your life. I killed the man who got Luis. I killed the other two in their car. When you were still running for Lisbon I took a chance on the police and grabbed some ID cards. You know my room at the hotel. Send a man down there. He'll find the cards behind the bathroom mirror. He'll find Joao's gun in the cistern. Tell him to knock. There might be a lady in the room."

"Where will he find the heroin?"

"You'll get that when I give it to you. Not before. Now take these cuffs off me and pour me a beer before I get angry." He sat still. "Don't be an idiot, Carlo. You've laid out 100 grams of the stuff already and you've promised 900 grams more. That means you're dealing with a very big organization. You come up with supplies like that and they won't let you stop. You may not be injecting the stuff, Carlo, but you're still addicted. And I'm the only place you can get any more."

110

His eyes weighed me up. He wanted to beat the hiding place out of me but that would be the end of the supplies. No more after the 900 grams, even if I told him. He stood up and unlocked the cuffs and crossed to the bar. He came back with two bottles of Sagres beer.

"The heroin is taped to the inside of the cistern in the toilet in the Navigator Bar," I told him. "It's been on your property since the day I arrived."

"Who attacked us?"

"One was a local Communist. One of the others was a Spaniard who was attached to MSR. I think the other two were his friends. MSR knew nothing about it. My guess is that Spaniards infiltrated MSR. They might have been Communists. I don't know. What worried me is how they knew we'd be there. Either one of you three told them, or they followed us. And I don't believe they had the time for that ambush if they were just following. Who else knew about the meeting apart from you, Joao, and Luis?"

"Luis and I didn't know where it would be. Joao didn't tell us. It was either him or you who told them. Or you were followed."

"Tell me about these men you're dealing the heroin to," I said. "What else do they do?"

"They run Lisbon. I run part of it for them. They are very pleased about the heroin. They want it to continue. I think it's going to the States. There isn't much heroin here. There's a lot of *liamba*, hashish. They control that too."

"Are they the same people who ran Lisbon before the revolution?" He nodded. Governments come and go. The hoodlums are forever. But Carlo was based in the Alfama, one of the little plums of the city. He also owned a bar in Estoril. Joao had said he was getting into tourist villas and real estate. He also used that bar on the waterfront where Phil had seen him last night. Hoodlums only drink in places they can trust. So Carlo ran more than the Alfama. He was young enough to be ambitious. If he wasn't one of the top three or four bosses, he would be.

"How much of the waterfront do you run, Carlo? How much of the docks?"

"Enough. I get what I want in, or I get it out. If I don't want a ship to unload, it doesn't unload."

"What about the dock unions? Who runs them?"

"They call themselves Communists. It doesn't mean very much. It's the same people who always ran it. Under Salazar there was a kind of union, an official union. Some of them are still there, saying they were Communists all the time. Docks are like that. The jobs go from father to son. Families are important, arrangements like mine are important. Politics are separate. Politics only matter when it suits the families. When it suits me."

"How do the Communists suit you? You've got other investments, other responsibilities. What do the Communists do for them?"

"In the docks, the Communists suit me. They are people I know. We have worked together for a long time." He shrugged. It was simple to him.

"So if it suited you to call a strike in the docks, even if the Communists opposed it, there would be a strike?" He nodded. "And if the Communists wanted a strike but you said no, there would be no strike?" He nodded again, smiling.

"So why don't you like the Communists, Carlo? If they don't bother you?"

"There are Communists and Communists. I have land, farmland I bought in the Alentejo. The south of Portugal. I bought a big farm. An investment. The Communists took it over, gave it to the peasants. Down in the Algarve I was building villas. I bought the land, laid roads, built apartment villas. All honest business. The builders go on strike, the wages double. The villas that are finished are taken over by poor people. They pay me no rent. There are no tourists. Here in Alfama, young girls come around to the whores, tell them to stop working. Communism is bad for me. I want tourists. I want my land back, I want to finish my villas. If the Communists take the government, we'll have new Communists in the docks. There'll be no room for me. That's why I'm talking to you, Ingles."

"What do the big men say, the ones who run Lisbon?"

"They said it was okay to work with you. The heroin is nice.

But they would work with you anyway. They lost money in Angola and Mozambique. They have lost land in the Alentejo. These are very rich people. They are with you and the Americans."

"What do you know about the Americans, Carlo?"

"I know who you saw this morning. At the Military Club. He was in the Alentejo at the landowners' meeting."

"What do you know about the north, Carlo? Joao said last night people in the north expected the guns."

"What everybody knows. We have family up there. The *caciques* don't like the Communists. There are very few Communists in the north. People are poor, but they own their own land. If the Communists come, they will lose their land. And the priests hate the Communists. The north will throw them out. The poor farmers will do it. They want to do it now, but the *caciques* say they must wait for the right time."

"What's the right time?"

"That's up to you, Ingles. You and the American. You want to weaken the Communists in the city. The American wants to weaken them in the Alentejo. If the north throws the Communists out too soon, they will still control Lisbon and Setubal and Santarem and the south. That would be a civil war, like Spain. I will help you because I want to keep my land and my villas. But also because I don't want a civil war. I have a nephew who is a Communist. He is a fool but he is a nephew."

"Do you realize that you will have to fight a lot of little civil wars to stop a big one?"

"Yes. And I also want the heroin."

"You'll earn it. There are two Russian ships in the port. They're waiting to load some wine. They should stay empty. It would be nice if they could be damaged. We're going to ruin their demonstration this Saturday in Lisbon. Their newspapers are talking about another meeting in Benfica tonight, in the stadium. Can you out the power lines just as they begin, cut the lights and the loudspeakers?" He nodded. I asked him if he had any suggestions.

He walked back to the bar and pulled out two bottles. One

113

was brandy and the other a clear white liquid. Anis. He poured a measure of each into a glass and brought it to me, and went back to the bar to pour his own.

"*Sol y sombre*," he said lifting the drink. "Sun and shade. There are three Communists at the docks union. New Communists. They lived in France until the revolution. Then they came back. They have no family. Nobody likes them. They can go in the river." He looked up. "I have some friends in the police. They like to make arrests. Perhaps we could spare some heroin. The police like to catch heroin. Some in a Communist office, some in a man's home."

"I'll arrange for another kilo. Can you help Joao and the Retornados?"

"They can meet at the docks. We can arrange a demonstration in their favor. A march on the ministry." He sipped at the drink. "Can you get dynamite?"

"Yes, but you'll need people who can use it."

"We have conscription in Portugal. Most men were in the army. Some of them learned about explosives. That's where I learned. Keep the detonators simple—fulminate of mercury. When can you get it?"

"I'll need two days. Where do I get in touch with you? If it's urgent?"

He passed me a card. It was the same one I had pulled from his purse last night at the stadium. It called him the manager of the Bar Beira, the one on the waterfront. There was no home number.

"Call there and leave your number. I'll call back within five minutes." He stood up. "The truck will take you back to Rossio. More comfortably than they brought you."

I put 500 escudos on the table. "For when you bury Luis," I said. "Some flowers. A wreath." He picked the note and spread it in his hands. "When I find who ordered the ambush I will tell you."

"Thank you, Ingles. I would like that. Luis would have liked that."

Carlo was still careful. I climbed from the cellar bar into the back of the truck. The door was locked and we drove off down the hill. The truck stopped. The back door opened and I climbed out, blinking in the sudden sunlight. A figure jumped into the back of the truck, closing the door from the inside. The van pulled away. I hardly saw him.

I crossed the square to the row of phone booths. I called Otto first. He was at his desk. I thanked him for last night, and said I wished his man had been a little faster in his reactions. Otto said the man had done his best, but he had been warned I might use the phosphorous first. He said the leaflets were all fixed. I asked him to clear the Angolan demonstration for the following Sunday and to tell the printing shop about the Retornados' magazine. I told him tonight's Communist meeting at Benfica was taken care of. We arranged to meet the next day.

I called Major Antonio. He said they were still trying with the Spaniard, and to call him later. He sounded tired. He asked if I remembered what I had said about newspapers and printing machines. I remembered I had suggested them as targets. He said he hoped my sleep would not be disturbed. I asked if there was any news about a change of government. Rumors, he said. Only rumors.

Then I telephoned the hotel. Marianne was not in her room. I paged her. No Marianne. I walked out of the phone booth and took a cab to the presidential palace. There was a knot of journalists on the steps, looking hot and bored. Phil was lying back, his head pillowed on his shirt, his brown chest getting browner.

Four ministers had gone in, he said. Interior, Justice, Defense, and Finance. That was the heavy mob. What about Foreign Affairs? Two carloads of journalists had driven over to the Foreign Office to try and find out where he was. Phil said two officers had gone in. One was the military governor of Lisbon. The other was the guy who was going to govern the Azores. That was the one I had seen with Marianne's father at the club that morning. It was a long time ago.

It was mid-afternoon when I got back to the hotel. No sign of

Marianne. On her bed was a sheaf of notes of the Reuter's tapes and a piece of notepaper saying I had missed lunch and she had gone sightseeing. Love, Marianne.

Love, Marianne, I thought, and pulled out my typewriter and sat down to justify my press card. The story I wrote for the London agency referred briefly to the rumors of the change of government but focused on the way in which the Communists were steadily gathering the reins of power into their hands. I pointed out their weakness in the north and the possibility of a series of popular risings against them. I wrote what Major Antonio had said about the *caciques*, and said the Communists were likely to face trouble in the docks and from their extreme left rivals in the trade unions. I added a paragraph about the Americans bringing in the men from Chile, and named Major Thayer, called him a man of mystery. I concluded on the note that worried me—if the Communists were getting ready to take power, or if they felt their slow accumulation of control was being threatened, what would the Russians do?

I sent the story off to London by the hotel telex. Within an hour of its arriving on the foreign editor's desk, a copy would be in Chisholm's office. It was almost as good as giving him a live briefing. He'd like the paragraph about the Yanks, and if the Resident had sent a report of our conversation, Chisholm could worry a little more. He liked worrying about the Americans.

There was one thing I kept to myself. The guns. Only Joao and Carlo knew I had the guns. And only I knew where. I pulled the blinds and slept.

# 11

The explosion rattled the windows, and it was enough to wake me. I was still dressed and I crossed to the balcony and looked at the red flare in the night sky. MSR was taking its revenge. It was just after 2:00 A.M. No sign of Marianne. Suddenly I thought of the way Phil looked at her and I felt my jaw tighten. I loosened it. She was a big girl. She was a girl I picked up to look innocent when I crossed the border with a kilo of heroin. The note was still on her bed. Love, Marianne.

I undressed, showered, and went back to bed, half-expecting not to sleep. I used the old soldier's trick, forcing myself to keep my eyes open until they tired and I slept. The light woke me, just before eight. I telephoned for breakfast and the papers and climbed back into the shower. Her panties were still on the rail. I shaved, remembering to change the blade. Her talcum powder stood on the side of the sink. Something occurred to me. I went to her bedside table and opened the drawer. Her pouch of birth control pills was there. She took them at night. The last one had been taken on Tuesday. This was Thursday morning. Girls do strange and foolish things, but they usually remember to take their pills.

I worried through breakfast and through the papers. The big news was the tragedy at the Communist meeting at Benfica. The lights had failed, there had been an explosion and the crowd panicked. Two dead and many injured. There was a photo of the platform, trampled and broken. Red flags were torn and flapping. There was no copy of *Diario*, the first paper the Communists took over. I flicked on the radio for the morning news. Eleven dead at the *Diario* atrocity, it said. The printing presses were beyond repair, but the valiant workers' paper would continue. The unknown bombers had left a painted slogan on the wall of a building opposite. It said "The Secret Army of Liberation strikes—Communists out of Portugal." There was no change of government. I checked behind the bathroom mirror. Carlo's man had taken the cards I'd put there. I checked the cistern. He'd taken the gun too.

That pulled me up short. Carlo's man had been here. I had even warned them there might be a woman in the room. I looked around the room more closely. Her shoulder bag and purse had gone. So had her passport and her travelers' checks. Her clothes, toilet things, and birth control pills were all still in the room. I sat on the bed and tried to think it through. By the time Carlo sent his boys up here to get the ID cards, he and I were friends again. Or were we? He had tried to grab me, and it could make sense for him to try and put pressure on me through Marianne. But Carlo did not know much about her. As far as he was concerned, she was a chick I was screwing. He could not know about the complications with her father. Nor about the complications with me.

The thought of Phil drifted into my head again, a spike of jealousy. I dismissed it, angry with myself. If I had taken the decision to trust her over her father, I'd be a fool to suspect her about another man. She couldn't have faked yesterday. I walked out to the balcony, rechecked the bathroom, and even looked at the thin film of dust under the bed. There was no sign of struggle. She would not have gone with Carlo's men willingly. I composed myself. I had a meeting scheduled with Carlo for later in the morning. If he had Marianne I would find out. If he didn't have her I would think again. Maybe Daddy had warned her off me—I was back again to my basic trust in her, to the sound of her voice saying my name.

I dressed and went down to the street and over the road to the phone booth. I used the double-ring code to reach the Resident. I said, "Nine o'clock. The occasional place." The phone went down. I thought about Otto. I had thirty minutes. Germans start work early. When I opened his office door he was going through his mail.

"Benfica was nice," he said. "I suppose you knew about the *Diario* bomb?"

"Who?" I said. "Me?" He asked me if I had any 2½-escudo coins. I gave him two. He went to the corridor and came back with two plastic cups of hideous coffee and began to drink them both.

"I want two cases of dynamite, unmarked, and some mercury detonators. We'll need some more heroin and some walkie-talkie radios. I need the radios for the demo on Saturday. I'd like a tail on that American I told you about, Thayer. Hire a detective agency. Tell them it's a divorce case. He's been busy with landowners in the Alentejo. We want to know which ones."

"How much heroin? How many walkie-talkies?" He was scribbling on a note pad.

"Two kilos and six walkie-talkies. I hope you burn that pad every day."

"Just as soon as I make up the accounts and forward them. In triplicate." He laughed, and the windows blew in. We both dived on the floor under the desk before the glass hit the wall. Our heads bumped.

"You have a very loud laugh," I said. We got up and went to the blasted window. The smoke was still rising two blocks away.

"That's the *Republica* building," he said. "You should have warned me. Now I'll have to buy some more coffee. I didn't get a morning paper today because of you. Now I won't get an evening paper. I like the crosswords."

" 'History is a cruel goddess,' " I said, " 'and drives her chariot over mountains of dead men.' "

"Quoting Engels at me," he said. "Before nine in the morning. You ought to be ashamed. Give me some more coins for the coffee machine."

"I'm sorry, Otto. I hoped you'd think it was original. I've got to go." I gave him the coins and he gave me some proofs of the leaflets we had planned. I stuffed them in a pocket.

"Your Angolans have permission for their demonstration next week. All the churches in five dioceses will be distributing the leaflets on Sunday. I have the tear gas for you."

"Deutschland uber alles, Otto." He waved and bent down to pick up the broken glass from his window.

I took the Metro to Campo Pequena and got to the road junction by the kiosk at two minutes past nine. The Bedford truck came up with the side door open. I climbed in and we drove away again.

"This is most inconsiderate, Maddox. You arrange a meeting at less than an hour's notice and you are late. I had to drive around the block."

Nine in the morning and the Resident was perfectly dressed. The hand that held the cane wore a gray glove. The other was holding a pocket watch. He slipped it back into his waistcoat. He smelt of Pears' soap and bay rum.

"I was delayed by an explosion. One of the evening papers won't appear today."

"Is all this really necessary? There are adequate resources

within Portugal to restrain the Communists without adventures such as yours."

"That's what people said about Czechoslovakia in 1948. If the Russians are going to back the comrades here, Portugal will need all the help it can get."

"The last time we met you inclined to the view that the Russians would not be active here. You suggested an agreement with the Americans."

"I still don't know, sir." There came that "sir" again. It suited him. "I'm running some operations against the Russians themselves, some of their offices and personnel here. If they are under orders to soft-pedal in Portugal, they won't react. If they strike back, we'll know they're serious and we can plan future strategy accordingly. I was hoping you would have some news for me."

"I do. You will fly to the north, to Oporto, this afternoon. You will meet three people. One is a policeman, another is a churchman, the third is an Anglo-Portuguese wine merchant. You are expected for dinner at the English club there at eight. I recommend the Infante de Sagres hotel."

"What about our American friends? Do you think they are talking with the Russians?"

"I informed London of your concern. The Russians have increased their presence here, primarily in their trade mission. I am more concerned by the activities of the Czechs and Poles. In this part of the world the Russians traditionally work through their satellites. The Czechs are negotiating a textiles agreement and the Poles have increased their commercial staff, ostensibly to discuss Portuguese requirements for trains and buses. The Poles are not known for their expertise in these fields. None of the new personnel is known to London."

"The Americans?"

"They seem to be relying on their Portuguese friends in the army, but I hear that a little discreet assistance is being given to expropriated landowners."

"London told me to stay away from the army. Is that wise, sir?"

"Probably not. But if those are your instructions they should

121

be obeyed. Did your instructions extend to this little bomb wave that has descended upon Lisbon? Or are you being over-zealous?"

"I'll tell you when I get back from Oporto. Can we meet on Saturday morning?" He nodded. "These rumors about a change of government—can you shed any light on that?"

"Nothing momentous will happen until the army council meets next week. The objections being voiced by the civil service, which led to the rumors you are hearing, will be joined by those of the army. A change of government may appear to follow. I suspect that the change will be of personalities, not of policies. Quite simply, Maddox, nobody knows what to do except the Communists. The Communists are applying the rule book. They have the trade unions, they have the press, they gain control of more and more ministries, but nowhere is there any sign of political intelligence."

"I suppose that's why London set us to work."

"Don't be a fool, Maddox. You flatter yourself and you flatter your masters in London. All Portugal needs is a simple, clear statement from London and from Washington that Communist domination in Portugal is unacceptable. Once that statement were made, the Portuguese themselves would kick out the Communists. You and I have to operate in our devious little way because our masters in London are too timid to say clearly and publicly what the national interest requires. We are not an arm of British policy, Maddox. We are an excuse for the fact that there is no policy. So we must do what we can and so convince our masters that the battle is already won that they will announce they are ready to fight. You will give my regards to the gentlemen you will meet this evening. They have my confidence. You have my good wishes. I will expect you on Saturday morning."

The Bedford truck dropped me by the cathedral. From habit I walked quickly into the crowd, not looking back, but my mind stayed in the truck, still dominated by the extraordinary force of the old man. Again and again, when they trained us, our teachers said that policy was not ours to make. Our job was to do what we were told. They showed us a country and pulled it apart so we could see how it worked and where it was weak and where it could be made to fall. We could do all this, but we did it when we were told.

They had an imaginary country at the big house in Somerset where they held the courses. They called the country Erewhon, and said we should think of it as Nowhere spelled backward. It had trade unions, police forces, roads, bridges, industries, armies, docks, political parties, ministries, local governments, postal services, international alliances, crops, and even a climate.

Day in and day out, we played with Erewhon. How do you cause a financial crisis? What would you do to provoke a strike here? A political demonstration? A closure of the universities? How would you raise the price of this? Look for the simplest way, they always said, the way that leaves least to chance. That was why they distrusted assassinations, unless you could be certain who would replace the dead man. They liked strikes, they liked bombs, they liked small and gullible political parties that needed money. They liked using organized crime and manipulating the stock exchange. They reckoned all that was quite predictable.

But what they taught us was the methods of carrying out the orders we received. Create this kind of crisis; undermine that kind of opposition; promote that cause; wreck this policy. The Resident came from another era, from simple times when agents acted as they saw fit and when policy was made by the man on the spot. I was just a very highly trained messenger boy. I did the job very well, but as the Resident had told me, I didn't know if it was the right job. And neither did men like Chisholm and the politicians back in London.

I should be driving to Estoril and checking out the house where Joao lived. I should be calling Otto. I should be at MSR Headquarters, giving some well-trained advice on extracting information from the Spaniard. I should be arranging the trip to Oporto. I should be seeing Carlo, drafting more leaflets for Saturday, delivering tear gas, deciding what to do with the guns in the garage at the villa.

Instead I was drinking coffee at a cafe overlooking the cathedral and wondering where Marianne had slept last night. She was a child. A well-fed, healthy American girl with clear skin and a neat figure and a tongue as slim and pink as a cat's, and I was worried about her. Balls. I wasn't worried about her. I was worried about me because she was all right and I wasn't, and I didn't know where she was or what she wanted.

She had a very dainty way of eating. She would lean forward, and the wings of her hair would fall to either side of her face, and when the fork was raised to her mouth she would flick her head so the hair fell back and the morsel popped into her mouth. Her eyes would widen a little and suddenly focus onto me as the fork lowered to the plate. I ought to be seeing what Carlo had done about the Russian ships. I had to persuade somebody to throw petrol bombs at the Polish Embassy. Maddox, the government of Erewhon has a balance of payments deficit—how do you make it worse? Raise insurance and shipping rates, strikes in the transport industry, place smear stories in the foreign press about contamination of key food exports. Very good, Maddox.

I forced myself to the cafe phone and called Major Antonio. His men weren't getting anywhere. I said I'd be with him in twenty minutes. I called Carlo at the bar. He was in. I said I'd see him in two hours at the Beira. I called the barman at the Navigator bar. Joao had been there last night. No sign of him today. I asked if he had a truck I could use and he said it would be ready at noon. I called the airline and booked a flight for 5:00 P.M. They said they could also handle hotel reservations, so I reserved a room at the Infante de Sagres. I was back in gear. Love, Marianne.

My instructors were right. It was all in the training. It was training that took me to the basement at MSR to look at the bloodied mess they had made of the Spaniard. I wasn't surprised he wouldn't talk. His mouth was too much of a mess. They had pulled out some fingernails, and his genitals were a mass of bruises. They were idiots.

It was training that made me send a man down to the Rossio statue where the hippies hung out, with an order for two tabs of

124

acid. It was training that made me bathe the poor bastard, bandage his fingers and clean up his mouth. It was training that made me put a black hood over his head, thick gloves on his hands, and wrap him in foam rubber. It was training that made me put a TV set in the room tuned to an empty channel. I turned up the volume. The pure white noise of the even static would be the only sensory input the poor bastard would have. Apart from the needle. I told Major Antonio how to crunch the LSD tablets when they arrived, and how to mix them with 20 cc of alcohol. An injection of one cc every hour on the hour. After each six hours, remove the hood, a bright light in the face, and very soft, very gentle questions. Tape record everything he said. It's all in the training, Major. Satisfaction guaranteed. In return MSR would petrol bomb the homes of the Polish second and third secretaries, the Russian chargé d'affaires and the offices of the Czech commercial mission. Blame it on the secret army.

Training took me through the meeting with Carlo. The dockers were demanding stand-by money for the work they were not doing while the Russians finalized the wine deal. The ships were lying outside the docks. The dockers had all the work they could handle, but the dock authorities had informed the Russians that the stand-by money would be added to the harbor dues. The Russian captains had refused. The dock authorities had refused to let any more Russian ships in or out until the money was paid. The deputies for the Ministers of Commerce and Transport were at the dock offices trying to work it out.

Carlo was a genius. A natural. We'd never thought of that in Erewhon.

He did not mention Marianne at all. All he wanted to talk about was the clever way he had stopped the Russian ships. I raised the matter of the guns again. He said he was happy with the arrangement, so long as I kept the guns safe and they were ready when needed. Casually I asked him if the girl had been in my room when his men went to collect the ID cards on the previous day. He said he didn't know and went behind the bar to make a phone call. He came back shaking his head. The room had been empty, but full of clothes for two people. He asked if I had woman problems. I said only the usual. If you ever want a girl, he said, gesturing at the bar and the nightclubs around him. I said I'd remember that.

"Carlo, there is one thing that puzzles me." He looked blank. "One thing I do not understand," I explained. "I know why you hate the Communists, but how do you feel about the old regime? Salazar and Caetano, the old fascists and the government that went with them. You prospered under them. Do you want to see them back?"

"You don't understand business, Ingles. It was time for them to go. They held back a lot of things. Old laws and old customs that they wanted held back tourism, where my money is going. Salazar had a dream of an old, rural Portugal or brave peasants and country virtue. He wanted that to last forever. But he was the only one who did. I don't want him back, or his system back. I want a Portugal where people make money, can build and expand as they choose. More industry, more tourists, more prosperous Portuguese to spend money in my bars and clubs at the weekend, to rent my holiday villas when the tourists go home. Besides, we can't go back. Angola and Mozambique are independent now. We can't reconquer them, and we have to get a living and a place for our families who have been thrown out of there. Portugal has to make its own living. So there is no room for fascists or Communists or any other politicians. I want customers, wealthy customers, and so do the men who run my kind of business here. We are realists."

So he was, in his neat little moustache and his two-tone shoes. The very clothes he wore and the style he adopted were twenty years out of date. He was like some petty tribal chief in an underdeveloped country who knew the world was changing and wanted to change with it. If I came back in a year, Carlo would have lost his moustache and be wearing a formal black mohair suit and drinking malt scotch. Maybe I misjudged him, maybe he'd be wearing jeans and a sweat shirt and a medallion around his neck and a beard and his hair curling over his shoulders. Whichever he thought was smarter, Carlo would wear it. He was a survivor and I found myself liking him too. He was my kind of hoodlum.

"But you are becoming a politician yourself, Carlo. You will have to make alliances and deals and live with the rest of them. Some of the old fascists will always be around, and so will some of the Communists. How will you handle that?"

"I don't see the problem, Ingles." He poured us two more beers. "Politicians aren't people, they just represent different kinds of power. I've been dealing with different kinds of power all my life because I want a part of it. And then there are politicians who are family and some who are friends. That is different. The friendship and family come before the politics. The Angolans are going to give me some kind of power, so is my money, so are all my old businesses like the docks and the unions. You like the trick for the Russian ships, eh? You like that kind of power?"

"Carlo, I love it. It's brilliant and you know it. And I know you are dealing with me only because of the power I represent. I have no illusions about that, Carlo."

"Nor do I, Ingles. But let us see how our powers work out. There may be room for friendship if we work well together. If that happens, maybe you will tell me what troubles you about this girl, eh?" I nodded as I left the bar. Maybe I would.

I telephoned Otto for the address of the warehouse where I was to pick up the supplies. I told him I approved the leaflets and that I was flying to Oporto later in the day. He asked me how many newspapers there would be tomorrow. I told him to get used to using the radio.

I took a cab to Estoril, to the central square. The driver waited while I checked the bar. It was empty. He took me to Joao's street and I paid him off. Joao's house was a grand, three-story affair flanked by mean, single-story buildings. I checked the doorbells. Joao was the second-floor apartment on the left. I walked around the back and climbed into a garage yard. I used a garbage can to get onto the roof of the low building on the left. A window was open, so I tapped it twice and crouched. No

127

reaction. I climbed in the window and I was in a bedroom. There were photographs of young men on the wall, some of them nude, some of them lewd, some of them old and faded and with black censor's oblongs at the crotch. This was Joao's room, unless he had a boyfriend who kept his own room. I checked some envelopes on the dresser. Joao's room. One drawer was locked, and I picked it open. Dirty magazines. Men and little boys. Note for London; change the file to read "Definite pederast leanings."

In the other drawers were some transparent shorts, conventional underwear, shirts, sweaters, a flick knife, and a heavy Browning automatic with 9 mm ammunition. On the floor of the wardrobe were two kinds of shoes. Mens' and boys'. Little boys' shorts and shirts on a shelf. From the sizes, Joao liked them about twelve years old. There was a little girl's party dress for special occasions. There were three bottles of baby oil. I unscrewed a cap—scented.

Why should I feel superior. I grinned, remembered pouring the oil onto Marianne as we made it in the bath. Marianne. The training took over again and I checked the letters in the envelopes. Two from family, two from boyfriends, a bill for electricity and a government check for 1,600 escudos from the ministry that provided welfare for the Retornados. Under the bed was a plastic bag with about three ounces of marijuana, very green. The bed sheets were creased.

On the wall was a little framed picture of the Virgin Mary and above the mantelpiece was a crucifix. Photos on the mantelpiece. Three of Joao in uniform, once with his parents, twice with his arms around other soldiers. All laughing. One of Joao and another young man in swimming trunks lounging by an expensive swimming pool. A black servant in the background. One of two old people; the woman had Joao's eyes. A pile of cigarette packets and one loose brick in the fireplace. Behind it there was a roll of notes: 6,000 deutsche marks and 3,000 dollars; 1,200 French francs. I put it in my back pocket. If Joao was working for me I didn't want him feeling financially independent.

I went back to the Navigator bar and picked up the keys for the truck. I drove to Otto's warehouse and signed the invoices in triplicate for "underwater diving equipment." We loaded the crates onto the truck, and I drove the truck into a yard behind the bar and walked around to the front and gave the keys back. Joao was sipping a beer. I paid for it and bought another for myself. We sat down at a corner table and went through the plans for Saturday's demo and for the Angolans' meeting.

Joao said he wanted to go around the camps and centers where the Angolans were being temporarily housed, and I gave him 10,000 escudos for expenses. I told him he had permission for the rally the following week, and to make arrangements for a press conference to announce it and the formation of the refugees' association. I told him the leaflets and the tear gas were in the truck and Carlo knew about it. Luis was to be buried the next day, he said. I said it was a very sad thing but he would be revenged.

Joao said as soon as we needed more men he could get two hundred from the refugee camps. Men with army training. Even some ex-Paras. I asked where he could keep them in Lisbon but he hadn't thought of that. I said it was a good idea and he should bring them into the city for Saturday's rally. I gave him more money to hire two coaches and told him to get somebody to rent a big warehouse somewhere in Estoril. When the time came, we would have to keep the men somewhere. Carlo might know of a place, and he should lay in food.

Was anything special planned for Luis' funeral, I asked him. No, but there would be a lot of mourners. Luis was well known and well liked among the Angolans. An idea began. I asked Joao about the cemetery, about the way the Portuguese conducted their funerals, how many mourners there would be, and so on.

By the time I left to go back to Lisbon, we had planned a great funeral for Luis. Joao promised three thousand mourners, a rousing memorial speech from the steps of the church, and a march from the cemetery to the ministry for the Retornados. Joao had liked the phrase "We are here to show that Luis is not forgotten by his friends. We are here to show that the Retornados will not be forgotten by his countrymen." I would pass the word among the foreign press that there would be a political

129

funeral—so far none of the journalists seemed to have written about the returned Angolans. We had called Carlo, who had promised to lay on a delegation of dockers and customs officials paying tribute to a fallen comrade. I left Joao drafting a leaflet that would claim Luis had been shot by the Communists and had fallen for Portugal and the rights of the Retornados. Training.

# 12

The plane was only half full. I stretched out on the three seats to try and doze for the forty-five minutes it took to reach Oporto. Sleep would not come. There had been no sign of Marianne at the hotel in Lisbon. Her birth control pills were still in the drawer, her cosmetics and toothbrush still in the bathroom. I had thought of calling her father, but dismissed the idea. I knew I would soon have to start facing the possibility of a kidnap. Pressure on me, pressure on her father. In a way, I'd almost prefer that to happen. At least a kidnapper would have to let me know he had her. There would be a target, there would be the knowledge that she was somewhere. There would be a rational explanation.

The other explanation was that she had gone off on her own accord, too briefly to collect her belongings, or too urgently. It could be another man, it could be an impulse. I checked back. She had been at the hotel at lunchtime on the previous day, expecting to see me for lunch, delivering the notes from Reuter's. She had been missing for a day. The hotel had no message from her, and nobody at the bar or at reception had seen her since. She was just gone.

I had last seen Phil yesterday afternoon, outside the presidential palace. Nobody had seen him around since then. Maybe the two kids had gone off together. She was twenty-four. He was about the same age. I was thirty-one. Maybe she thought that was too old.

At twenty-four I was old enough to have been in Aden, old enough to volunteer for a transfer into the SAS. Not that you could volunteer—you had to be asked. I had let it be known that I wanted to be asked. One story had it that you let it be known by hitting an officer and then out-fighting every other bastard in the detention camp. I never heard of anybody getting in that way. There was a woman in Aden too. She had disappeared. The sergeant she was married to had gone to the chaplain and got her sent home on compassionate grounds. Then he'd come looking for me with two friends. They had broken my nose and two ribs, but I put all three of them into hospital. Only after that did the invitation come from the SAS. I had forgotten the wife's name. I never knew if the sergeant went back to her.

The evening papers were full of pictures of the bomb damage at the two newspapers. The inside pages carried the story of the trouble with the Russian ships at the docks. The union negotiator, who was supposed to be a Communist, had told the papers that the dockers were demanding the stand-by money out of solidarity with Portuguese wine workers, whose livelihoods were being imperiled by Russian delay in the wine negotiations. The COPCON security force announced that it would put special guards onto all newspaper buildings. The police were investigating four murders near the National Stadium. They said it looked like a gun battle between criminal gangs. There was nothing about Luis being a customs man. There were big advertisements for the Communist demo on Saturday and more photographs of the chaos at the Benfica stadium. The plane banked into the landing circuit.

The cab took me straight to the hotel. From the outside, it was less than imposing. The entrance was in a side street, but the brasswork shone and the doorman was impeccable. A porter scurried out to take my overnight bag. As I checked in, I could see a restaurant the size of a ballroom dominated by a tiered central table piled high with fish and fruits. The central courtyard was filled with fountains. The woodwork was black with age and polish. It was all very pleasant but I preferred the room with the balcony back in Lisbon. The thought of Marianne stabbed again. All I had decided on the plane was that everything would be explained when I returned to Lisbon. Either there would be a message from a kidnapper, a message from her father, or her things would have disappeared from my room and there would be a note saying good-bye and Phil and I, or Tom and I, or Dick and I wish you luck. Love, Marianne.

I showered and changed and turned on the radio. Nothing new. I called room service for a cold beer and worked on an article about the bombs. I left the hotel at seven thirty, handing the story to the reception desk for telexing. Back in Lisbon, the Reuter's wire and the American agencies were all headlining the mysterious secret army of liberation that claimed to have placed the bombs. I had speculated on there being an arm of the ELP, the Portuguese Liberation Army that was supposed to be mobilizing in Spain. Even if my agency didn't use it, the story would amuse Chisholm.

The British Club in Oporto was as dark and grim as the ones in London. Like them, it smelled faintly of brass polish and cabbage. There were old copies of *Punch* on the tables and the

*Times* on a huge old lectern in the library. The porter took me up the library stairs and along a corridor lined by cabinets containing silver captured from the French by Wellington. I was shown into a small and private dining room with a table set for four at one end. Two men stood by the empty fireplace, before a portrait of General Beresford. At the other end of the room was a portrait of Sir John Moore. The walls were lined with prints of British uniforms of the Peninsular War. The two men had glasses of white port in their hands. There was a decanter on a small table between them.

"Mr. Maddox, I am Jorge-Luis Beresford. Might I present Police Commandant Silva Gomes." We all shook hands and I was given a glass of white port. I was told we were expecting the bishop. I was asked if the weather had been fine in Lisbon. I said it had been Talavera weather. The police chief looked blank. Beresford explained how the Light Division had walked forty miles in a day in full battle kit to try and reinforce Wellington for the battle of Talavera. They marched in the heat of a Spanish summer day and thereafter the British Army spoke of Talavera weather. The police chief still looked blank. We all looked at our glasses. Beresford said he hoped to get back to Scotland in time for the grouse. I said that was nice. The police chief said there would be better hunting in Portugal. Beresford said that was interesting. I asked Beresford if he was any relation to the general on the wall. He said he was a great-great-grandson. I said that was very interesting.

The bishop arrived. He was introduced and given a glass of port and asked if he had had a pleasant journey from Braganza. He said that he had been in Oporto for two days on diocesan business but the journey had been most agreeable. Beresford asked how the weather had been in Braganza. The bishop said that the weather had also been agreeable. Beresford led us to a table and rang a small silver bell. Two waiters entered with soup.

The soup was drunk. Or maybe it was eaten. I used the spoon Beresford chose. The police chief used his bread. I was asked if I could shed any light on the rumors of a change in government. I repeated what the Resident had said that morning. They all nodded sagely.

"We will be joined after dinner by the military governor," Beresford said. "I thought you might find it valuable to hear his views. He wanted to join us but it seems that he had to attend a meeting at the barracks."

I asked the police chief in what sort of circumstances would he call upon the army to help maintain order.

"I can maintain all the order I want," he said. He broke off to sniff the wine. "But it might be useful to say that I cannot. In that case I would call in the army. Officially I should call upon the Ministry of the Interior in Lisbon, who would send police reinforcements. But they might send COPCON. Left-wing troops. So in practice I would call upon Pedro." Beresford intervened to say that Pedro was the military governor. The police chief continued.

"They might try and send COPCON anyway. But COPCON would have to rely upon me for its intelligence. If I said I expected trouble in a town a hundred kilometers away, across the mountains, they would go there."

I asked if he had the kind of problems with the police that Pedro seemed to have in the barracks. He snorted.

"My policemen are old soldiers. They obey orders. They don't try and tell me what to do. All good Catholics, good family men. Good Portuguese. Am I right, your Grace?" The bishop nodded. The souls of the police were safe. His nod guaranteed it. I asked the bishop if his diocese had received any leaflets for distribution in the churches on Sunday. He smiled and said that he had. His flock were already alerted to the dangers of atheistic Communism. But he thought the leaflets could prove most valuable. The police chief added that his men were distributing more copies around the bars and clubs. Beresford tinkled his bell.

The sole was excellent. The police chief and the bishop attacked their fish with energy and appreciation. Beresford supervised the withdrawal of the cork from the new bottle of wine. The waiter hovered with genuine concern as Beresford then observed that Pedro had seen the leaflets and was having more copies printed for the army barracks. He particularly liked the one with the mug shots and criminal records of the four Communists arrested for trying to smuggle the guns from Angola.

"Wish we knew where they are," the police chief said."We're going to need them."

"Why would you need them if you have the police and Pedro and the army?" I asked.

"It is more than a year since the army made the revolution," Beresford observed. "In a conscript army such as Portugal's, a year can make a great deal of difference, particularly if the troops no longer have the prospect of a shooting war in Africa. A majority of the younger officers, and a terrifying proportion of the NCOs, are no longer prepared to obey orders without questioning their political motives. The conscripts have caught the same disease. It is less serious here than in Lisbon, because the conscripts here are northerners. The Church still has a great deal of influence, and the north is still largely conservative. But Pedro's authority has to be exercised with a great deal of care."

"Men's minds are giddy," the bishop said gently. "Portugal has undergone a year of change. The empire has fallen, the government has fallen. There are new forces, new politics, new ideas; the old authorities will return, because man needs order and he needs guidance. In the north here, the forces of order still reign, although today we must reign discreetly. So what news do you bring from Lisbon? We read of bombs and rumors. What can you tell us?"

"The counteroffensive against the Communists in Lisbon has started, and it will grow over the next two weeks. There are three separate spheres of action. The first, but this will take time, is to threaten their hold on the trade unions. This is being done by other left-wing parties and by less formal groups. There are criminals and gangsters who are influential in some unions. They are now moving against the Communists. The object of this is not to take over the unions but to put the Communists on the defensive.

"The second is more direct, and is partly designed to win

publicity and bring the eyes of the world onto Portugal. Direct attacks upon Communist meetings, upon their offices and their newspapers and homes, and upon their allies. We are working on the assumption that the Russians are not prepared to risk a war to support the Communists in Portugal. So a further motive for the direct attacks is to probe the reaction of the Russians.

"The third action is to build a political force based upon the refugees from Angola and Mozambique, the Retornados. A political party for them is being organized, and a newspaper. This party can either join formally with one of the centrist parties or it can play an independent role. It will need your active assistance, your Grace"—the bishop nodded vigorously—"and your blessing. It will also need your cooperation, Commandant. Its early meetings must be protected, its parades given police permission, its recruitment encouraged.

"There are other ways you can help. The wine deal with the Russians must not go through"—I looked at Beresford. "Any commercial deals being planned with Eastern Europe must be aborted. This can be done by restricting bank credits, by demonstrations, by the kind of delays in the official paperwork that I am sure you can organize, Commandant.

"The Church can help by persuading all good Catholics to join their trade union and to oppose the Communists from within. It will have little impact, but if the employers start to recognize an alternative force in the unions, the Communists will be severely weakened." Beresford nodded.

"This will need money, organization, and determination. You three clearly have it. What I basically offer you is the opportunity to let the Portuguese people of the north speak for themselves against the Communists. If the people of the north choose to throw the Communists out and burn their offices and expel their workers, then they need not fear that Lisbon and the industrial zone around it will be solidly behind the Reds. We will frighten the Communists in Lisbon, and you can throw them out of the north."

The three of them sat stunned. I had felt the same way at the end of my first day at the course in Somerset, when the instructors had built up the nation of Erewhon and showed us how to take it apart.

Beresford shuddered and cleared his throat. He picked up the little bell and the waiters came with the meat course and the red wine. This time the waiter opened the bottle on his own. The commandant and the bishop picked at their food until the waiters left.

"We have a hundred thousand Retornados in the diocese of the north," the bishop said. "They will be with you. I will declare a day for them, a march through the holy city of Braganza with the relics of the saints at their head. Your Retornados party will swell with their numbers. In every village, the Angolans have come home to their families. They can be reached through the priests."

"We can hold up the trade deals all right," Beresford said. "But I'm worried about losing the work altogether. There's a lot of unemployment."

"I told you this would cost money, Beresford. Something else to remember. This crisis with the Communists may pass this summer, but we're not just thinking about this summer. If you build an anti-Communist crusade and then people stay unemployed, and the Retornados stay unhoused and the unions do nothing for their members but get rid of the Communist leaders, then you'll have another Communist threat in five years' time that you won't be able to meet.

"You have a long-term job on your hands. You have to reconstruct a country. You and your businessmen friends, Beresford, will have to invest and reinvest. Build factories, train workers, build a new economy. You can do it in your own wine trade. Hire the best marketing man in the world and start to export. So far you have stuck with your port wines and their safe little market in the British upper class. You can do better than that. Look at Mateus rosé. It sells all over the world. One company did it. All the rest can too. And don't give me that crap about Portuguese wines not traveling—Mateus travels.

"The Church has a new role to play as well, your Grace.

Portugal needs you, but it doesn't need the Church that stifles education and set its face against all political change. You've had a revolution here, and we're trying to save you from its excesses. We also have an interest in keeping a non-Communist Portugal. But the Portugal we want to see is rich and prosperous, a member of the EEC and a modern democracy. All that Britain and your friends can do this summer is to buy you time so that you can begin to make the reforms that Portugal needs. If you don't, we can't save you. Nobody can. It's your country and your problems. Do you know why the far Left are helping us fight the Communists? Because the far Left knows that when Communism fails, a centrist government is likely to fail too and open the way to another kind of revolution. Is that what you want to see?"

Fuck them. It was as clear as day. They wanted the Communists stopped, for ever and ever, Amen. But that was as far as they saw into the future. I pulled out my Rizlas and rolled a cigarette. Their eyes watched, fascinated. I asked Beresford if there was an ashtray in the room. He tinkled his little bell.

"You are right. You are right." The police chief sank his glass of wine and pulled a pack of villainous local cigarettes from his breast pocket. "As long as Portugal is a poor country, it will be either fascist or it will be Communist. Poor countries need strong governments. So we need a rich Portugal. But that's our problem, Ingles. Let us return to this summer."

Beresford looked nervously at the waiters, who were hovering with cheese and fruit. They had been trained not to listen. One of them wheeled a trolley into the room. It tinkled with bottles of port, liqueurs, and brandy. Another brought a silver salver to Beresford. It contained a note.

"Pedro sends his apologies, gentlemen. He writes that a soldiers' meeting and democracy have delayed him at the barracks. A pity. I would have liked him to hear that, Maddox. When he came back from Mozambique two years ago he said much the same thing. You and he would get along well. Would you prefer a cigar to one of those rolled things you smoke?" I stuck to my rolled things.

"Very well, gentlemen. To this summer. When can you start your popular uprising?" I smiled as I said it. A bishop, a police chief, and a businessman and their popular uprising. "Tomorrow night, if you like," the police chief said.

"Fine," I replied. "That will give the Communists something to talk about at their Lisbon rally on Saturday. Can you arrange for simultaneous attacks in two towns? Or even three?" They nodded. I asked if we could arrange a regular channel of communication and the bishop gave me the name of a priest in Lisbon. The commandant gave me the name of his brother, a police divisional chief in Lisbon.

"The last thing, gentlemen, is to make sure of the army. I do not like the fact that Pedro could not join us tonight. I cannot help you with the army. You must arrange that yourselves, but I must be informed of the likely outcome of the army council next week." Beresford promised to arrange it.

We parted, Beresford leading us in a toast to the friendship between the British and Portuguese peoples. Very touching. I left first, the others would follow. A cab was waiting and began to drive me back to the hotel. I directed him to go past the main barracks. There was a guard at the gate, squatting on his haunches in a sentry box. His hair was long and he was smoking. The building was quiet, but lights blazed everywhere. I wondered how Pedro was getting on with his troops. The cab took me back to the hotel. I drifted to sleep, wondering if Marianne was taking her pill tonight.

# 13

As soon as I woke up I called the hotel back in Lisbon. No Marianne and no messages. I skipped breakfast and took a cab to the airport, conscientiously trying to read the papers and prepare myself for the day. The funeral for Luis, the last plans for making chaos out of the Communist demo tomorrow. My mind could not concentrate. I had to put the woman out of my head. Christ, there were some rules so basic nobody ever thought to pound them into our heads. Like keep your mind on the bloody assignment, Maddox. Don't get involved with women, Maddox. Not on duty, Maddox. If I were back in London running this job and my agent swanned off on a love affair, I'd terminate him. I bloody would. It doesn't happen, it must never happen.

They served coffee on the plane and that helped a little. The flight was half empty so I had three cups and stared out of the airplane window, wondering where the hell Marianne was. All I had to convince me she had been kidnapped was my own faith. That and the pills she had left in the hotel. She had gone willingly because there had been no struggle. She had gone reckoning that she would come back because she had left her clothes. So the presumption was she had gone with somebody she knew. Which brought me back to her father and the old suspicion that she, too, was a professional. And if she was a pro then she could say she loved me and make love like an angel and make me believe it. But she would not have gone with Daddy or anybody else unless she had something of value to take with her. Even if she suspected what I was doing she could not know. Christ, in a way we were on the same side.

As soon as the plane landed I telephoned the hotel again. Still no Marianne. I clubbed my brain to try and work out the logic of why I had lost her. If she wasn't leaving with my plans and contacts, and I was sure of that, she was leaving because somebody who held her could put pressure on me. And that brought me back in the old circle of Joao and Carlo knowing I had the guns.

I drove straight from Lisbon Airport to the MSR building. Major Antonio looked as though he had slept in his clothes. We went down to the basement and looked at the foam rubber lump rolling in the middle of the floor. If it was speaking or sobbing you couldn't hear. The TV set still blared white noise.

"It's all on the tape," Antonio said. "There's a lot about his mother and more about his sisters. Does this treatment always affect them like that?" Always, I told him. I had seen it used on Irishmen, Arabs, and a Russian. They all talked about the moth-

142

ers. The psychologists said it was something to do with the womb environment of the foam rubber.

"He worked for Spanish Intelligence," Antonio said. "So did the others. Their mission was to infiltrate the Portuguese Left. There are some also in the Communist Party. The objective was to cause controlled chaos in Portugal."

"How do you mean, controlled chaos?"

"The Spanish Government wants enough left-wing chaos in Portugal to frighten the Spaniards, but not enough chaos to threaten the stability of Spain. Very simple. This one worked for DGS, the General Directorate of Security. So did the other Spaniard. The two Portuguese boys were recruited, thinking they were working for the Spanish Communists and infiltrating MSR on behalf of the Portuguese Communists. It's a mess."

"So's he." I was unwrapping the thick gloves from the hands and looking at the crude dressings I had put on the places where his fingernails had been. Antonio brought me the first-aid box. I changed the dressings and took the hood off the face. The eyes were squeezed tight and the lips had swollen from the beatings. He had vomited and it was sticking in his hair. Antonio brought a bowl and we cleaned him up. He breathed like a fish, taking gulps of air into his mouth. We took off the foam rubber and he lay on his back, his legs bent up against his chest.

"If he's DGS he'll recover. They train people to survive this kind of thing. We could dump him outside the Spanish Embassy. They'd get him back to Madrid—but they would know we had broken his cover. And we still don't know who told him to ambush me at the National Stadium. He's your prisoner, Major. It's your decision."

Antonio grimaced. He looked a mess. His shirt collar was open and dirty, he hadn't shaved, and his hair was lank. Three days ago he had been elegant and well-groomed, the very model of the model politician. Now he was much older, and from his eyes came a look of deep pain. As though he had been the victim of the torture he had supervised. I liked him the more for it, but I had to know who gave the orders for the ambush that had killed

Luis. I handed him the flashlight. He flicked on the switch and shone it into my eyes and I turned my head away. He sighed and bent to the Spaniard, flooding those swollen eyes with the beam of light.

His questions were gentle and he cradled the Spaniard's head on his lap. I switched on the tape cassette, holding the microphone to the thickened lips. It didn't take very long.

The four of them had been ordered to the stadium by another Spaniard, another DGS man who had infiltrated the Communists. They had been told I would be meeting somebody, they didn't know who. The job had been assigned to them because the guy who guarded the door at MSR could recognize me again. They were told to find out who I had met, to recover some heroin, and if any of us got hurt that was too bad. The Spaniard retched again, dryly. There was nothing left to vomit.

"Ask him why the shooting started, why he ran, and how he got away," I said. Antonio shook his head, but he asked the questions. I bathed the Spaniard's lips with a damp cloth. He looked very bad.

He had been posted halfway up the hill. The shooting had started and he had joined in. His Astral had jammed and by the time he had cleared the round the fight was over. He had gone to the top of the hill where his car was. There was no sign of his partner, the man I had shot. The orders had been to leave no traces, whatever happened, so he had worked around their rifleman and shot him in the back of the head. Two single shots. Then he had driven away.

"Who was the rifleman? Who sent him? When were the Spaniards told about him?" I asked urgently. "What happened to the rifle?"

It had been part of their briefing. When they were told to make the ambush they were told they would have a rifleman in cover. A local man. Expendable.

This was serious. Only Otto had known about the rifleman. He was supposed to be one of Otto's men. Unless there had been two riflemen, one from Otto and the other with the Spaniards. But why had they started shooting? Why not just shadow me and the men I met? It made more sense to find out what I was doing and whom I was seeing than to take me out of the game.

The rifle was in the river Tagus, the Spaniard said. He had taken it from the grip of the man he had shot and then got rid of it. He did not know why the ambush had been ordered. That was how the order came. He had ditched the rifle, returned to base, and was still trying to reach his control when the MSR guys picked him up.

"Have you got enough from him now?" Antonio's voice was savage. "Are you satisfied?"

"I'm satisfied, Antonio. Now what do we do with him?"

"We'll have to dump him somewhere. We can't kill that."

Antonio looked down at the Spaniard. He had rolled onto his side, still curled like a fetus. His bandaged hands were pawing at his crippled face.

"We can dump him outside a church hospital. They can look after him and he won't be lucid enough to call for the DGS or to get back to Madrid," he suggested.

"Have you thought what he'll want to do to you when he recovers?" I asked.

Antonio looked at me and then looked down at the man. The Spaniard had crawled to some of the foam rubber that littered the floor. He looked as though he was trying to burrow into it. Antonio roughly pulled him away and picked up one of the heavy gloves. He placed it firmly against the Spaniard's mouth and nose, cutting off his air. The Spaniard kicked feebly. Antonio knelt his weight across the curled body, pressing both hands to the smothered face. The Spaniard tried to roll but there was no strength in him. At last, Antonio rose.

"We'll get rid of the body," Antonio said. "Then we start cleaning up. He told us a lot last night. They killed our man in the bank workers union. And they have other contacts in our group. They will have been arrested by now. It's been a long night."

"Are you going to tell the Communists about the Spanish infiltration?" I asked. "Let them clean up their own mess. It will take them time and effort to question their own people. An

145

anonymous phone call will do it. Just give some names, and say they need checking as Spanish DGS. The Communists will have to check and it will tie up their best men for days."

Antonio nodded. "With any luck they'll blame the Spaniards for everything that has gone wrong for them in the last week. Maybe the Russians will blame the DGS too. After last night."

Antonio told me of the night operation. Just as we had agreed. The homes of the two Polish diplomats, the Czech commercial mission, and the Russian chargé d'affaires had all been hit at 3:00 A.M. as I slept in Oporto. For good measure they had put a thermite bomb in the car park of the Intersindical building. There were no cars there but there had been a petrol pump. The morning radio said the fire was still out of control. The newspaper offices were too well guarded for any more attacks, but they had blown the main transmitter of RCP, the Communist radio.

"Can you tell the Communists the Spaniards did it?" I asked. Antonio shook his head. They had left slogans on the walls. The secret army of liberation again, he said. Rumor had it that all the members of the Communist central executive had gone back into hiding, just as they had before the revolution.

We left the basement room with the curled body of the Spaniard in the corner. I looked back. The glove was still stuck to his face. Antonio gestured upstairs, and said most of his men were asleep and he was tired enough to join them. I asked him to remember the phone call to the Communists and he nodded. I stopped at the door and turned to him.

"You remember the girl I was with? The one with the father at the U.S. Embassy? She's disappeared. Have you heard anything?"

He shrugged his shoulders and shook his head. He almost said so what. I suppose I should have said the same, but I looked at him, trying to see if he was lying. I didn't think so. He looked too tired.

I couldn't find a cab back to the hotel so I walked. Three streets were blocked off by police jeeps and COPCON armored cars. Cameramen were taking pictures of a burnt-out building. It had been the Czech commercial mission. Four times before I reached the hotel I was asked for my papers. There were few cars on the streets, even fewer pedestrians. There were police and soldiers everywhere, armored personnel carriers drawn up along the Liberdad Avenue every hundred yards. The city was reaching a state of siege.

At the hotel, I went straight to my room. No Marianne. Her pills were still in the drawer. I went down to reception and they handed me a small flat package. It had been delivered the night before. I asked to use their photocopying machine and put the package under the flap. I pressed the button and the photoflash flared and the copy paper never came out. It had taken a flare negative of the package and I could see it contained an oblong thing, with evenly spaced ratchet holes. It was a tape cassette, with none of the trailing wires you need for a booby trap letter bomb. I took the cassette up to my room and played it.

It was Marianne's voice. "They" had her. She didn't know who "they" were. She was being fed and was well cared for. If "they" didn't get the guns she would be killed. I would be contacted. She missed me. Love, Marianne.

Then came a man's voice. Good English, with a Portuguese accent. They knew I had the guns. There was no point in denying it. They wanted the guns and they wanted them by Sunday. If I agreed I should hang a red towel from my balcony. Then I would be telephoned. The tape ended.

I glanced out of the window. There were about five thousand windows a man could watch from and see if there was a red towel on my balcony. I would have to tap the phone.

I looked in my Oporto air ticket for the name I had scribbled and the numbers I had underlined. I telephoned my police contact, the brother of the commandant from Oporto. Yes, he would put a trace onto any calls that came to my hotel room. I told him to have it ready in thirty minutes and rang off and went down to the lobby to buy the newspapers. The ones that had appeared. I needn't have bothered. I had already been told the headline. On the back page of two of them was an item about a Retornado funeral that afternoon. It was for Luis. Carlo and Joao had done well.

Back in my room with a red towel borrowed from the hotel kitchens. I hung it over the balcony and sat down to wait. After eight minutes the phone rang. I was hoping it would be Mari-anne but it was the male voice on the tape. Still speaking English. He asked me if I knew the beach road at Guincho. I said yes. He said there was a car park beside a modernized castle that contained a hotel. I could not miss it. The exchange would take place there. Sunday night at dusk. The girl was well. He rang off.

I lay on the bed and waited. After four minutes the policeman called. The call had come from a public phone booth in the Avenue of Viscount Valmor. A police patrol car had just reported it empty. I thanked him and asked him if there was any news from the north. He said no, but he was expecting great events that night. His brother in Oporto had already asked for police reinforcements but had been turned down, because of the crisis in the capital. The crisis of the bombs, he added. I said I understood and would call him again. He said the phone call sounded as though I might need discreet assistance at Guincho on Sunday. I said that might well be the case. He would be the first to know. We rang off.

The bed I was lying on had been her bed. Her things were still in the bathroom, still in the wardrobe. On the balcony was the suntan oil she had used. In the drawer, her pills.

First question—who had kidnapped her? The candidates were many. Major Antonio of MSR, the Communists, the Spaniards, even Carlo and Joao. It had to be somebody who knew I had the guns, and only Carlo and Joao could have known that. But Carlo and Joao knew they would get the guns anyway. Not yet, perhaps. They were bright enough to realize that I would hang onto the guns until I felt the time was ripe.

Ripe for what? Rephrase the question, Maddox. What do you want to do with the guns? I want to give the guns to Joao's Retornados, to those two hundred men he is recruiting. My little army. The guns are for them. And Joao and Carlo also want the guns to go to that little army. So it makes no sense for Joao and Carlo to kidnap Marianne and bargain her life for the guns. Second answer. Carlo and Joao knew me too well to think I'd give up the guns for a woman, even if her old man was the mastermind at the U.S. Embassy.

But who else would know I had the bloody guns? Major Antonio didn't know. Maybe the Communists had worked it out. The Spaniard we had tortured at MSR had said the orders came from a senior DGS man who had infiltrated the Communists. They knew about me—enough to try to kill me in the ambush. But who had told them I was in Lisbon? Who had told the Communists I was dangerous?

Back to the beginning again, Maddox. Who knew your mission? London knew and London often leaks, but it doesn't leak names of agents and it doesn't leak fast enough for them to be on my tail within twenty-four hours. Otto knew my mission but he was part of it. Besides, Otto hates Communists. Joao and Carlo knew my mission, but they would not set up an ambush in which they could die.

It was all still murky. There was somebody out there whom I did not know. Somebody who knew me and knew my job and was trying to stop it. Somebody who thought I could be bought with a girl's life.

A girl's life. Marianne's life. I looked across at the other bed, the one we had never used. Then I played the tape of her voice again. How much did I want those guns? Correction—how much did my job require those guns? Be objective, Maddox. The guns were not vital. They were an accident. You had no plan to set up a private army of two hundred men with heavy machine guns and grenades when you arrived in this bloody country. Do you need, really need, those men now?

The objectives were simple. Stop the Communists from taking over this summer. Build up a centrist party based on the returned Angolans, and use that as your base network to infiltrate Portuguese politics permanently. Work closely with the European allies so that we have a neat multinational operation. All in the

Common Market together. And stop the Yanks from doing whatever it is they're doing.

The Yanks—that was one more man who knew, or who guessed what I was doing here. Major Thayer: with his military contacts and his landowners' organization. And if this was a fake kidnap, then who else could have persuaded the girl to go along, if not her own father? It could be Thayer—but how would he know I had the guns?

Back again to the beginning. Yes, I wanted the guns, but I did not necessarily need them. I certainly would not need them until the two hundred men were recruited and assembled by Joao. I still didn't know who had the girl and the only way I could find out was to go along with the deal. So I would find out who wanted the guns, and who had the girl, and with my police contact we could stake out the Guincho rendezvous and recover Marianne and the guns. No. Cancel that. You may be friendly with the police, Maddox, but they still aren't going to like you sitting on that pile of military hardware. Besides, according to the Oporto commandant, the police might want the guns for themselves. Maybe I could borrow some men from Carlo. Maybe the girl would live. The phone rang.

It was Otto. He wanted to know if I had any respect. Did I know how hard things were for the Residents when diplomats . . . he broke off and started again. Did I know how difficult things became for the Residents when things started to go bump near the wrong people. I told him he wasn't being very clear. He sighed and asked me to meet him. If I could talk my way through the police checkpoints and army roadblocks everywhere.

Four roadblocks and three passport checks later I walked into Otto's office. The glass was still on the floor and the curtains fluttered through the empty windows. I was surprised at him. I thought he'd have had all this fixed yesterday. I said so.

"The windows were replaced yesterday," he said quietly. "They got blown out again last night when the Intersindical building went up. I tell you one thing, Maddox. These windows are not going on my expenses. They are going on yours."

"In triplicate," I said. He didn't smile.

150

"Do you think you've done enough damage yet, Maddox? Do you think you've blown up enough offices and houses? Do you think you have worried the Russians and the Czechs enough? Have you any idea what happens in every embassy when other diplomatic buildings start exploding. My ambassador explodes, Maddox. That's what happens. He doesn't know very much, Maddox, but he knows enough to start bawling me out when his dear colleagues start picking glass splinters out of their hair. Do you know who was staying overnight at the home of the third Polish secretary? The German commercial attaché, that's who. The Pole was away on business. Our commercial man is having a useful affair with the Pole's wife. They are now both in hospital. Severe burns. And I am getting the blame. The story is all over town. The Poles are furious. And the commercial attaché's wife is even more furious."

He paused for breath and I rolled myself a cigarette. His finger looked sore from where he had been banging his hand on his desk as he complained. I reached in my pocket and tossed him two coins. He picked them up and stormed out and came back in with two cups of the dreadful coffee from the machine.

"I ought to pour this down your stupid neck," he muttered, passing me a cup. "I ought to have you arrested. You know you're going too fast with all this, Maddox. There's no rhythm. This bombing wave just suddenly starts. One day all is quiet, the next day . . . poof. It's like a war. It's too sudden. People are suspicious."

"The rhythm is not mine, Otto," I said. "And you know it. This whole city was just waiting for it. Just like the north is waiting for it. I pushed it a little, Otto, but only a little. I don't even know who is going to blow what up next. The thing has taken off with its own momentum. We've got what we wanted— a state of siege. Now people have to move, they have to come into the open. We've imposed a pattern, Otto. It's the Communists against the rest. We've done very well."

"You mean you have lost control, Maddox. That's what you mean. You don't even know what's going to happen next. You've made an open season. Anybody can get blown up now.

This was supposed to last all summer. You've telescoped the schedule into a week. And nothing is ready yet. Nothing except you and your cowboys."

"Don't worry, Otto. I fixed things in Oporto. They are starting tonight. The faster we force the Russians to react, the better. We've got to bring the Russians into the open—and the Americans. The Communists are in real trouble now. They don't know what to do next. Their prestige is going. After tomorrow's demonstration they'll panic. They'll either try to take over completely or they'll retreat. I'm guessing they'll retreat because Moscow will say so."

There was a light breeze from the blasted windows, enough to stir the papers on Otto's desk. He shuffled them together and put his phone on top to weight them down.

"Otto, you've got your orders and I've got mine and we both know things are going very well. Is the copter ready for the demo tomorrow?" He nodded. "That plane we talked about—can it be ready on Sunday? For a four hundred mile round-trip flight?" He nodded again. "It will have to meet me at an airport at a certain time. I'll tell you where and when nearer the day—okay?"

"I'll fix that. There was one other thing." Otto rooted in his desk and tossed me a newspaper clipping. It was a copy of the article I had sent from Lisbon, and one of the paragraphs near the end was marked in red. It was the part that referred to Major Thayer as "a man of mystery."

"Are you trying to make an enemy, Maddox? You've just about blown him with this piece. He can blow you open too, you know. And if I were him, I would. This is just plain foolishness."

"It's okay, Otto. The journalists have been muttering about the ambassador and his playmate from Chile for the past week. It's not the only reference like that. And I keep telling you, we have to probe the Yanks as well as the Russians. I know what I'm doing."

Before I left I asked him if anything had come of the idea to hire a private eye to tail Thayer. Otto had little to report. Thayer had been either at home, at the embassy, at the Military Club, or out at the commando barracks at Amadora since the tail was first posted. He had seen no women, the detective agency reported. Poor Thayer.

I took a cab to the cemetery, and tried to work out who wanted the guns on Sunday. It was crazy. Friday afternoon, or probably Thursday when they let me know what they wanted. Tuesday when they grabbed Marianne. It could have been a grab. Just because there were no signs of a struggle in the room did not necessarily mean she had gone willingly. A gun in her face, an injection, a gas aerosol. There were many ways. But none of them made sense. They wanted the guns and they wanted me worried. But why wait so long before I handed the guns back? Unless they wanted me to be out of action on Sunday. That would point to Sunday night for something. They wanted the guns, and I was not so dumb as to think they would take them and say thank you and courteously bring Marianne to my car. I presumed they wanted to get the guns and me at the same time, and conveniently out of action for Sunday night.

At the very least I had to have someone watching at Guincho to find out who made the rendezvous and where they went back to. Even if I didn't go. The car stopped with a lurch. We were at a traffic light, alongside a dark painted truck. The car window-glass acted as a mirror with the truck behind it, and as my reflection leaped at me I knew in my bones that I would have to get Marianne back. I would have to lay on my own ambush at Guincho, and get there with the guns and then shoot my way to whoever held her. I had a private army of Joao's two hundred men. I had my own private arsenal of guns. I could do it if I could get the guns back up from the Algarve and put them into Joao's hands and stake out the rendezvous.

The lights turned green and we pulled away, and I was looking out of plain window again. Do you mean to say, Maddox, that you are prepared to jeopardize your mission, jeopardize the lives of your innocent supporters, bring your government into disrepute, and launch gun battles in the heart of a friendly nation, for a fetching wench who is probably an enemy agent? You bet your ass I am, your honor. The defense rests.

# 14

The earth fell onto the coffin like a patter of rain. I was surprised to hear it, twenty rows back where I was, but the whole vast crowd was silent. I saw the rifles of the customs guard of honor rise like pikes into the sky, and then they fired a last salute. Through the echo of the shots came the high wailing of Luis' wife, supported at the edge of the grave by two other women dressed in black.

I pushed back in the crowd to one of the tombs, and Joao hauled me onto the marble plinth. He had been taking photographs. Every tomb carried photographers. They were draped around stone angels and perched on granite crosses. I looked around the huge bowl of the cemetery and only at the top of the rising ground could I see grass. The rest was people. Ten or fifteen thousand people. I patted Joao's shoulder. He had done very well. I asked him what would happen next.

"Speeches," he said. "Some of the old men, the *caciques* from Angola. Everybody knows them. Officially, they run the Retornados' movement. Then we march in protest to the ministry. On the next block is the Communist HQ in Lisbon. We'll finish the demo there. Don't stay too close to me."

I arranged to see him and Carlo at the Beira bar on the waterfront at eight. Then I faded into the crowd and walked with them from the cemetery to the ministry. The procession was led by three priests, and then came a carved statue, the Virgin of Juanda, carried on the shoulders of the old men who had spoken of Luis and his qualities and the murderous Communists who had shot him down. Then came some two hundred gray-uniformed customs men, acting as a guard of honor for the widow and the mourners. And then came the crowd, lapping along the pavements, stopping the traffic and oozing ahead of the priests. The cops saluted and waved us through the junctions.

The banner I carried said "Justice for the Retornados." Around me other banners asked for jobs, for houses, for schools. Others said "The Revolution makes us live in tents." Joao and Carlo had organized this well. Joao had been different on the plinth—more confident, sure of himself. I grinned. This was how it should be. They could run their own bloody politics and I could stay well in the background. With any luck all they would need from me now were regular supplies of heroin. And the guns. Even the guns were theirs by right.

At the ministry, we filled the huge square and flooded over the COPCON armored cars that had been posted in front of the building. No problem, the soldiers fraternizing with the crowd. The troops and civilians probably knew each other from Angola;

that was how it looked. The minister, said an aide from the balcony, regretted that his duties called him away from the office. He would not be able to address this fine crowd of Portuguese citizens, but he assured them that he was working night and day on their behalf.

"On the Communist behalf, you mean."

Fifteen thousand heads turned to look at Carlo, standing on one of the armored cars, the amplified loudspeaker still at his lips. The soldier beside him looked nervous, but Carlo removed a flower from his own buttonhole and dropped it into the muzzle of his rifle. The soldier grinned and the crowd roared its approval.

"So where is this crooked minister? Is he hiding with his Communist friends?" The crowd roared again. Carlo was a natural rabble-rouser.

"Is he keeping fat on the money he steals from us? How much did they pay him for those old tents we live in?"

The crowd's roar sounded different this time—not just angry, but relieved, as though somebody were saying something out loud that they had only dared to think. Carlo was doing this well.

"We worked in Angola. We worked for ourselves and for Portugal. And now look at us. Living in tents, while these Communists get fat on what they rob from us."

Carlo had never slept in a tent in his life. As far as I knew, he'd never been to Angola. He certainly hadn't worked, but what the hell. He was getting across.

"What are we doing here? There's no power here. This ministry has nothing for us. We know who has our houses and our jobs. We know who the robbers are. We know why we live in tents. We know why our comrade was shot down. We know who killed Luis. Who was it?"

He turned to the crowd. Oh Jesus, I should have warned them about rhetorical questions to a crowd. Nobody knew what to say.

"It was the Communists. The Red robbers."

Another amplified voice, from the other side of the square. It

156

was Joao, standing on another armored car. He had his arm around a soldier and was wearing his camouflage cap. He too had a flower in the barrel of his gun.

"It was the Red robbers who stole our land. Down with the Communists. Death to the Red robbers." This was Carlo again.

"The minister is one of them. He's with his Red robber friends," Joao shouted back. It was like amplified Ping-Pong. One shouted a slogan and the other took it up. Soon the crowd was singing with them.

Far away across the square, at the back of the crowd, there was a movement, a stirring in the great pudding of people. The swirl of the movement attracted everybody. We all began to drift toward the movement. I jumped onto an armored car to see. The crowd was sprinting—not drifting—away. Behind me Joao and Carlo were still shouting their point counterpoint. "Get the Reds"—"Smash the Red robbers." There was another man with a loudspeaker at the back of the square directing the angry crowd to the Communist Party HQ on the next street. There was no way I could get through the crowd to see, but I heard the crack of gas guns and soon enough I caught the tickle at the back of my throat. Tear gas.

I pulled out my handkerchief and opened the tap on the water carrier that was fixed to the back of the armored car. I wrapped the wet cloth around my face and plunged through the crowd toward the sound of the gas shells. Everybody else was moving in my direction. The crowd was angry enough to go through the gas. It wouldn't last.

As I rounded the corner I saw two harsh yellow flares burst through the gray haze of gas. They were petrol bombs, splashing against the wooden shutters of the Communist building. Not all the shutters were closed. Terrified white faces on the upper floors were hastily pulling them closed. Another splash of yellow fire, and another, this time on the door. Behind me there were klaxons as the armored cars tried to bully their way through the crowd to protect the building. At the far end of the street, still retreating and firing their gas shells, was a small group of COPCON soldiers with the red and black flashes on their shoulders. Two petrol bombs burst in front of them and they retreated around a corner. I hoped Carlo's boys had sense not to try and petrol bomb the armored cars—there were too many people packed around them.

The Communist HQ was closed and shuttered, the petrol bombs flaring uselessly on the stone walls, charring the gaily colored Communist posters and licking at the stout old doors. The armored cars had nosed their way through and were taking up positions in front of the building, and COPCON reinforcements were coming around the corner. With the cunning of a mob, the Angolans were drifting away. There was no sign of Carlo and Joao, but the press photographers were still at work, and from a Land-Rover near me I saw a TV team with CBS emblazoned on the camera. The whole world was watching. I should have told Carlo to shout some of the anti-Communist slogans in English. I drifted away with the tail of the crowd.

I stopped at a bar and called Otto, telling him how it had gone. He said he was pleased, but he didn't sound it. He said the white powder had arrived, so I went back to his offices and picked up the black attaché case. The two bricks of heroin were packed with newspapers. We went over the plans for the Communist demo the next day. All was well.

Back at the hotel I wrote two articles on Luis' funeral and went to the desk to telex them. No chance. Half the reporters in the hotel were fighting around the operator, so I went down the Liberdad to the Ministry of Information, but their telex machines were just as busy. So I crossed the street and went up the side street to the Reuter's building and handed in the copy to the clerk and gave him 200 escudos. He said they'd be on the wire before I went downstairs. I believed him. I checked the watch: 7:05 P.M. Just time to see Major Antonio before I went to the Beira.

When I reached his office there were two new phones on the desk, and he was speaking into all of them. In front of him was a list of names. I walked behind his desk and glanced over it. There were thirty names and addresses, with the union affiliation of each man. Seven names had been ticked. Antonio ticked three more.

"This is revenge, Maddox. This is for what those Stalinist bastards did to our boys." He turned back to speak into another phone and yelled angrily down the mouthpiece.

"Fools, they missed him." He put a large circle around the name of a man from the railway union. "That was one we wanted. He was seven years in Moscow. One of their best, but he wasn't at home when we called. I called the Communists, Maddox, and told them about the Spaniards and the DGS. I gave them the names our Spaniard spilled to us and then I reckoned they would be rounding up the suspects about now. So I sent my squads in at the same time. Now it will look like Communists killing Communists.

"Do you know how easy it was, Maddox?" He was grinning, the fixed glaze of an exhausted man. "The ones who have gone underground, they are using the same old addresses, the same old safe houses they used before the revolution. We know them. My boys know every one. Half of them were Communists before the revolution. It's been like . . . like . . ." he broke off, his hands gesturing to show me how easy it was to kill Communists. "Like clay pigeons. Red pigeons."

A phone rang, and as soon as he picked it up, another. He made one more tick, then slowly underlined one name. He quickly fired questions down the second phone, and then turned to his radio transmitter and gave some more orders. He looked at me.

"Trouble," he said. "One of them came down the stairs shooting as my men were in his hall. I've just ordered our mobile squad along. I've told them not to bother to kill him, just to get our dead and wounded away. If we leave any bodies they can be identified, and then we're all targets. The mobile squad had a 105 mm recoilless rifle in the back of the truck. That should do it."

Another phone rang. I waved him good-bye and walked down the Liberdad once more, showing my papers at every corner.

159

The city was dark and listless, many of the shops closed long before time. At the pavement cafes, even the waiters hovered indoors. There were no customers. There were few cars, and those I saw were waved down at roadblocks every few hundred yards. There was still a memory of tear gas in the air. It began to feel familiar; it began to feel like Belfast again. State of siege.

I ought to get a medal. I was doing so well I soon wouldn't need to be here. On this afternoon's evidence, Carlo and Joao were hurting Communists and building their party. Major Antonio was clearly enjoying every phone call in his new role as the scourge of the Communists. Every phone call and every killing. And the city began to smell like Belfast. All I'd had to do was point people in a certain direction. Funny how fast they learned.

The Beira bar was brightly lit and garish. A real Portuguese bar. The tourists would hate it. The walls were tiled and the only decor was three half-carved hams hanging from the ceiling. There were three huge cheeses on the bar and a bin full of bread. At the bar, a bored-looking man in a white jacket juggled six glasses into line on the zinc counter. Without looking he flicked a five-liter jug of wine over the glasses, filling each almost to the brim. With one hand he swept the six full glasses onto the counter and skimmed them down the bar in different directions. I watched, unbelieving. In Britain, they'd put him on TV. Here, he was just a good barman.

"*Tinto*," I said. He glanced at me—the one word told him I was a foreigner, and therefore unusual in a bar like this. Others at the bar also turned. Heavy-set men with thick, clublike hands. I showed him the card Carlo had given me. He nodded his head to the rear bar, through a bead curtain.

Carlo and Joao were sitting at a table with two other men. One I recognized from the funeral. He had been one of the old *caciques* who spoke at the burial. The other I did not know. He looked like the man at the bar. Tough and short and heavy, his hands immobile and thick in front of him. He was a docker or a sailor. Other people don't get those hands, with the look of solid blocks, as though the individual fingers had never been spread.

160

Each finger was almost as thick as it was long. Carlo shouted "*Hola*" and gestured at me to sit.

"The Russians have persuaded the ministry to pay the dockers waiting time for the ships," Carlo said. "This is Jorge. He did the negotiations with the minister."

Jorge and I shook hands. Or rather, my hand shook his club. I smiled. Jorge grunted and poured me a glass of wine. I was introduced to the *cacique*, as just "the Englishman." That was enough. I dropped the attaché case beside Carlo. He nodded, and I said he had been very impressive in the square at the ministry. He and Joao should enter politics.

"We already did," said Joao, and he and Carlo flushed with pleasure. They knew they had done well. I asked who the third man with the loudspeaker had been—it was another of the Luanda network. The word had been passed around the Angolans that the Communist rally for tomorrow would see more action. Carlo said his boys would attack the platform as soon as the smoke bombs started in. I warned him about tear gas, and told him about face masks soaked in vinegar, and grease for the men's foreheads.

"We've got two hundred more," said Joao. "And we've got the warehouse in Estoril. All the men are ex-army. Most of them Paras. You know what we want now—some property of ours. Our guns. Now is the time."

"I thought you wanted the guns for the people in the north, Joao. Now you say you want them near Lisbon. What's in your mind?" I asked.

"We're agreed on this, Ingles," Carlo said. "From all that we hear, the north can take care of itself. Am I right, your honor?" he asked of the old *cacique*.

"There are no problems in the north, Ingles," the *cacique* murmured. "As I think you have cause to know—a certain man of the Church."

"So the north is safe—we'll know better about that later tonight. I think it's going to start tonight. But say you are right, and the north can do the job without our guns, why do we want guns near Lisbon? What are you trying to do, Joao? Pull a coup?"

They all smiled. But nervously. Joao shook his head.

"Look, lads. You've done very well. The funeral was brilliant. You've got the Angolans organized. You've got your men set up, but that's not enough. Right now you haven't even got enough men or enough strength to mount a putsch. You know what a putsch is?

They looked blank.

"A putsch is a little coup. A little military action that lets you take over the palace, the main government building. It's something that a small number of men can do if they do it at the right time and in the right way. The problem is they're dead within twenty-four hours. A putsch is a grab for power when you have nothing else to sustain power. When you have no political base, no allies, no support in the army and the police to keep you in the palace once you've seized it. Putsches do not work. And you haven't got the manpower or the support for a coup."

"We have friends in the police, friends in the army." Joao leaned forward excitedly.

"Okay, Joao. So you seize the presidential palace and you seize all the ministries in Lisbon and the police are on your side and your friends keep the army neutral. Then what? You get a general strike. Nobody goes to work. The Communists are still too strong for you in the unions. Then when you occupy the ministries, where are your civil servants? Are they going to come into work with the buses on strike and reports of shooting at the ministries? What about the radio, the newspapers? Do you stop them altogether—and have nothing to put in their place? What about the rest of Portugal? All the other industrial cities will be Red strongholds. Civil war in Setubal? Grow up, Joao. You're talking about the big league. You can't do it. We don't even have to try."

"This is our country, Ingles. We decide what we have to try," the old *cacique* said.

"There are lives involved, your honor." I had to be polite to him. "Portuguese lives that will be of value for the future. They

162

must not be thrown away to no purpose." I turned back to them all.

"You don't have to try to pull a coup because the decision is already being made. By the Communists. It is up to them now. They are at the crisis, or they will be by the weekend. They must decide whether to seize full power or whether to retreat. You now have the power that could prevent them from taking control. You have no more. What is your base—the refugee camps? They can be bombed. They can be shelled. Even if your two hundred ex-paratroopers were armed and equipped they wouldn't last five minutes in Lisbon. They've got no artillery— and the Left has the RA-LIS regiment."

There was a long silence. Carlo broke it. He lifted the attaché case I had given him and dropped it on the table. He opened it and looked at the heroin.

"Okay, Ingles. You're the boss. Tomorrow we hit them as planned, huh?"

"Carlo—we'll need a good radio," I said.

He took my arm and led me up some stairs. He opened a door and flicked on a light. Proudly he gestured me inside. A military transmitter. Where the hell had he got that . . . ?

"For the ships," Carlo said. "I like to know what ships are coming in. Now we use it to keep in touch with the Angolan camps and with the north. Telephones can be tapped—radios are safer."

"Balls, Carlo. Radios can be overheard and monitored."

"True," he said. "But how many people here speak Fanagalo?"

"Speak what?"

"Fanagalo. It's a lingua franca, a pidgin used in southern Africa. Most Angolans speak it, and some soldiers here. But since the revolution very few soldiers bother to monitor the radio waves like they used to. No more fascism, Ingles. A free country."

"Carlo, if I'm trying to reach you on Sunday evening from an airplane—what frequency?"

"The best is 24.9, but I wouldn't trust it. Not from an airplane, not without testing it and you being in line of sight."

163

"I want to fly in on Sunday. One hour before dusk. I want to land at the airport and have your boys meet me. Then I want to take the guns and drive—alone—to Guincho. To a hotel like a fortress. I want to meet some people there and I want to exchange the guns for somebody important. When I leave with this person I want your men to kill the people I meet. Can this be done?"

"I know the place you mean. It's a *parador*—a state hotel. There is no cover. You can see the road both ways from there. And how do we kill the men except by gunfire? And if you have the guns there can be no gunfire. And once Joao's men get the guns at the airport they will not give them up to you. And if they did, and if the ambush could be made—once Joao's men start to shoot they will hit the truck with the guns—and it also contains grenades. One big explosion. No ammunition. No guns. You are mad, Ingles. Who is this person you want to exchange?"

"It is someone involved with the Americans, Carlo. It could be important."

"For God Almighty it could not be done, Ingles. Even if you could reach me on the radio. This is not possible. Think again and we can talk of this tomorrow, after the Communist demonstration. Now come down again."

We went down the stairs and joined the others. There was food on the table. Slices of the ham I had seen in the bar and plates of cheese. In the middle of the table, a huge bowl of the biggest prawns I had ever seen.

"*Gambas*," Joao explained. "*Gambas* piri-piri. It is a great dish of Mozambique—and Angola. The sauce is hot—but the wine cools."

He gestured to three bottles of the green wine on the table. We ate with our fingers. The Portuguese ripped the thin shells from the prawns and tossed them onto the floor, sucking at the heads of the prawns to take each morsel of flesh. As we came in, Carlo had pressed a button on the jukebox. A sentimental ballad sounds the same in any language.

"Do you like our celebration, Ingles?" said Carlo, spitting the head of a giant prawn to the floor. "It is a celebration of farewell to the Communists."

"This afternoon was very good, Carlo, but it was not a farewell to the Communists. More like a warning."

"Not those Communists. The three I told you about. The new Communists at the docks. The three new ones who were in exile who nobody knows—I told you about them. They went into the river tonight."

He laughed, and the other three Portuguese toasted his raised glass.

"If they stay in the river, Carlo, that's fine. But I don't want to be attacked by any angry wet men."

They all thought that was very funny. It wasn't meant to be. The prawns and the wine disappeared. The *cacique* and Jorge took their leave. Joao and Carlo and I settled over our coffee, and Carlo said he had a surprise for us. He took us to his car and drove up to the Alfama, to his Montegordo bar. Yes, I said when he asked me. I remembered the place.

At night it looked better. A three-piece band, two guitars and a drummer. The place was almost full and Carlo led us to the only empty table by the dance floor. Three girls joined us, all blonds, and the waiter brought us champagne. Real champagne. I looked at Joao, who was ignoring the ladies. Carlo's girl was already on his knee. I smiled at mine—her hand was on my thigh. Joao's girl put her hand on his shoulder and whispered to him. They began to talk. Carlo clearly didn't know Joao's tastes in bed.

"You enjoying yourself, Ingles?"

Carlo was standing beside me, swelling with good humor. The natural host. The nightclub boss having fun in his club. Good times for everybody. He dragged me onto the dance floor, and the girls came too.

"Ingles, you see the door beside the band." Carlo gestured. "My offices—a sleeping room. My present to you, eh?" He gestured at the girl and put the fingers and thumb of his left hand together, making an O. He poked the index finger of his right

165

hand in and out. "You enjoy it, eh?" He grinned and danced away, his hand on his girl's buttocks, his mouth clamped to her neck. She had slipped her hand under his jacket at the back, and down the waistband of his trousers. The band played "Yesterday."

# 15

I woke at dawn and left the girl sleeping. The black roots of her hair showed clearly in the morning light as her long fair tresses fell across the pillow. She had been very good and very professional. I had wanted to leave early, but she danced excitingly, rubbing her hips against mine until my erection made it clear we would go and use Carlo's little room. Not that we used it—she took me out of the club and around two corners and up some stairs to her room. I consoled myself with the thought that Carlo would have punished her if he thought she had failed to please me.

Before we slept I had told her of Joao's tastes and the problem for the third girl. She had laughed in the dark, her cigarette glowing beside me. Joao was well known. The third girl had been a man. One who liked dressing in women's clothes. We smiled at that before we slept.

I walked down the hill, ticking off the day's tasks. First, to talk to the Resident. Then a last check with Otto. A check call with Major Antonio. The Communist demo. And then a meeting with Carlo—which meant I had to dream up some new scheme for getting an aircraft from the Algarve up to Lisbon, to a safe airport, and keeping the guns to myself. While getting Marianne back and finding out who had kidnapped her and why.

Walking through the Rossio Square I bought the newspapers. *Diario* was on the streets again. Its front page shrieked about assassination squads killing good trade unionists. They blamed the right-wing secret army, with its "well-known base in Spain, financed and supported by the might of Spanish Fascism and the DGS secret police."

Good for Major Antonio. The DGS infiltration had got the Communists chasing their own tails. The Spanish Embassy would love this. There was a whole story about DGS infiltrators.

Back at the hotel, I ate a quick breakfast and skimmed the rest of the papers. They all carried stories about unrest in the north, but nothing specific. I switched on the radio.

"Two men killed and three wounded as a Communist local office was attacked and burned late last night in Famalicao. The police had arrested three Communists fleeing the burning building for illegal possession of arms. Two other Communist offices burned without casualties in other towns. The police were seeking Communist officials to explain arms caches found in the ruins. Police reinforcements were being sent to Leiria and Torres Vedras in anticipation of anti-Communist demonstrations called for the afternoon. In Lisbon, leave had been canceled for troops on COPCON internal security duty who would be guarding the

168

mass meeting called in the center of the city by the Communist Party. Narcotics police had arrested five men in a bar in the Alfama and charged them with possession of heroin. The five men were Communist Party members. The drugs were hidden inside a toilet cistern . . . And now the international news. In Beirut . . ."

I switched off the radio, grinning at Carlo's use of the cistern for the planted heroin. In the rooms on both sides of mine, toilets flushed. The hotel was full again, with more journalists and TV crews arriving by every plane to cover the story of Portugal's Red summer. They would all be at the Pombal statue for the afternoon rally.

I climbed into the shower, mentally composing the story I would file for the agency that day: The tightening Communist grip over Portugal was threatened . . . no. The tightening Communist grip was loosened last week . . . no. The Communist dream of controlling the future of Portugal has been rudely awakened in the past week . . . no. The Portuguese revolution began last week to turn on its Communist heirs and devour them . . . maybe. I began to towel myself dry.

I walked behind the hotel to a small cafe and used its phone to reach the Resident and arranged to meet him in two hours. Then I called Otto at his home, but he had left. I called the MSR office. Major Antonio was still sleeping. The phone went back on the hook. At the bar, I ordered a *carajillo*, a big coffee with a slug of anise, and sipped it slowly. There was no point in any more check calls. Everybody knew what to do this afternoon, and they would do it well enough. My job was shrinking with every day that passed. The north was rising, the Angolans were organized. That left Marianne and the guns.

I could forget about both of them. Just leave the guns where they were in that garage in the Algarve. Forget about the rendezvous with the kidnappers on Sunday evening. But there was one other thing I could do, another point where I could exert some counterpressure and maybe get somebody else on my side. I went back to the phone and called the American Embassy. Thayer was in his office.

"Well, hi there, Dave. Been playing any more squash with old men?"

"This is no game, Major. Your daughter has been kidnapped. She's been missing for three days. I got a tape yesterday with her voice and a ransom demand."

"What is it, Maddox? What are they asking?"

"They're asking for something I haven't got, Major. They're asking for those guns that went missing from the docks. I don't know who they are and I don't know what makes them think I know where the guns are. That's more your line, Major."

"They must have a good reason to think you have those guns. They must have. You don't pull a kidnap on suspicion—how long are they giving you?"

"Major Thayer, anybody who kidnaps Marianne knows he's putting pressure on two people, on you and me. Maybe there's a reason to think you have the guns. Work that one out."

I replaced the phone and went back to the office. There was one more piece of pressure I could apply, one more surprise spanner I could throw into the works. I walked up to the Reuter's office and borrowed a typewriter for twenty minutes, and gave the story to the telex clerk for my London agency and for the Australian papers. I catch-lined the piece "Exclusive."

"Lisbon's war against the diplomats escalated last night from the bombing of homes up to kidnapping. Marianne Thayer, twenty-four-year-old daughter of the American military attaché in Portugal, has been seized from her Lisbon hotel . . ."

I kept the rest of the story vague, nothing about any ransom demands—just the fact that the kidnappers had sent a tape of her voice. I ran over Thayer's background in Chile, called him a "mystery man" again, and added that the Portuguese police had not been informed of her disappearance.

One more thing would help. I asked if anyone had seen Phil, the young photographer. I called the Tivoli Hotel and was put through to him in the lobby. He had some shots of Marianne, so I told him they were worth money now she had disappeared. He gave me the names of six papers and two agencies to telex, advising them he was air-freighting the photos. Enrico, the Reuter's bureau chief, checked the telex copies and started to follow up. There were going to be a lot of people looking for Marianne apart from me. I left as Enrico was on the phone to the embassy, asking to be connected with Major Thayer.

Twenty minutes later, when I climbed into the Resident's truck by the Gulbenkian center, it was empty. The driver angled the mirror so I could see his face. It was the usual man. The Resident wanted me brought to him. We drove under the bridge and along the coast road, turning inland by the Belem tower. There were troops drawn up at the railway station, and we passed three busloads of police heading for the city. The driver did not speak again until we turned into a quiet lane off a shopping street. It was like the wide entrance to a London mews, but the gates were still there, opening silently as the truck approached.

Once we passed the rear of the shops, we were surrounded by tall trees, and a gravel drive stretched ahead. The trees shortened gradually and became bushes; on the left opened a formal, classic garden with statues and symmetrical flower beds and a raised pond with a fountain made of porpoises and a mermaid. To the right, the ground fell away down wide steps to the house. In the middle of the modern block of shops and apartments lay a private park and this old, elegant palace. It had an English look, wide and low and plain, without the curving cornices and pillars and false fronts the Portuguese love. At the bottom of the steps, cutting roses, the Resident turned to greet me.

"It appears that your discussions with our friends in the north were most fruitful. My friends warn me, however, that you appear to be a committed young man. Are you committed, Maddox?"

"Yes, sir, just as you are. Just as we have committed London. The process has started here, the Portuguese themselves have begun to take over—in exactly the way we hoped they would. In that we have all been committed."

"I understand you, Maddox. Come inside. I have another guest you must meet."

The other guest was Chisholm. He was sitting in the library, fifteen feet above us on the gallery, examining a huge old painting that was a map of some unfamiliar coastline. He turned and saw us enter, and rose to his feet. He leaned on the gallery rail, enjoying being able to look down on us.

"Very sharp off the mark, young Maddox. You haven't been gone a week and a half and the bloody city is blown up. Blood running in the streets, bombs everywhere, tanks all over everybody's TV sets, and the cabinet is having fits. Are you trying to be a one-man IRA, Maddox? Make another little Belfast for you to play in?"

"Mr. Chisholm, I am an old man and you are in my house. I am not accustomed to discourtesies between my guests and I do not intend to become so. Perhaps you will rejoin us in my study when you have recovered your temper."

The Resident gave Chisholm a last, reproachful glance, and took my arm to guide me through the hall. The old portraits that hung at intervals by the grand staircase even looked like the Resident. The study windows looked onto the sweep of steps I had descended from the truck. I was handed a glass of Madeira and looked around. What part of the room was not lined by books was covered by aging photographs, all of them portraits and all of them signed. Side by side between the windows were formal poses of the German Kaiser and Britain's King Edward.

"My father knew them both," the Resident explained. "In the First War we had to take down the Kaiser, and in the Second War we had to banish poor King Edward. Now, of course, they are both harmless, my dear Maddox. As harmless as that old ship over there, on which my brother served as a midshipman."

He pointed to an old photograph of the first dreadnought, taken at a review of the fleet in 1908, the caption said. The first of the modern battleships, with her twelve-inch gun and her heavy armor and her twenty-four knots.

"When I was a boy, Maddox, the dreadnought was thought to be so powerful that she could sink all the rest of the navies in the world by herself. She had the guns with the longest range and she was the fastest ship. Logically she should have been able to use her speed to keep at extreme range and blow the enemy to blazes before his guns could reach her. In the event, of course, they were a tragic waste, ships useless for any purpose other than to provoke other nations to build similar mastodons. Their purpose was to pound each other to pulp, but most of them were sunk by mines or by submarines or by aircraft. Theirs was a short reign, Maddox, and it was less than glorious . . . Ah, my dear Chisholm. A glass of Madeira, perhaps?"

Chisholm took the drink graciously and joined us by the window, jingling the coins in his trouser pocket. He was wearing a double-breasted blue blazer with a club crest and brass buttons. It made him look like the secretary of a seedy old boys' rugby club.

"The Minister is concerned about the pace of events here," he began.

"So are we all," the old man murmured. "So are we all."

"But I think you're right about one thing, Maddox. You're right about the Yanks and Russkies. There's a deal on and I'm sure of it. It's not Yugoslavia though. I think you've guessed wrong there. If the Russkies are going to give up in Portugal then they've been given a free hand somewhere else. That's why I'm here. We've got to find out where the Yanks will sell us out next.

"Anyway, Maddox, I told the Minister you had my full backing. That you were kicking over the ant-heap to see what crawled out of it. He took the point. Old Otto's been backing you up, you know. The cables from Bonn have been very flattering. Us and the Jerries together, eh? Showing the Yanks what this business is all about."

"How do you know the deal isn't a straight swap, Portugal for Yugoslavia?"

"Because Yugoslavia was settled years ago. They settled it themselves when they began training their people to fight a guerrilla war against invaders. The Russians aren't fools. They're not going to put their head into that noose. No—there's something else being bargained for here, and that's what we have to find out. Still, that's the big picture. Mustn't lose our perspective for today, though, must we chaps? Maddox, let's hear a report."

I told him everything—except about the guns. I told him about Marianne being with me, who her father was, and that she had been kidnapped. I suggested that she had been kidnapped to put pressure on her father, and had moved smoothly on to talk about the way we had mobilized MSR to use against the Communists in the unions when Chisholm interrupted.

"Just a minute, Maddox. You say you picked her up in Madrid by pure chance? That she just happened to be the one your lustful little eyes lit upon? Because I don't believe it. I just don't believe it. Are you sure she wasn't just planted there, planted on you by the Yanks?"

"The only people who knew I was in Madrid were your London staff and the Madrid Resident. It was on his suggestion I picked up a girl—and we only planned that in the afternoon. It was a coincidence."

"Well, I suppose it's not impossible," the Resident said. "But I share your misgivings, Chisholm. But all this is detail."

I continued with the briefing, running through the whole campaign in the unions, with the Angolans, in the north, and for the bombings. The Resident then gave his report, beginning with the news that the Portuguese Treasury were desperate for a major loan. They had approached the Russians—and the result was not yet known. The Americans had not been asked to help. Chisholm added that there had been no approach to London or Brussels. The loan was for $800 million.

"There is another matter that troubles me," the Resident said. "Two of my great-nephews telephoned me this morning to regret that they would not be able to attend a family dinner this weekend. It is the kind of occasion they would usually be at pains to attend. I fear that they are expecting their military duties to engage their time—with what purpose, I know not. And I had a note yesterday from one of my managers who farms near Santarem. For the past four months the cavalry school there has not been training—the government had deliberately restricted the supplies of petrol to ensure that the tanks and armored cars would not embark on a surprise visit to Lisbon. As a result, there was no petrol for exercises—but the exercises have started again. Therefore they have been given petrol."

"Are you saying the military are getting ready to move?" asked Chisholm. "That could be a disaster—Maddox's Angolans aren't ready, the parties aren't established. Do you hear these rumors, Maddox?"

"There are always rumors—but my Angolans are ready. They've got themselves a party and they've got some strong-arm boys. Politically, they can take care of themselves, and I think the army is too divided to try a move. But I don't really know."

Chisholm looked at his watch and stood up. He was lunching at the embassy, he informed us, where he would expect my report on the Communist rally before dinner. The Resident was asked to see what else he could find out about the army's maneuvers. We were both told to relax. The Resident was thanked for his Madeira. The Resident gestured me to a chair.

"What was that badge on his blazer?"

"I think it was a cricket club, sir. I really didn't see."

"Extraordinary. Almost as extraordinary as your tale about this young American lady, whose adventures you related with an unconvincing lack of concern. I assume that you have become attached to her."

I thought it best not to reply. He looked at me, his eyebrows raised and waiting for my confirmation. I nodded.

"And I presume that her kidnappers may be seeking to bargain with you over her, as well as with her father." This time he didn't even bother to look at me for confirmation. "So what are they asking from you, Maddox? Or have they already asked?"

I told him the whole story—how I had got hold of the guns and how I had been able to hide them and about the two hundred men Joao had recruited who could use them. And about the phone call to my hotel and the rendezvous for Sunday evening at Guincho. That made three people, I added, who knew I had the guns. Joao and Carlo and now the Resident.

"Well, you will have to find out who wants them. You have to keep the appointment at Guincho. You might even recover the girl."

"Sir, that's my problem. I'm more concerned now about this idea of yours that the army is up to something. These great-nephews of yours—are they being specific?"

"No, and it is most unlike them. Every other move by the army has been known to me, but not this one. My friends in the northern and central commands report nothing unusual. The unrest seems to be limited to the Lisbon area. It is not even unrest —simply a series of straws in the wind at some key military bases."

I told him of Major Thayer's meeting with the commando colonel at the Military Club, and the private detective's report that the major was spending time at the commando barracks. We digested this, and at the same second we both reached for the phone. The Resident passed it to me and I called Major Antonio, simply repeating what the Resident had said about petrol being delivered to the cavalry school and officers canceling other engagements. He said he would start to check. Then the Resident called someone who sounded like an old friend and rattled off a burst of questions.

"That was the adjutant at the staff college. There's a meeting called for this afternoon with Lourenzo. He's a conservative general. Well-liked and trusted. He was number two in the Portuguese mission to NATO, did two years at Fort Leavenworth in the States. All the staff college personnel have been advised of a night exercise tomorrow night. Leave canceled and live ammunition to be issued. I think this is it, Maddox."

I turned to leave and he walked me up the long steps to the truck that would take me back to the city. As he closed the door behind me he paused. "You realize the implications of this for those guns of yours, Maddox? They could be more valuable tomorrow night than your young lady."

# 16

When I got back to central Lisbon the crowds were already drifting from the Plaza d'Espana over the hill toward the great park where the Communist rally was to be held. The green truck dropped me at the bullring and I took the Metro down to the Liberdad Avenue. The trains were crowded, and when I walked up the stairs into the open air I could hear the tinny sound of amplified voices. The speeches had started. Two police helicopters were beating slowly up the avenue toward the main platform where the speakers were warming up the crowd. Through the heavy throbbing of the engines I heard the odd phrase . . . liberty for the working man . . . the final defeat of fascism . . . the solidarity of progressive forces . . . the last despairing counterattack of reaction.

I went into the hotel and took the elevator to the penthouse floor, squeezing through the pack of other reporters to look down the avenue to the Rossio Square. The marchers were beginning to appear, wide ranks under their red banners, women and kids coming up the sidewalks on either side of the columns.

There was a tap on my shoulder. It was Phil, smiling. He'd sent off the pictures of Marianne, and his pictures of the Angolan funeral and riot yesterday had been widely used. I told him there was no more news of Marianne.

"I've been asking around my friends on the Left, Dave," he said. "Nobody seems to know anything about it. It's not a Portuguese thing, kidnapping. People are angry about it. You got any ideas?"

I shook my head and he followed down in the elevator to join in the rally. The marchers were still coming from the Rossio, and the columns of the Communists trudged slowly up the hill, their banners advertising each factory they came from, each union they represented. The helicopters were much higher now; the sound of their engines muted and the speeches were audible.

On either side of the marchers, the crowd had formed into layers. There were older men with red armbands acting as stewards and marching on the flanks of the column. Behind them were women, some of them with kids, taking up the slogans chanted by the marchers. Behind the women, pressed against the shop windows and lounging between the parked cars, were row upon row of silent men. They weren't chanting, they weren't shouting counterslogans. They just lounged and watched.

"Trouble," said Phil. The camera was by his side, and I heard the sound of the motor drive as he took pictures of the silent men. People still think you can't take pictures without having the camera pressed to the photographer's eye. I looked at my watch

—another thirty minutes before all the marchers were due to assemble around the statue for the main speeches. Phil and I squeezed our way through, showing our press cards to the cordon of police, and reached the huge plinth of the Marquis of Pombal's statue. He was famous for dragging Portugal into the eighteenth century. Like every other available surface in the city, his statue was a riot of political posters and slogans, hammers and sickles and red fists squeezed between the endless patterns of capital letters for whichever group of party militants had last been at work with the paint spray. Phil and I shinned up the statue and perched astride the stone maidens who clustered around the base of the old nobleman. Phil nodded to other photographers.

Below us, the platform had filled with Communist notables, and on each side of the platform was a platoon of COPCON troops. There were more soldiers on the platform, their eyes continually scanning the crowd. Three maidens away from me on the statue was a guy in plain clothes with binoculars slung round his neck and muttering into a walkie-talkie. Phil took a picture of him too. As the ranks of marchers reached the statue, the stewards funneled them around to the sides of the park, where the columns lost their cohesion and the people were crammed together.

"The police estimate is eighty thousand, including the people still to come up from the Rossio," the man from UPI said as we hauled him up to our vantage point. "The Reds sure pulled out the stops on this one."

It was a huge swell of faces and red banners. The dips and slopes in the ground made for bumps and hollows in the crowd, not like a sea but like a huge heap of trampled gravel. Every single head was moving, but the whole crowd gave an impression of complete stillness, with odd ripples of the banners when the down-draft from the helicopters stirred their fabric.

One of the speakers came forward, a new tone in his voice. He held up his hands for silence, and as if on cue, the police helicopters climbed higher, their clatter reducing as they rose.

"We are a hundred thousand already, Comrades . . . Viva!"

179

The crowd roared back at him, the two syllables stretching endlessly through the afternoon . . . "Vee-ee-ee-ee-var-ar-ar-ar."

"Viva la Liberdad!"—an echo of a hundred thousand voices poured back at him.

"Viva la democracia!"—and their response roared out and died away. Acia-acia-acia—the last syllable still tumbling from half the crowd as the others cried again, "Vee-ee-var-ar-ar."

"Viva, viva PCP!" Long live the Portuguese Communist Party. There was a rhythm to this chant, roared again and again as the marchers still joining the rally began to mark time, stamping their feet in time to the slogans. All around us on the statue, the cassette recorders were stretched eagerly out. The echo of these chants would be on radio waves around the world.

It was a good rally, a convincing rebuttal to the bombs and killings and Angolans that had threatened the Communist claim to the loyalty of the Portuguese working class. Around me I could see the other reporters mentally composing their stories for tonight: "100,000 Portuguese Communists rallied in the streets of Lisbon yesterday to assert that the revolution was still theirs . . ." I wondered how many other reporters had seen those silent, lounging men who flanked the marchers.

Then one of the helicopters began to sink, the sharp, fierce sound of its motor flapping the banners above the platform and drowning the speaker's voice. It came lower, the beat of its blades so close that their sound was picked up by the speaker's microphones and carried by the loudspeakers. The color of the crowd changed as a hundred thousand faces turned upward—a vast spread of pink and pale faces as people started to cover their ears with their hands. The man near me with the binoculars was focusing on the copter. Beside him, another man in plain clothes was muttering into the walkie-talkie.

I looked up. The helicopter just above us looked like a police one. The colors were the same, but scanning the sky I saw the two original police choppers moving our way. Clearly they were coming to investigate this intruder.

Then bundles started to drop from it, solid shapes against the sky that scattered in the wind from the blades into thousands and thousands of leaflets. Still low, the helicopter cruised down the avenue, just above the level of the lamp posts, scattering the leaflets as it went. The two police helicopters hovered just above the platform, as though to deny that part of the sky to the newcomer. Then one of the police craft cruised down the avenue to follow it.

The effect of this second flight was to rescatter the leaflets over a larger area, the new draft of its blades dancing the sheets of paper up side streets and down the Metro entrances. I glanced at the leaflet Phil had caught . . . it was one of the drafts Otto had shown me, with the mug shots of the four Communists who had been arrested for trying to get the guns from the docks. Another drifted down to me. It was a new one. This one carried mug shots of the Communists who had been arrested for possessing the heroin Carlo had planted on them.

The speaker below us was still yelling into his mikes, without success. All you could hear was the pounding beat of the copters. Then from both sides of the avenue there was a flurry of movement and hundreds of tiny objects were lobbed into the air, to fall in the ranks of the Communist marchers. Huge clouds of orange smoke began to billow from the corner into the Rossio Square up to the statue where we sat.

The first helicopter turned, dodged the following police craft, and came back up the avenue, still scattering leaflets, the wind from its blades spreading the plumes from the smoke bombs. The whole avenue, packed from side to side with thousands of marchers and spectators, was completely lost under the orange river of smoke. The helicopter passed right overhead, and dropped more smoke bombs into the crowd in front of the platform. Like huge orange flowers, the smoke bloomed as the packed mass of people eddied and swarmed, looking for ways to escape.

There was a familiar sharpness in the wind, not just the acrid dryness of the smoke, but the taste of tear gas. The copter was still dropping canisters throughout the maddened crowd. Suddenly the sound died. One of the speakers had the sense to turn off the microphones. The copters still lashed the square with their sound, but at least the loudspeakers weren't adding to the din.

There was a sharp whistle blast. One of the COPCON officers on the platform had at last decided to do something. Seizing a carbine from a soldier beside him, he began to fire single aimed shots at the strange copter. Another officer leaped up beside him and wrested the gun away, hitting the marksman over the head. He pointed at the crowd, indicating what would happen if the copter crashed. Orange smoke began to billow up around them, and through it came a surge of men with clubs in their hands, lashing out at everyone on the platform.

They were Carlo's boys, putting the final, ruinous touches to the chaos of the rally. Others with axes were swinging at the wooden supports of the platform. They were wearing masks, just as I had warned Carlo. Tendrils of the gas swirled around us on the statue, and I nudged Phil. Time to leave. He shook me off, still taking pictures, although there was little now to see but smoke.

There were odd shots coming from the platform now as the soldiers lost their nerve, and more shots from the avenue behind us. There was a crash from in front as half of the platform collapsed under the axes. From the side streets armored cars nudged helplessly into the crowd, as useless as the ones that had guarded the platform. In this crowd, they could only fire into the air.

I put my feet down to drop from the statue when I heard a cry and Phil fell across me. We dropped ten feet onto the heads of people who had huddled against the plinth for shelter. Phil landed on top of me, and I felt the moist warmth of his blood flooding across my back. He had been shot in the neck and the blood was bubbling around the exit wound, but it wasn't pumping out. The bullet had missed the artery.

My eyes squeezed against the gas and, the smoke swirling around us, I tried to carry him to one of the armored cars.

The helicopters had gone, but the sound of the ambulance sirens was almost as bad, mixed with the retching of a hundred thousand throats as the gas poisoned the afternoon. Phil was heavy on my back and still bleeding as I tried to climb over retching people and push my way through the wreckage of the platform. I half-fell onto the back of a masked man who was methodically beating a still old man with the blunt end of the ax. The old man was still on the ground, his shoulders jerking as the blows fell. He wore a red sash and there was blood in his hair.

I staggered away and reached the dull green metal of one of the armored cars. It was closed up and I could hear the pump of its ventilation system as the crew sheltered from the gas. I hammered uselessly on the huge rear door, trying not to breathe with my eyes squeezed shut. Two men staggered into me and joined me in beating on the armored car, joining me because all around us was smoke and madness. I was hammering on a closed door, and it made sense to them. There were eight, ten of us hammering on the car, two of them with baulks of wood from the wrecked platform. A woman used her stick to poke behind the wire grills on the rear lights of the armored car, breaking the glass and the bulbs, hurting something, getting her revenge for the hurt done to her. The lights and the bulbs made as good a target as any.

When the ambulance came and I dragged Phil to the shadow of its red cross the armored car had almost disappeared under a heap of people too hurt and too angry to ask why they were hammering at this lump of military metal with its cowering conscripts inside. They had smashed the headlamps and ripped off the radio aerials.

I left Phil with the ambulance and staggered back to the hotel to clean up. The street was pooled with vomit and scuffed leaflets.

# 17

I had showered and changed and gargled with vinegar to clear my throat of the smell of the gas. The water in my shower had turned orange from the smoke particles when I washed my hair. I had called Otto, and he was jubilant. The copter had got back to base while the two police craft had tried to coordinate the rescue services. Otto's copter was being repainted back to its civilian colors. I told him I wanted the cargo plane to meet me at Portimao airport at midday tomorrow.

"The runway is too short. It's a landing strip, Maddox, not an airport."

"It's big enough, Otto. It takes the Air Force Nord-Atlas. Can you do it? The pilot has to land at noon precisely."

He sighed and complained, but he could do it. I called the hospital. Phil was in the operating theater. I debated calling the fat man in Madrid, but decided to tell Chisholm instead. He could tell Phil's father. I called Carlo to congratulate him on the afternoon's work.

"It went well, Ingles. We stopped them cold. It's the last rally they'll ever hold. Have you seen the television?"

"No, Carlo. I'm sure it's terrific. Look, you remember what I said about the airport and Joao's men. I want you to forget it. Something has come up. We need new plans—we have to meet."

Forty minutes later we were in the back room of the Beira bar. Carlo had got Joao to join us. They hadn't found the time to shower, and they both had orange tints in their hair.

"Everything points to tomorrow night," I began. "We're getting word from all over. But we don't know who. It could be the bloody Jesuits. We just don't know, but somebody is going to try to pull a coup tomorrow night."

"You sure you don't mean a putsch." Very funny, Joao.

"Yes, I probably mean a putsch. And if we can't stop it we want to be part of it. We want to have some of the action. So we have to take something and hang on to it."

"Wait a minute, Ingles," Carlo interrupted. He wiped his hand over his face. "There's going to be a putsch, right? We don't know who it is, right? But we want to control something important, so no matter what happens we end up on the winning side. Is that what you mean?"

"That's what I mean. And we are going to take something that everybody needs. Something that you'll need if you're going to win. Something you can't win if you don't have it."

They looked blank. Carlo wiped his hand over his face again.

"We're going to take over the bridge tomorrow. And we're going to keep it. We're going to take it with Joao's men and with my guns. Then we stop anybody else using it."

"You're crazy," said Joao. "So we have the bridge and two hundred men guarding it and machine guns and grenades and all that shit and then we get a squad of tanks wanting to use the bridge. Are the machine guns going to stop tanks?"

"You've got enough dynamite to blow up the bridge. You set the dynamite. You keep the detonator by your side. And you put a big notice on both sides of the bridge saying it's closed. If a tank wants to argue, tell them about the dynamite."

"That bridge cost $40 million. It's one of the longest bridges in the world," said Carlo.

"So if you blow it up you can be first in line for the contract to rebuild it, Carlo. But you won't have to blow it up."

"How long will we have to hold it?"

"No longer than Monday morning. If the coup doesn't work by then it isn't going to work. And we've got the bridge."

"Bazookas and mortars. We'll need them. Just in case the tanks don't believe us about the dynamite."

"We'll get them. Somehow. Carlo, have you got any friends in construction companies?"

"Sure. Three or four."

"So borrow some bulldozers. You can block the bridge with them, dress up some of your men as builders, and put big contract signs at both ends of the bridge. Workmen's lights. Official signs saying 'No entry'—'Bridge closed for repairs.' You see what I mean? So people don't get suspicious too soon. If you move in about thirty minutes before dark, take out the telephone lines so the guys in the toll booths can't call out and check about why nobody's told them about the bridge repairs. And you just hold on to the bridge. No tanks get across, no troops, unless we say so. We're in control."

"I see what you mean," grinned Carlo. "If the putsch wins, they only won because we stopped reinforcements crossing the bridge. If it fails, it fails because we stopped its reinforcements crossing the bridge. Either way we're heroes."

"Right. And they won't dare send in the air force and they won't dare send in artillery because they don't want to damage the bridge. It can't miss, Carlo. Can you do it?"

"Can you get bazookas and mortars?" Carlo countered.

I asked for the telephone and called MSR. Major Antonio was worried. He said something was happening but he didn't know what. The army had put the regular signals clerks onto new duties and brought in new men to handle military communications. The signals clerks had been Major Antonio's first line of defense. Whatever was happening in the army, they were the first to know. Now they were in the dark, and so was MSR. He was hearing other things that frightened him. Leaves had been canceled at some camps, and reserve NCOs had been called back to their regiments.

"It looks like we were right about it, Antonio. Everything points to Sunday night. But we still don't know who is behind it. You got any ideas?"

"Lots of ideas, but none I'm sure of. I'm sure of one thing. It's not the Left. The signals clerks prove that. The signals clerks have always been Left. Communications is technology, so most of the signals people are ex-students, drafted from the university. They're Left. So this thing is being pulled by the Right. It still leaves a lot of candidates, but it means we can start alerting the Communists and the Socialists. And we can alert RA-LIS. Their guns command the airport and the main approach to Lisbon."

"Antonio, RA-LIS is light artillery, right? And they are based by the airport—would that mean they would be equipped with mobile heavy weapons? Antitank stuff and mortars?"

"Yes, they are part of the mobile reserve. Part of our NATO fast reaction force. They have an arsenal at the base so the equipment can be moved onto the planes and flown with the troops direct to forward NATO positions. What's on your mind?"

"Have you got any friends at RA-LIS who would let you borrow some equipment until this coup fever is over? I'd want mortars and bazookas and some 105 mm recoilless."

"What for, Maddox? Our interests only coincide up to a point, remember."

"What's the most important single chunk of this country's transport system, Antonio?"

"The bridge . . . the bridge. It's one of the first things they'll go for. They have to have the bridge, Maddox."

"So how do I get the antitank equipment?"

"We'll go for it tonight. Meet me here at midnight. You'll need a truck. And Maddox—where are your men from?"

"Leave that to me. They're ex-paratroops. They'll hold it. See you at midnight."

Carlo and Joao were bent over a map of Lisbon, Carlo's fingers stubbing at the point where the bridge met the southern shore of the river Tagus, just below the huge statue of Christ.

"You know something, Maddox," Joao said. "We've only to hold one end." He laughed. "Easy. Me against the army. It's still crazy."

"We'll pick up the heavy weapons tonight. It's all fixed. I'll bring the truck here about 1:00 A.M. Maybe later. You can take the truck on to the warehouse at Estoril and brief the men. I suggest you spend the evening checking the access points to the bridge and choosing your positions. Carlo, can you fix the bulldozers and the workmen's clothes—and one last thing. You know that long stretch of open road between the far end of the bridge and the tollbooths? You'll have to keep that clear. That's going to be our private airstrip."

"Why do we need a landing strip?"

"So I can join you—with the guns."

We left Carlo on the phone to his friends in the construction business, while Joao dropped me at the British Embassy before going across the bridge to take photographs of the approaches. The meeting with Chisholm was short and formal. He already knew about the ruin of the demonstration—the TV was still screening the traffic of the ambulances and the COPCON roadblocks. The pro-Communist Minister of Justice said a major inquiry was under way to find the owners of the rogue helicopter.

Chisholm turned off the set and led me across the main hall to the commercial section, where the Resident and the military attaché were studying a large-scale map of the Lisbon region while the young diplomat who was our liaison with the Foreign

Office wrote out the order of battle of the Lisbon garrison on a large blackboard.

"We're both agreed, Chisholm," the Resident said. "Tomorrow night."

"So we know when and we know where—but who the hell is it?" Chisholm asked, mildly enough.

"That's what puzzles me, sir," the military attaché said. "I thought I knew the political leanings of every unit in the army, but some of the indications we have just don't add up."

"Explain," said Chisholm.

"The decisive units are these, sir. First, the cavalry school at Santarem. They have tanks and armored cars, and the school is just beside the main reserve pool of military vehicles. Being professional officers, mainly young subalterns, they are mildly on the Right. Certainly anti-Communist, but also anti-fascist. Now the air force and the navy are both right-wing, dedicated anti-Reds. They have been more involved in NATO than the army. But the marines are leftist, and they are based here, just across the river at Montijo." He pointed on the map to a point on the far side of the river from Lisbon. "Their heavy guns would be able to hit Lisbon, and to cover the RA-LIS base here by the airport, on the eastern flank of the city.

"You see the pattern," he went on. "The Left holds the main artillery strongholds that cover Lisbon, while the army units are based farther out. The commandos at Amadora, to the north of the city, are leftish with conservative officers." His pointer moved northward up the map. "Here at Tancos is the paratroop base, shared between the right-wing air force and the leftist Paras. The Paras should be seen as more Communist than left wing. They have their own commissars in some platoons in the regiment."

"So normally if there were going to be trouble, you'd expect it first at Tancos, to see whether the Right or the Left try to take control," said Chisholm.

"Exactly so, sir. But Tancos is the quietest base. Nothing unusual there at all. In fact, the whole camp is half empty with people away on weekend leave. And moreover there is the coastal artillery at Cascais—they're pro-Communist too, and the best guarantee against the fleet trying to sail up the Tagus. But half of them are on leave too."

"The Tancos base may be half empty," I interrupted. "But aircraft from the rest of the country could still fly in and fill it up quickly enough."

"That's true," the attaché conceded, "but there are no unusual reports from the other air bases. The picture simply isn't clear yet. There is one other thing. . . . Part of the central command are on weekend maneuvers. Two brigades of motorized infantry are moving north and west of Beja—but they are south of the river from Lisbon. They have an armored car detachment. Of course, if they could neutralize the marines at Montijo, then the RA-LIS base could be shelled from Montijo. With a bombardment and an airstrike, the tanks might break through the RA-LIS base. Then if the infantry brigades could cross the Salazar bridge —I mean the 25th April bridge—then Lisbon would fall."

"So the bridge is vital?" Chisholm broke in.

"Only if these southern brigades are part of the coup. And if the RA-LIS base falls. Yes, sir."

"Who's commanding those brigades?"

"Lopes Veroso, sir. He was deputy commander in Mozambique—about to go off to become governor of the Azores. A career soldier, not a politician."

"You won't like this, Chisholm," I said. "But he's a friend of the American military attaché. I saw them together at the Military Club. They were joined by the commander colonel. A man named Lores. That's a bit too coincidental for my taste."

"The Americans again," Chisholm frowned and turned to the attaché. "Any U.S. Navy movements?"

The attaché leafed through his files. "Supplies convoy en route Newport-Naples, should pass Gibraltar Monday midday. There's a carrier in at Cadiz with usual escort, destroyers and frigates. They would all be in range, sir."

"I'm convinced. I don't know about you but I'm convinced the bloody Yanks are at it again. It'll be another bloody Chile, right on our doorstep. Army moves in, a new strong man, protect

190

private property, NATO solidarity. I can see it all now." Chisholm was pacing beside the desk. He stopped and looked at the Resident. "I'm going to cable London and urge formal representations to Washington, asking the Yanks to call it off. It'll be chaos. Portugal's part of Europe, damn it. It's not the bloody Yanks' pitch. It's ours, it's a European pitch. I want your support, sir," he nodded to the Resident. "And I'll want your assistance, Colonel, to persuade the ambassador to concur."

He turned to me. "Your role is dormant for the moment, Maddox, but we might need you to spread the word around your friends on the Left. Tip them off in time and we can stop this thing in its tracks. In the meantime, just stand by."

"I can't do that," I said. "In the first place, the Left is already tipped off—but if the paratroops are all on leave there may not be much they can do. In the second place, I'm going to make sure nobody uses that bridge."

"What the hell do you mean?"

"I've got two hundred ex-paratroopers who are going to take over the bridge tomorrow evening. I'll need the next twenty-four hours to get the equipment for them to hold it."

"These are your Angolans?" asked Chisholm. I nodded. "This could be just what we need. So we can go to the ambassador and say that local Portuguese people are already mobilizing to stop this coup, could we? So we needn't ask London to complain in Washington—we could just watch the American ploy collapse."

"We have to be certain that it does collapse," the Resident murmured. "Absolutely certain."

"So we warn the Left. If they can get their troops back to Tancos and alert RA-LIS they'll be sitting waiting as soon as the Right starts to move."

"With respect, sir, that might not be enough. I don't know what the Left can organize in twenty-four hours, but they will have to contend with the tanks from Santarem—and the air force." The military attaché knew his stuff.

"We'll have to see what London says. In the meantime, we alert the Left and hold the bridge." Chisholm was enjoying himself, holding his back straighter and sucking his stomach in.

"We're going to have to be careful of one thing," he said. "When we're briefing the Left we'd better be a little careful of the Communist Party. If the Yanks and the Russians have come to a deal, then I should imagine the Commies will be keeping a pretty low profile this weekend."

I looked at the man with respect. But if the Communists were on the other side, we'd lost already.

"If I might make a suggestion," the Resident murmured. "No matter what the Communist leadership may have agreed to do with their Russian friends, the Communist rank and file are hardly likely to welcome direct army rule. I think we should tip off some Communists, so long as we choose the right ones."

"I think the Resident is right, and I've got a suggestion," I said. Chisholm gestured; the floor was mine. "Why don't we bring in my MSR contacts? I mean bring them into this room. Give them our full briefing and leave it up to them to coordinate the Left's response. They'll know which Communists to tip off."

We agreed. I called Antonio and told him I was coming to see him, and drove off in one of the unmarked embassy cars while Chisholm got onto London. I took Antonio back to the embassy, back to meet Chisholm. The briefing lasted for two hours, with Major Antonio making copious notes. It was the U.S. Navy movements that finally convinced him we were right. I drove him back to his HQ, and asked him to have four good MSR men from the Algarve to meet me with a car at Faro airport the next afternoon. He made a note of it on his pad, asking what the hell I would be doing two hundred miles away from Lisbon.

"I'm going to hijack an airport. Only a little one. Portimao."

# 18

I got some sleep on the plane flight down to the Algarve. The night had been too busy. Chisholm had got a reply from London, and it wasn't good enough. London wanted to wait and see what happened, suggesting a "strong representation" to Washington on Monday morning if the issue was still in doubt. But in the meantime they wanted total security and no consultations with the Germans or anybody. Chisholm fumed and sent more cables, finally wringing the concession that the protest would be made at midnight to both Washington and NATO HQ in Brussels. But only if it looked as though the coup were faltering. London was not going to argue with success.

I had gone round to see Otto and cajoled him into delaying the rendezvous with his plane. I thought he would complain, but he agreed to have the plane at Portimao at four thirty, rather than noon. If he'd asked for an explanation it would have been a lame excuse. It meant that when the kidnappers were waiting for me, with a gun in Marianne's back, I'd be in mid-air over Portugal. The Resident had been very nice about it. We had strolled in the embassy garden just after dawn, hoping to revive a little in the morning air.

"The girl will be safe, Maddox, I am convinced of it," he had begun. I was silent. "Whatever happens tomorrow night will change the political situation so much that there will be no point in keeping her. And not much point in having the guns."

It didn't help. I could have retorted that the girl could be dead by dusk—hours before the coup began—but there was no point. The decision was taken. It had been taken back at the bar with Carlo and Joao. Once it was clear that we needed the guns, there had been no choice. I asked the Resident to change the subject, and he started to talk about the embassy's roses. That didn't help, either.

When it came to it, there hadn't even been time to agonize over my decision. It was already made for me by the logic of the timing. We had to hold the bridge to stop the coup. To hold the bridge I had to bring up the guns from the Algarve. But the guns had to be brought to the bridge at the right time. If I stayed with the original plan of meeting Otto's plane at noon, then we would be in Lisbon long before Carlo could take the bridge. As soon as I made the offer to hold the bridge with my Angolans, I realized that I had to betray Marianne. They had probably told her of the deal. Perhaps even now she was awake and thinking of seeing me in the afternoon, giving up some silly military hardware so I could get back to the serious business of being with her again.

The Resident and I strolled through the garden in silence, and when we stepped off the path onto broken ground he took my arm. "Like many old men, Maddox, I have spent a good deal of time pondering the wars I have fought in," he suddenly observed. "Every time I walk I think about my bad leg and why the devil some German youngster felt the need to shoot at me. And the more I have read, and the more I have thought of it, the more convinced I become that the reason for the First World War was the overwhelming importance of the railway timetables. The German plan was to use almost all of their army to crush the French in six weeks, and then move some two million troops back across Germany to defeat the Russians. When the Russians first started to make angry diplomatic noises about one of the unusual minor affrays in the Balkans, the Germans were trapped by their own logic. They could not face the threat of a Russian invasion, so they launched their own attack on the French. From what I gather of your kidnappers' arrangements, you have been forced to foil them because of similar considerations of timing. It is not a pleasant thought, my dear Maddox, but it is a philosophical one and it is all the consolation I can offer."

I made no reply. It didn't help. We picked our way over the fresh-turned earth, where the gardeners had been at work. They wouldn't dare to skimp on the job, not with the ambassador as their boss. The soil smelled rich and moist, darkened by decades of conscientious manuring and compost. The ambassador had been here a long time. The garden would reflect his good stewardship long after he had gone.

"Much of it is my fault, you know," the Resident said quietly. His hand was still on my arm and suddenly he tightened his grip. "Don't misunderstand me. We thought it was for your own good."

I turned slowly to face him, not brushing his hand away. "Go on," I said.

"You have to understand that we have worked together for a long time, Derwent and I. The Madrid Resident, the one you call the fat man. It's that Andaluz cooking he likes that does it. When I first knew him he was as slim as you. And as efficient."

"Tell me how it was your fault," I said. I heard my voice, toneless and flat. His grip was still tight on my arm.

"Derwent went out to Mexico for us some years ago. He knew Thayer there, the girl's father. In the course of one of our regular meetings he told me that Thayer was being posted to Lisbon. That was one of the reasons, one of the many tiny facts that built up the picture and persuaded London to send you out here."

"So the fat man knew her father. So what?" He took his hand from my arm and bent to the ground, picking up a clod of earth and crushing it with his hands, savoring the smell of it.

"The girl was on holiday in Madrid and looked up her father's old friend. The fat man," he added, his eyes on the earth, avoiding mine.

"So he arranged for the two of you to meet. He took her to the bullring, telling her to follow the man who had sat beside him. He told her you could be persuaded to take her to Portugal. That was where she wanted to go."

"So she was acting on orders?" My voice was tight, like my chest, like my fists.

"Nothing so simple, my dear fellow. Life never is." He picked a stone from the clod and threw it away, toward the garden wall. "She knows her father is more than a simple soldier, and she knew Derwent wasn't the boozy expatriate Englishman that he seems. And I have no doubt she guessed that you were a most unorthodox journalist."

"So the fat man told her to pick me up and screw me—just like that? For a lift to Lisbon? Bollocks." I thought back to the night in the disco, the way she danced.

"It was a little bit of extra insurance. Not for you. For us. For me and for Derwent. We do that kind of thing a lot, you know. You would be surprised at the little tricks we have, we Residents. We tend to be suspicious of firemen like yourself, sent out by London to do the jobs you people think are beyond us." He stood upright slowly, almost painfully, showing his age.

"Derwent told me that he had advised you to take a girl with you, to cross the frontier. He planted the idea in your mind at the bullfight—is that not true?" I nodded. And I remembered the way she had looked at him and then at me when the bullfight ended.

"It was a double trace. We wanted a trace on you, and we wanted a very discreet line to Major Thayer. I knew the man was up to no good as soon as he arrived at the embassy. He replaced a friend of mine, a colonel. He was very fond of roses. We got on terribly well."

"So what did the fat man tell the girl? That I was the shy, retiring type?" His eyes were on my face now, not a trace of regret in them.

"I don't know what he told her, except that it was successful. You took her to Lisbon with you. You had direct access to Thayer. We had a trace on you through the girl. We knew, roughly, what you were up to."

"You mean she was reporting back to Madrid? On me?" He shook his head at my question, sighing. I felt very stupid.

"You aren't a fool, think before you jump to conclusions. Of course she wasn't keeping in touch with Madrid. She didn't have to. I knew the two of you had checked into the Tivoli within an hour of your arrival. It was just an extra check for Derwent and for me. Keeping an eye on you. I'm sorry it worked out like this."

"So what do you know about the kidnap?" A bird squawked and flapped away, disturbed by my voice. I had almost shouted the question. The Resident watched the bird dart over the garden, soar above the embassy roof.

"Nothing at all, I'm afraid. We hadn't expected that." He turned back to me. "I do regret that events have taken this course. But there we are. Would you help me back to the path?"

Numbly, I gave him my arm and we picked our way across the new-turned soil. "He keeps the gardens very well, wouldn't you say?" I didn't reply. "Odd how you can always tell an ambassador by his garden. A good one, I mean." He broke off and chuckled. "I suppose I mean the ambassador's wife. They are the ones that matter, after all." His voice was almost a whisper, as though talking to himself. "The girl would have come to Lisbon in any event," he said suddenly. "You know that."

197

I nodded. Yes, I suppose I knew that. There was no more to say. We went back into the embassy and got on with the day.

The trip to the RA-LIS base had been simple enough. I showed the guard the pass Major Antonio had given me and they waved the truck through to one of the warehouses. We took eight bazookas, eight 81 mm mortars, and four recoilless. The RA-LIS boys even helped us load up. There were three other shadowy trucks driven into the warehouse while we were there, removing the same kinds of weapons. The Left was preparing to put up a fight. Carlo had asked if there were any small arms, but the stores sergeant said they had been moved out of Lisbon months ago, wanting to make sure nobody armed the workers. Then he grinned. The workers aren't defenseless, he added. We told him we were glad to hear it, and Carlo gave him the clenched-fist salute.

About breakfast time I managed to get three hours sleep, but when the stewardess shook me awake as the plane came in to land at Faro airport, I knew I was still weary. There wasn't much more I could do. Carlo was getting the bulldozers moved up during the afternoon, and Joao would ensure his men took the bridge at the right time. The schedule was very tight. I had to get the plane and the arms to them by six-thirty. Until I got there they would only have Carlo's handful of small arms to hold the bridge. They had the heavy weaponry to stop armored cars, but it was the infantry weapons that would count. The machine guns and grenades in the Algarve villa.

When I got off the plane there were two men waiting by the door to the arrivals lounge. They both wore MSR buttons in their shirts. They escorted me to the car park where two more men sat waiting in a Seat saloon. I asked them to take off the MSR badges and throw them away. Then I asked them to take out their wallets and any identification papers and leave them in an airport locker. As we drove back along the coast road to Lagos I told them what we had to do. Easy, they said. The airport isn't even guarded.

They were wrong. Any other day but this we would have driven straight into Portimao airport and waved to the three civilians in the control tower and driven the truck straight to the end of the runway to load the guns onto Otto's plane.

Getting the guns had been easy enough. The villa was still empty and the truck was still there. So were the guns. We used a tire lever to force the garage door open and then I crawled under it to cut the ropes that tied the door to the truck. We checked the truck, replaced the rotor, and siphoned some of the Seat's petrol into the tank. She started first time. Two of the MSR men climbed into the truck with me. The car followed. The drive to Portimao airport was just as easy. We turned off from the main road to Faro and drove past the head of the runway before sweeping around to the entrance gates. The runway was deserted, and there were no planes on the field.

But the gates were closed and there were three bored sentries beside it. The driver of the car got out and chatted to them. Then he walked back to me in the truck.

"There's some kind of alert," he said. "The airport is closed. I told them we had arranged to meet an aircraft here but they said they've got orders. He says all the airstrips all over the country have been closed. There's a sergeant and five other men at the control tower."

I looked over to the tower. All six of them were lounging in the open, but they had their automatic rifles with them. So did the three on the gate. I climbed out of the driver's cab and went to the back of the truck, where two of the MSR men sat beside the crates.

Quickly they prized open one end of the crates and mounted the NATO general purpose machine gun on its bipod, aiming over the tail of the truck. They set the gun up deep inside the truck and then passed out some grenades and two FN rifles.

I sent the car driver back to the sentries, to tell them that we were going to turn around and drive off. He got in the car, turned it neatly in the narrow lane and drove in front of the truck so the car was shielded from the soldiers. I passed the grenades into the car and gave the MSR men in the passenger's seat one of the FN rifles. I took two more grenades and put them into my shirt and climbed into the cab of the truck. I turned it slowly, trying to keep the rear in the shade of the trees so the soldiers would not see the mounted machine gun.

Then I put the truck in reverse, gunned it, and charged into the locked gates. One of the sentries was fast enough to grab his rifle and start firing. As I went past them I tossed one of the grenades into the little group of them and I heard the chatter of our machine gun firing through the wire mesh of the gates at the group of soldiers around the control tower. We hit the gates and they began to give. With a wrench of metal they came off the support rails but then I was slammed into the back of my seat, and bounced forward onto the windshield. The truck hadn't burst through the gates. We were tangled in the wreckage.

I slammed into first gear and shot forward, slamming into the tail of the Seat saloon, which was still reversing, hoping to follow me through the gates. At the side of the car, the grenade I had thrown suddenly exploded and I saw the driver and passenger slump forward into the smashed windshield. I shuddered to think what the collision had done to the little machine gun nest in the back of the truck, but I slammed the gear into reverse and charged back through the tangle of gates. We bumped and lurched our way over with a grinding of metal and thuds on the floor of the cab. As we bullied our way through I heard the truck's machine gun start firing again. I spun the wheel and tried to keep the truck reversing straight for the control tower. Then they shot at our tires.

I was crouching low in the cab and trying to steer by the wing mirrors when the near-side mirror exploded into smithereens. The truck was lurching and swaying and losing speed. Then the machine gun stopped firing. I swung the wheel to turn the nose of the truck toward the control tower. I'd rather be shot at than have a rifle bullet hit the crate with the grenades.

As the truck lurched around I dropped out on the blind side and ran back. One of the two men was lying on the floor with a gash in his head. The other had been shot in the face. I picked up the machine gun and dragged it to the back of the truck. Then I dragged it off, with a cartridge belt looped around my shoulder, and dropped to the ground, hugging what was left of one of the wheels for cover. The tower was still too far away for a grenade. I gave them a short burst, just about ground level, and they stopped firing. I didn't know how many of them were still alive.

There was total silence. I kept glancing at both flanks of the control tower to see if the sergeant had the sense to send men out to the sides where they could catch me in a crossfire. But nothing stirred. I gave them another burst and two shots came back, one of them close. The other hit the cab of the truck. My ears were ringing with firing the gun and I held my nostrils and blew hard to clear them. They were still ringing but I heard another sound—I glanced around and there was a Nord atlas, Otto's plane.

There was no way it could land while the soldiers held me off. Takeoff and landing are a plane's most vulnerable moments. I took out a grenade, primed it, and tossed it as far as I could toward the control tower. It fell far short but the explosion must have been seen by the aircraft. I had to stop it landing. I gave the ground where the soldiers hit another burst and saw the plane circling.

The stupid bastard was losing height, coming in as if to land. I glanced back to the gate, where the wreck of the saloon was still burning. The pilot must realize that he couldn't land. Almost desperately I put a long burst toward the soldiers. This time three shots came back. I wasn't even keeping their heads down.

Then I heard the sound of another rifle, much closer. I spun to see if anyone had worked around behind me and then it fired again, firing from the truck. Maybe the guy with the gash in his head had woken up. He fired again and I heard a cry from the ground by the tower. Up on the truck, he could look down onto their positions. I gave them another burst and looked again at the sky.

I glanced up but couldn't see it, but I heard a sound like twenty generations of thunder, and the truck shook as the plane came over at about fifty feet. It climbed away. It must have seen the firefight. It went into a wide turn at the end of the runway and started coming back. Suddenly there was the sound of another machine gun, and the base of the control tower disintegrated into smoke and dust. The plane went low over the truck again, still firing, as the control tower began to sag over toward us. The dust was still rising as the glass upper story collapsed, falling directly onto the position where the soldiers had been.

The plane was turning again and coming in. I put a last burst of fire into the rubble heap of the tower, just to make sure, and then I crawled around to the back of the truck. The MSR guy in the back was as stunned as I was by whatever heavy artillery the plane had mounted. I looked at the guy with the bullet in his face. He was dead. The one who had woken up and started shooting looked in bad shape. He said he had been thrown forward when I hit the gates. I told him he had done very well.

The plane landed, and as it turned to start taxiing toward us I tried to start the motor of the truck. Nothing. It wouldn't even turn the motor over. I climbed out and went back to the machine gun as the plane came to rest, swinging its tail around so that the huge entry door in the fuselage was as near the truck as possible.

I looked through the plane to the other entry door where the contraption stood in silhouette against the sky. I walked around the tail to look at it. It was a twin mounted heavy machine gun, an old Browning firing heavy 0.5 slugs. With two barrels, that was almost two thousand heavy rounds a minute. No wonder the tower went down. I leaned in to look at the mounting when I heard a chuckle and Otto's familiar voice welcomed me.

"Do you like my little toy, Maddox? I thought you might find some difficulties, so I decided to come myself." Stiffly, because of his leg, the old German edged to the door and climbed out, hanging onto the Browning mounting as he dropped.

"Thanks, Otto. You were very timely. Somebody had been tipped off that the airstrip needed guarding, but where in hell did you get this?" I gestured at the twin Browning.

"The Portuguese sent a mission to Vietnam and came back very impressed with gunships. This is their version. They bought the guns cheap off the British after the war. You used them in your heavy bombers. I import the swivel mountings—you see, the gunner gets into this harness, then he can almost lean out of the plane. It's not as good as the gunships, but it's cheaper. The Portuguese used it a lot in Africa. I sold them forty, so I had one spare. Useful, eh?"

"Terrific, Otto. Now all we have to do is load up. The truck won't move—you'll have to get the pilot to juggle this thing across to the truck. Otherwise we'd need a fork-lift truck."

"That's okay. I brought rollers. We can slide them under the crates and roll them aboard." Otto gestured to two men who still sat inside the plane, and they jumped out with the rollers and climbed onto the truck. Otto went up to speak to the pilot.

I turned back to the MSR man with the gashed face and started trying to clean him up. I told him he'd have to come with us. The car and the truck were wrecked so he had no transport, and more troops would probably arrive soon to investigate the gunfire. He shrugged and I helped him clamber into the plane, then I joined Otto and his men in manhandling the crates onto the rollers. They came aboard fast enough, and the pilot began to juggle the plane again to get the tailplanes clear of the truck. One of Otto's men was chattering to him and looking at the wounded MSR man. I saw Otto nod and pull out a Walther automatic. Coolly, he shot the MSR man in the back and the force of the bullet knocked him off the plane. I turned back to Otto in disbelief, and the gun was aimed at me.

"I very much regret the necessity of this, Maddox, but you will move to the back of the plane. To that little perspex bubble in the tail. There, that's good. My regrets are not based on any regard for your clumsy self, but upon the job I now have to do."

He shouted for one of his men to keep me covered while he went forward to supervise the tying down of the crates. They had been stacked forward, right between the wings. The rear half of the plane was empty, except for Otto's guard and the two cargo doors. And me.

# 19

The takeoff hurt. I was crouched in the glass bubble at the back of the fuselage, the slope of the plane's tail above me and the tail-wheel bouncing its way through my spine as we bumped over the runway and climbed away from the field. Looking back I saw the collapsed tower, the ruined truck, and the car still smoking by the gates. By the truck was a white smear—the body of the MSR man Otto had shot.

"Why am I alive, Otto?" I asked when we were airborne. He had walked down from the cockpit, his gun still loosely in his hand. He stood beside the guard he had left to cover me.

"Because you have a noble purpose to fulfill. You will die, of course, but not yet. You have to be killed heroically by one of my men. You are going to become a famous corpse, Maddox. The filthy gun-running British imperialist. Stealing weapons, fixing coups. You are to be exposed, Maddox, and your body will be found beside the guns. Your death is all arranged."

"Where is this event to take place? And when?"

"At Tancos Air Force Base, later today. You will be found with your precious guns and with the bodies of some Portuguese traitors beside you. You will be shot by Portuguese patriots who will reject your bribes, and then we will call in the TV cameras and all your erstwhile comrades of the press. Front-page news, Maddox. British SAS spy uncovered with his trousers down. Surrounded by stolen guns. It will be a very good story, Maddox. And it will explain everything that follows."

"You mean it will explain tonight's coup, Otto. That's what you're involved in. But what's an old Kraut like you doing with the Yanks? Tonight is their operation, Otto."

"Not wholly, Maddox. Not wholly. Your own contribution to the events of the next twenty-four hours was dreamed up by myself. It will be an amusing part of a distressing series of events. The only amusing part. I am going to make you famous, Maddox." He grinned at me and walked back to the cockpit. "Ninety minutes flying time, Maddox," he called, and sent a second man to guard me.

The sun was beating down strongly on me through the perspex bubble and I tried to shift position. The guards waved their guns and made it clear I was not to move at all. I tried to work out where I had gone wrong. The answer was simple enough—I went wrong when I first met Otto at the briefing back in Britain weeks ago. When he had been flown in as the German end of a combined European operation. Chisholm's brain wave. You don't ask too many questions about people who've been friendly Residents for twenty years, and who share your assignment.

Otto had done everything right. He'd got the supplies I asked for, he'd laid on the copter at the demo, he'd sent a rifleman to cover me at the National Stadium. I trusted him like a bullfighter trusts his *banderillero* . . . and as I thought of it a little red light flashed in my head. My memory flashed back to a killing sword snaking out from an oiled leather sheath, the curl of it as the blade came free.

This was close, this memory of the leather, of the sheath. There had been somewhere else I had seen that curled leather, something else that had been scratching at the door of my memory ever since. I closed my eyes and saw a photograph, a small room, a woman, a child crying . . . the mantelpiece. On the mantelpiece was a leather case. It was the case for a night-sight. I had asked Otto to send me a rifleman with a night-sight. The case was on the mantelpiece. He was a Communist.

I checked the chain of logic back. Why would Otto use a Communist unless he had an arrangement with them? But Otto hated them, he was a professional Red-hater because of what they'd done to him when he was a prisoner of war. Ten years . . . you can do a lot to a man in ten years. Convert him, train him, set him up as an anti-Communist and then run him as a sleeper for twenty years until the time is ripe to use him.

"Otto!" I yelled it as loud as I could. "Otto!" The two guards had the guns pointing down my throat. "Otto!" His familiar shape limped back.

"What is it?"

"How does it feel to work with the Yanks, Otto?"

He shrugged and turned away.

"You've hated them for thirty years, Otto, and now you're helping them. How does it feel, Comrade, to sell your Portuguese comrades down the river? You waited thirty years for this, Otto. Thirty years to betray your own people. That's quite a life story. You know there'll be an Order of Stalin in this, Otto. The man who sold out the revolution." I spat the last words out.

He turned slowly around and came up to me, his hand dragging along the high rail down the roof of the plane. He looked very sad and very old.

"So you worked out how it is, Maddox. Not fast enough, but you did it. You finally worked it out. Does it shock your precious morality, Maddox? Is that it? I should stay loyal to my comrades no matter what. Is that what you think?"

"It's not what I think, Otto. You've got the thinking problem. You're the one who believes in the workers of the world. You're the comrade who is working with the Americans for the military coup. You're the comrade who is going to make this country safe for colonels and the capitalists again, Otto. Comrade Otto, the Portuguese workers' friend. The revolution you can trust."

"You're not very clever, Maddox. I might even have doubted my orders, but they offend you so much they must be right. The policy is Moscow's—they know more than I do. We lose in Portugal to win somewhere else. I am unimportant."

"So what's the deal with the Yanks, Otto? It is Yugoslavia for Portugal? So Moscow can march into Belgrade when Tito dies, you have to let the Americans pull their coup here? Or is it somewhere else, Otto? How about Berlin? Maybe that's it. As soon as they get through shooting all the Communists in Portugal, Russia marches into Berlin. How's that one, Otto? That near the mark? Hey, how about China? Maybe it's China. Maybe that's the deal. We get Portugal and you get to drop the big ones on China. Am I right, Otto? Come on, Otto. There has to be another victim of this deal. This is the big league, Otto. Yanks and Russians . . . the detente duo. There's got to be another sacrifice. These things balance out, Otto, you know that. You get Cuba and we get to kill all the lefties in Chile. You wipe out your Jews and we wipe out our Red Indians. Your morality, Otto. Somebody else's eye for somebody else's eye."

"There's panic in your voice, Maddox. What is it? The thought of dying? Is that what you're thinking about, about that last long moment when you see my finger tighten on the trigger? It will be me, Maddox. With great pleasure, I will fire very slowly. Is that why your voice is so high? Or is it just because you British are so minor now? Are you jealous of us and the Americans, Maddox?"

"The only people I'm jealous of are these poor dumb comrades on this plane—the ones you're going to sell down the river. I suppose you'll have to shoot them when you shoot me—just to make it look good. Like those Spaniards and that Portuguese comrade who got shot up by the National Stadium when you tried to kill me. They all died, Otto. They all made it look good. You really had me fooled."

"So it gives me the pleasure of shooting you later." He spun on his heel and dragged himself back along the high rail, the one to which the parachutists attach the static lines.

"God help you, Otto. You wait thirty years for the big job and they give you this one. Is this what you dreamed of when you were training? Working with the Yanks to sell out your own?"

He turned around again, slowly, and studied me. "The long training—yes, it was long but it was good." He smiled. "That's how I knew you had the guns. One day they disappear and the next day you ask me if I can make a cargo aircraft available. You thought they were your little secret. You didn't train long enough."

I looked at my watch. Somebody else who knew I had the guns would be bundling Marianne into the back of a car somewhere. Driving her down to the coast to Guincho and waiting for me to come and save her life. And Carlo and Joao and two hundred men, about to occupy a bridge with some bulldozers and antitank weapons and not enough rifles to drive off a platoon of boy scouts, Major Antonio and all the others who would go out tonight to stop a coup, and they would fail. All because Otto was smarter than I was.

"You know, you did only one thing that surprised me, Maddox. You know what that was?"

I shook my head. I didn't know and I didn't care, either. I didn't even particularly want to hear it.

"You betrayed the girl. That surprised me. I thought of it when you looked at your watch. You were supposed to get her back today, weren't you? You asked me to get the cargo plane for midday—that's when we were sure it was you who had the guns. And then you surprised me. You changed the time and betrayed your woman. I thought better of you, Maddox."

How in hell had he known about the evening rendezvous with the kidnappers? And what was that about "we were sure it was you"?

"I thought you knew the day after I got them, Otto—the day I asked you for the plane. What's all this about being unsure?"

"I was sure, Maddox. I was very sure. But the American—he wanted to be certain. So when the girl disappears, we tell you that on Sunday you can have her back. So then you come to me and say you want the plane on Sunday. Even Thayer was sure then."

"Major Thayer—so he kidnapped his own daughter."

"No—I had her kidnapped, but with his knowledge and approval. We set the trap and you walked into it. Just like a British amateur. Then it was simply a matter of devising a way to make use of you and your guns and your foolishness. You already know how we intend to dispose of you—fame at last, Maddox."

"Otto—can I move from here . . . I'm sick. Airsick."

"So your courage also fails. Vomit in your lap for all I care." He lurched back to the cockpit.

It had been an idea, a ghost of an idea. If they let me to one of the cargo doors to vomit I might just get the chance to grab the double Browning and shoot the wing off. Take Otto and the guns down with me. Better than let Otto shoot me and use my corpse to blame the British for the coup. Three seconds on those triggers and the wing would be cut into shreds.

"Otto!" I yelled again. He poked his head through the cockpit hatch.

"The girl—was she told it wasn't a real kidnap? Did she know her own father was behind it?"

"You're sentimental." He grinned with some warmth, the first sign of warmth since he'd pulled the gun. "No, Maddox, she didn't know. We wanted her voice to sound authentically frightened. It worked, eh?" He winked at me, and muttered something in Portuguese to my guards before going back to the copilot's seat.

One of the guards withdrew to the cargo door, the one with the gun mounting. The other helped me to my feet and pushed me toward the other open door at the other side of the fuselage. He grinned at me, pointed at the door and then at me and shook his head. No, they weren't going to throw me out. He put his hand to his stomach and brought it up to his mouth with a retching sound and pointed to the door. I was to be allowed to be airsick through the door. I lay down and inched forward, while one guard held my legs and the other trained a gun on me. It was a small gun, no bigger than a .32. It would slow me but it wouldn't necessarily kill me.

I gripped the edge of the door, the airstream quickly chilling my fingers, and slowly pulled myself up the plane so my head could rest against the side of the door frame. This pulled my torso across the threshold of the open door, and the guard hanging onto my legs turned his head away from the airstream. I put one finger down my throat and tickled. I retched, feebly, and tickled my throat a little more. I retched again, most of it being blasted back by the airstream onto the shoulders of the guard holding my legs. His head still turned away, he hadn't noticed. I retched again, a whole gutful, and it streamed onto the back and shoulders of the guard once more.

I looked across at the other guard. His mouth wrinkled and he put his fingers to his nose. I put my arm onto the other guard's shoulder, as if to wipe away my vomit.

Then I grabbed a handful of the stuff and hurled it into the face of the guard with the gun. I grabbed back for the edge of the door and swiveled my legs, slamming the vomit-covered guard against the cargo hatch, and his legs fell out of it. He clutched tightly at my legs, half of him already in the slipstream, thousands of feet above the ground. His head burrowed into my lap and I used the full swing of my arm to slam the base of my hand upward into his upper lip, driving his nose back through the weak part of the skull into the brain. Before his body left the aircraft, he was already dead.

I pulled myself up by the door frame and grabbed for the high rail, meaning to swing through and kick the face of the second guard. But my hand was still slimy with vomit, and instead of swinging to kick him I tumbled at him, tangling both of us into the gun mounting of the Browning. My left hand had gripped his gun hand, while with my right I tried desperately to hang on.

I had seconds before Otto came through the cockpit door firing. Even cargo aircraft are light enough to respond when passengers start getting hurled out of them. I was punching his gun hand into the mounting of the Browning, where the shells went into the breech, where the metal was sharp and solid. Once . . . twice, the gun dropped and his knee came up to my crotch. I doubled up forward and drove my head down into a crude butt to his nose, driving him back to the edge of the door. He was hanging onto the plane with one hand, the hand that held onto the Browning mounting.

I had one hand on the mounting and one hand groping for the gun the guard had dropped, so I sank my teeth into his hand just at the base of his thumb. In the same instant I whirled with the gun in my hand, the guard ripped his hand away and hung in the doorway, and Otto came into the fuselage, his gun ready.

Then I fired once; the slipstream blew the guard away, and Otto fired at the same instant as my second shot. My first had got him in the elbow and my second had missed. His shot had gone wide, unaimed, the trigger jerked when my bullet bit his arm.

His eyes looked for the two guards as I walked toward him, and then his eyes focused on the doors. He was speechless as I patted him down and picked up his gun from the floor. It was a big 9 mm Walther. If it had hit me it would have blown me through the back of the aircraft. I led him back to the cockpit.

Otto took the copilot's seat, and I put one gun in his ear and the other gun in the pilot's ear and savored the words I had always longed to say.

"Pilot, take this plane to Cuba." Then, very carefully, I wiped the vomit off my hands and onto Otto's neck.

# 20

"The wind's wrong—I can't do it." The pilot's voice rose but his hands were very gentle on the controls. Otto had his head on his knees, his good arm cradled over his head, the other hanging straight to the floor. Blood was still seeping through the rough bandage I had let him apply. Below us, at the far end of the huge bridge, was a 1,200 yard stretch of tarmac running up to the tollbooths. It was eight lanes wide, and Carlo and Joao had lined up cars with blazing headlights on both sides. It looked like Heathrow at Christmas.

"You either die trying or you die," I said as calmly as I could. He probably didn't understand my words but he understood the gun pushed into his neck. He crossed himself and dropped his flaps. He was a good pilot, losing height as we flew parallel to the bridge, his eyes flickering to a coastal steamer to check the wind direction by the smoke from her funnel.

As we passed the main strut for the bridge he edged out, away from the landing strip, heading toward the hillside. I jammed the gun at him more urgently. The pilot groaned and Otto opened one eye.

"He's going to sideslip in—the only way," Otto muttered. The pilot moved the stick to the right and pushed the left rudder, keeping the nose high, and we sideslipped, losing height rapidly and drifting back toward the line of headlights. Support struts flashed past beneath us and the plane leveled out and we landed, running tail high, on the wheels and barely slowing. Faces flashed past the windows and the pilot stabbed the rudders for braking. He looked calm, and we came to rest a good fifty yards short of the tollbooth. It was six twenty-eight.

I stayed in the cockpit, covering Otto and the pilot until Joao came, grinning inanely and thumping my back before he turned to direct the unloading of the guns. I told him to try and dismount the heavy double Browning and to get my two prisoners tied up and put away. He was wearing a bright orange hard hat and an orange fluorescent jacket. Carlo rushed up in a yellow hard hat. He carried a third one, blue. Now I knew my color.

"I saved you a tommy gun, Ingles," he grinned, and I punched him gently, with affection, high on the shoulder. He rolled with the blow, laughing, and then he wrinkled his nose when he smelt me.

"I get airsick easily," I said. "How long have we got?"

He showed me a walkie-talkie strapped to his belt. "We've had the 'Bridge Closed' signs up for thirty minutes. We've turned cars back, told them to go the long way, by Santarem, or take the ferry. We had two cops, but we showed them the contract."

"What contract?"

"The contract to repair the bridge, from the Ministry of Public Works and Construction. Official. It cost 50,000 escudos but it means nobody suspects us unless they talk to the minister. He is supposed to have signed the contract. If any troops are on the road, I have men with radios spread out on the approaches. I'll have almost an hour of warning. Who are the prisoners?"

"The old one is supposed to be the German Resident. He's a Communist. Been waiting for twenty years to do his work for the cause. He's part of the coup tonight. I want him kept safe—if you can, get him away from here to a safe house. I want him alive tomorrow. The other one is just the pilot. But he's a good one. Look after him too."

I told Carlo I had to get back to the city to liaise with my embassy and get reports from the other base. I asked him for a spare walkie-talkie and he passed me his own, saying he had another back in his command post on the bridge. I promised him I'd come back if there was trouble. He shrugged and walked me down the ramp to the barricade of bulldozers that blocked the end. We squeezed between them and the suspension cables, and he waved me off. He said he'd save me a tommy gun.

The walk across the bridge took me twenty minutes and at the far end, behind an effective but unobtrusive barricade of two sand heaps and a small dump truck, were Carlo's advance guard on the Lisbon side of the bridge. They were mixing concrete, but the guns were handy. They had bazookas at this end too. I went on through, squeezing past a long line of cars that was slowly reversing down the lane from the blocked bridge. One of them was a taxi, and he took me back to the hotel. If I went to the embassy I'd never get to change my clothes. The taxi driver didn't like the smell either.

Something very strange had happened in my hotel room. All of her clothes had disappeared. I checked the bedside drawer—the pills were still there. That meant that somebody else had removed her clothes for her, and it had probably been a man. I showered and changed and called the lobby to get me a taxi.

Marianne was safe in her father's hands. Just before we reached the MSR building I stopped the cab and went into a cafe for a coffee and a sandwich. Then I had another coffee with brandy in it. To celebrate. I walked around the corner and tried the door of the MSR building. It was locked, so I hammered. Through a grill I was examined and the door opened enough for me to slip through. At the end of the hall was a barricade with loopholes and an armory behind it. They helped me climb over and I went up to Antonio's office.

He was on the phone and there was a man at the transmitter, talking urgently into his mike. Antonio waved me to a chair and pointed to a pot of coffee on a tray. I rolled a cigarette and flicked the walkie-talkie button to Carlo. He was well set. Still no complaints from the public, and his guns were posted.

Antonio put the phone down, smiled, and reached for the coffee.

"How goes the bridge, my friend?"

"The bridge is safe. But the Communists are not."

"I know—we have got about three hundred of the paratroops back to Tancos. They had all been given leave by the adjutant— a party member. His own commissar has threatened to shoot him. The commissar believes us about the coup—he's pulling men back to base from wherever he can find them. A lot of the Communists are with us. But I'm still worried about Santarem. I know we've got antitank weapons, but it takes a lot of training to stand up to armor."

He stood up and crossed to his cupboard, stripping off his suit as he moved. He went down to his underwear and reached into the cupboard for his uniform. He took a long leather belt off a hook and threaded it across his shoulder, through the epaulettes. On his belt he hung a walkie-talkie and a heavy revolver. He clipped some small ammunition patches onto his leather strap and pulled a canvas small pack from the cupboard. Filling it with grenades from a shelf, he put a webbing strap around it and slung it over his shoulder. He tossed me an assault rifle and a canvas pack containing magazines and followed them with a camouflage smock. I put it on and looked at the Kalashnikovs. I

215

asked if he had got them in Africa and he nodded. He showed me out.

We drove first to the embassy, where the night guard held us at the door, aghast at our guns, until Chisholm came to escort us through.

"Planning on stopping this thing by yourself, Maddox?" he asked. The usual charm. The Resident was still there, still looking fresh, and there were more of the military attaché's staff. They had a radio installed to get reports from the consuls in Oporto and the Algarve.

"Situation hasn't changed much, except I'm a bit happier about the Tancos base," Chisholm said. "We've had one of the juniors in a cafe by the main gate. Says he's seen a lot of Paras checking back into the barracks. The infantry brigades are definitely heading our way. They were seen on the Evora road, about fifty miles away. They've got an armored car regiment in tow. Montijo is on defense alert, but the coastal artillery at Cascais is still empty. NATO orders simply have the Portuguese ships cruising in home waters—they could be just around the corner, waiting to sail up the river and bombard. We can get no sense out of Amadora, and the Minister is standing by in London. The U.S. Navy is moving in our direction, but we won't know exactly until after midnight. What have you got?"

Briefly, I said that we had the bridge occupied, and I told him about Otto. He said I must have made a mistake. I said Otto was in custody and he could interrogate the man himself. I confirmed that Thayer and Otto had been working together, Americans and Russians working for a coup by the Right, working to wipe out the Communists in Lisbon. Antonio confirmed that senior Communists were still refusing to mobilize against it, but that many of the rank and file had already joined the rest of the Left.

"Do you know what we are calling ourselves?" he grinned. "It is very funny for revolutionaries. We are Loyalists."

Chisholm cabled London again, with the confirmation of the Russo-American agreement. Again he urged London to complain in Washington. While he worked with the cipher clerk the

216

Resident debriefed Antonio, who confirmed that he felt Tancos base was now safe, and the cavalry school was solidly behind the coup. The Resident asked about Amadora and the commandos.

"That is why I am in uniform—I am going there now. There has been a meeting of officers and a meeting of the men. There will then be a meeting of everybody. I am a commando, and I am an officer. They know me and perhaps they will listen. But I am worried about Santarem. One thing we must have is some armor. We have some armored cars, less than a regiment. But with armor coming from Santarem—they can attack all night and attack again tomorrow. And I don't think the bridge will hold beyond tomorrow." He turned to me. "We can skim over and look at the approach roads, before we go to Amadora."

"How do you mean, skim?"

"Helicopter—from the RA-LIS base at the airport. That's how we are traveling tonight. We'll need to look around."

"Any indications on timing?" asked the Resident. "It's one of the things that troubles us."

"We think the assault is meant for 2:00 A.M., but they have to get the infantry and the armor into position. The armor must start to move by 1:00 A.M., which means they should be fueled and loaded before then. Then they will have to fuel up the tankers they will need. Tancos will make it clear. If they want to use Tancos as a base for aircraft they must seize it by midnight."

We all turned away to our walkie-talkies. There was no move from the bridge, and Antonio's radio operator said he was still trying to get another report from Amadora. Four of the main bridges from Santarem to Lisbon had been mined, and the detonators were ready. Antonio said it could only delay them—they could use the old roads. The naval attaché got off the phone from Brussels and said the latest NATO reports had the U.S. Navy steaming up from Cadiz, heading for Lisbon—or Britain, or France, or home. He said he would keep checking.

"The Minister was very impressed." Chisholm was back, rubbing his hands. "Very impressed. He's called in the German Ambassador and the PM has arranged an immediate meeting. The ambassador is talking to the secretary-general of the Socialist Party. There's a prospect he could formally ask Britain and Germany to intervene—or at least to force a cease-fire. Our lot might even go for that. Germans very upset about old Otto. After the Guillaume scandal, it's just what they don't need. Riddled with the other side, you know, those Krauts. Riddled with them. No security. All that American influence. Anyway, the Germans will probably tell their embassy to cooperate with us. I'd better go and brief the ambassador. Hang on to your bridge, Horatio."

The Resident had closed his eyes, as if in pain. Chisholm left and I walked over to the whiskey bottle on the side table, wishing I'd thought to take a drink while Chisholm was there to be offended. I took a slug and handed it to Antonio, who drank and passed it on to the Resident. He paused, and then accepted the bottle and put it to his lips. He swallowed twice.

"I haven't done that since 1918," he said. "What do we do now?"

I said I would go with Major Antonio. The Resident solemnly gave me another walkie-talkie. That was three strapped to my belt. It began to sag.

The copters were small Bell scouts, with just room for Antonio and me and the pilot. He took us first to the far side of the bridge, where I radioed Carlo that we were coming in. He said there was a police inspector who was very suspicious of his contract and was trying to reach the minister. The minister could not be found. He showed us the work so far—a long wide ditch in the tarmac beyond the bridge, with a ditching-machine still gouging at the soil.

"Looks good, eh?" said Carlo. "We got a pilot here and we still have the plane with the guns—but not enough runway. I was thinking what we could do to trucks full of troops stretched out on a road at night with their lights on. Pity about the runway."

We commiserated and climbed back into the copter, taking a long sweep down to the south and east to look for the lights of the infantry brigades. We flew south for almost twenty miles, and Antonio began to mutter about getting to Amadora when we turned east and saw them. We swooped very low to see if we could make out the dumpy silhouettes of the armored cars, but all we saw were trucks. The jeeps began to flash the lights as we flew slowly down the column.

"They think we're with them," said Antonio, reaching for his gun. I held his arm. There were too many guns in the convoy. And anyway, we knew where they were. We flew beside them checking their speed and then radioed Carlo. We gave him their location and said they could be with him in less than an hour.

It was while we were coming down to land at Amadora that I thought of it. Antonio was keen to climb out and find out what was happening in the commando barracks. He kept glancing over his shoulder at the men running from the guard room to the helipad.

"The Brownings," I shouted. "Why can't we fit them onto the copter and go and shoot up the columns. A real gunship."

Antonio nodded and turned away to greet the first of the soldiers who ran up. A sergeant, he saluted Antonio as soon as he saw the uniform.

"Antonio," I yelled. He turned back to me. "Tracer—have you got any tracer, caliber 0.5? That's your 12.7 mm. Get me some of that and I can hit Santarem." He heard the word Santarem and came back to the copter.

"Tracer," I said. "The fuel dumps at Santarem. Get me some 12.7 mm tracer for the Brownings and I can hit the fuel tanks."

He turned and snapped a question at the sergeant. He shook his head. There were no such things as 12.7 mm tracer. There were tracer round of 7.9 mm and even some high explosive 12.7 mm, but that was all. We told the pilot to turn off the engine, and at last we heard ourselves speak. Antonio sent off the sergeant to gather up what tracer and 12.7 mm explosive rounds he could find. We then radioed MSR, who radioed the RA-LIS base, asking for three fitters with portable welding gear, to be put into three copters and flown to Amadora. A fourth man was to be standing by at RA-LIS. I flew straight back there in the copter, radioing Carlo that I was coming in for the guns. I picked up the fitter, and within fifteen minutes of the idea he was starting to mount the double Brownings into the copter. It took him just over an hour, and as we were loading the belts of high-explosive shells one of Carlo's scouts reported seeing troops.

"They'll be twenty minutes away and they still don't know we're here," Carlo reported. "Go and hit Santarem first. Then come back." We checked our watches—we both had 11:05. I said I'd see him before midnight and he walked away, stooping beneath the blades as the pilot pressed the starter.

It was a simple flight, straight up the river Tagus for forty miles, and there was Santarem, the lights of the town spilling widely out beneath us. The pilot had the map on his knee and pointed at the cavalry school site. As we swooped in, a flare ignited, almost as high as we were and bathing in light the ant-heap of the parade ground. The armored cars were all drawn up in line, waiting to fuel up, but there were no tanks. They must have left already. The pilot scribbled on his knee pad: "Tank slow. Cars catch them." I nodded and we scanned the sky for the other copter, the one that had beaten us to it and had thought to pack some flares. I should have thought of it.

Suddenly we saw it, or at least we saw the source of the tracer bullets that began to curl down from the copter. It was aiming at the huge petrol bowsers that stood at the head of each line of armored cars. I saw two jeeps hit; and one armored car near the middle of the line exploded as the tracers poured down its open hatch. But the bowsers were unscathed, and already we could see the tracer shells leaping back up at the copter as the troops recovered from the surprise.

I signed to the pilot to go down low and to the side, hoping to creep in close while the troops were firing at the other copter. But somebody must have seen our exhausts, because a stream of tracer began to arc toward us. I swiveled in my seat to take the handles of the Browning and yelled at the pilot that I was ready. He boosted power to counter the gun's recoil and I sprayed the first line of the armored cars from back to front.

The first three cars exploded—those were the ones that had been hit at the back, where the armor is thinnest, designed only to stop rifle bullets. One other car began to burn—I must have hit some ammunition being loaded—but I missed the petrol

220

bowsers. As a dozen streams of tracer began to curl in and catch us, the pilot gave full power and leaped up, curving away above and over the armored cars, forcing their gunners to maximum elevation. Another burst of tracer spurted down from the sky behind us—the third copter had made it. He was good. His first burst hit one of the bowsers we had missed and then, in the sudden flare of the explosion, we saw that it had blasted two of the armored cars onto their sides, blocking the main exit from the parade ground.

The pilot dropped us like a stone, and I started firing again, hosing the front of the line, looking for another bowser lurking in the long, flame-lit lines of the cars. I saw another two cars explode, and we swooped low over them again, the pilot steadily dropping grenades out of his side door. As we swung away, we saw two streams of tracer coming from the sky, and another bowser exploded.

We turned to come in again, this time through a concentrated counterfire of tracer and turret-mounted machine guns. The pilot jinked and weaved, putting us in the cover of the building and swinging out to the side, darting above the roofline, giving me seconds for each quick burst before we went back to cover. The cars near the back of the parade ground had already started to disperse to other parts of the camp, hugging walls for cover while firing back at the choppers. One of them was lucky and caught one of the two high in the sky with a stream of tracer that must have hit the copter's ammunition. It blew apart in the sky while I was threading the two last belts into the guns. Each belt gave me twenty-five seconds of firing. I showed the pilot that this was our last charge, and he nodded and swung us away once more.

He swept us around the camp in a low curve, coming up the main driveway into the parade ground so we were hidden by the flare from the two burning cars that blocked the gates. He juggled us higher until I could see above the flames that there were three bowsers left. I took the first one with a short burst, shot all around the second without hitting it, and moved onto the third for the last few seconds of the ammo belt. I shot its tires and cab away and they began to burn, but the bowser failed to explode. I grabbed the Kalashnikov and started putting single shots into the bulk of the tank, hoping to cause leaks that would ignite, but without success. We began to swoop away when the surviving copter above us put another whole belt into the third bowser and it blew at last, taking the two armored cars still attached to it.

I reported first to Carlo, then to the embassy, and finally to the MSR radio man, asking him to get a message to Antonio. If there was one piece of news that would sway any uncommitted minds in the commando barracks it would be the news that there would be no armored cars coming from Santarem. The MSR radio man came back. He could not reach Major Antonio, but the Tancos base had been secured by the Loyalists. The men coming back from leave had already worked out their plan—they man-handled the aircraft in the hangars onto the runway to block it. Then they chained the aircraft wheels. Tancos base was neutralized.

I got the pilot to fly back to the south, looking again for the infantry brigades. We spotted them about four miles short of the bridge, stopped on the road, with smaller lights, probably jeeps, driving up ahead to investigate. I wanted to reload with more of the explosive bullets, so I told the pilot to head back for Amadora. As we flew I kept badgering the MSR radio man to contact Antonio. I wanted to have the cartridge belts ready on the ground when I landed.

We couldn't even land. There was a gun battle going on across the landing zone, and some of the huts were on fire. The pilot shrugged and swept us away to the RA-LIS base, where we loaded up with ordinary 12.7 mm belts and took some more aviation fuel and cruised back along the bridge. It was hard to reach Carlo by radio this close to the bridge. I kept yelling at him "four miles," but it didn't get through. I signaled to the pilot to land in as sheltered a position as he could and first reported back to the embassy and to MSR that a gun battle was going on at the commandos' base. I suggested to the MSR controller that with the armored threat gone from Santarem he could move some reserves up to the commando barracks. He reported back that we hadn't got the tanks at Santarem, just the armored cars. I saw his point.

We found Carlos and told him the column had stopped four miles away. He said he knew where they were and he'd already spoken to a colonel in a jeep. Told him the bridge was closed, then went back to rig more arclights for the bulldozers to work by. By now, he had built a second antitank ditch. Carlo had everything under control, and asked me not to use the gunship against the column until we were sure it was attacking.

"After Santarem and Tancos," he explained, "I think we've won." I asked him if he had anybody monitoring the radio for news bulletins. He had—there had been no word of any fighting or military activity. I radioed the embassy and asked the Resident to start telephoning the story through to my agency in London. Within five minutes of being on the wires in London, the Reuter's and AP and UPI boys would be onto it, the BBC would report it, and if any wavering soldiers were still thinking of joining the coup I wanted them to know we had taken their armor. The Resident agreed and we overed and out.

We went back to Amadora, and there was still fighting, but by now it had moved away from the helipad. The MSR radio man was still unable to locate Antonio; we landed and I quickly ran under the blades to an emergency aid post. The sergeant who had saluted Antonio was propped against a fire bucket while a medic worked on his thigh and a private held up the emergency blood transfusion kit.

I asked for Major Antonio and the sergeant shrugged. The private muttered something about "commandants" and signaled toward the fighting. I sprinted back to the copter and we took off to circle the fighting to see what was happening. It had focused around one main building, and from the flashes of the guns it looked as though one force was trying to encircle the building and was being held up on the flanks. We swooped low to see who was who, but it was impossible. The man at MSR still reported no contact.

The Resident buzzed me on the radio to say that there were

reports of fighting at Montijo. We took off and climbed high and we could see it. Glows of flares in the sky, and the MSR radio said there was a full-strength attack going on in the marine base, led by armored cars. We swooped across and were over mid-river when we saw, rather than heard, a big explosion in the countryside, about twenty miles east of Lisbon. The pilot looked at his map and his finger stubbed one of the road bridges. The tanks must have turned up. We radioed the news back to MSR and dived around the rear of the Montijo base.

The base entrance was being pounded by mortars firing smoke bombs, which probably meant the armored cars were forming up to attack through it. This time we had some flares on board, and I dropped one on the infantry side of the smoke clouds. The armored cars were there and we swooped behind them to hit their rear armor. This time I lacked the explosive bullets and only one of the cars exploded. But three had been badly shot up.

The pilot took me away from the armored cars and we began to seek the soft-skinned troop trucks. They had been well dispersed—the most we saw together was eight, and we left them all burning, though most of the troops reached cover. The last one exploded in a sheet of pure white flame. Ammunition truck. We found two more groups of four trucks and shot them up and then swooped over the mortar positions, the pilot leaning out to drop his grenades.

That was when the tracer hit us. I saw it curving in toward us but was sure it was going above us. The pilot kept us low, but then two bullets ricocheted away from our landing skids and the next two went into the pilot's legs. He kept us low, jinking left and right, zooming through the smoke and over the marine base. I saw him look for a landing ground, but mortar shells were still coming in and he swept away while blood began to puddle on the floor by his feet.

I looked helplessly at him. I couldn't fly a copter—there was nothing I could do. He took us straight over the river to the RALIS base. It was his base too. He brought us down in the center of the helipad, and I leaped out to bring the doctor. We took him off in a stretcher and I trotted beside it and looked at the mess the bullets had made of his left leg. The doctor said he would be okay and told one of the artillerymen to get me a drink. They had some cheap brandy and I asked for coffee with it. They had that too. I asked if they had another copter pilot, but no. I sat down to my walkie-talkie.

The embassy had put out the news story and had already been called back by Reuter's and the BBC. The Minister was even more impressed. The ambassador in Washington had been instructed to request an immediate inteview with Kissinger. The German Ambassador would be there too. The MSR man came through with the news I didn't want to hear. Major Antonio had been killed at Amadora barracks. Fighting continued.

# 21

There was still no spare pilot, so I asked them for a car. I was offered a motor bike, and they promised to send the gunship copter back to the landing ground on the tarmac by the bridge as soon as another pilot arrived. I took the river road and the streets were totally deserted between the airport and the end of the bridge. Across the river, by the Montijo base, I could see the sudden sun of flares and hear the dull thudding of the 75 mm cannon on the armored cars. I stopped at the approach to the bridge and radioed Carlo, asking him to warn his guards that I was coming over. He had still not heard back from the colonel he had seen, but the flares from the Montijo fighting made him think they would attack soon.

I drove slowly over the bridge, watching the battle for Montijo. There was another helicopter over it, firing tracer, and I wondered what had happened to the Portuguese Air Force. They could have blasted our little copters out of the sky. I thought of the runway at Tancos, blocked by their own aircraft. I began to think we had won, as long as Veroso continued with his assault on Montijo, and as long as the tanks did not break through the RA-LIS defenses at the airport.

When I got to the far side of the bridge, I had to climb the hill toward the huge cross to find Carlo's command post. His ex-Paras had told him not to worry about a frontal attack up the tarmac road to the bridge. They knew that armored cars were not going to get past bazookas on an open road with no cover. They were worried about infantry moving through the hills on the flank and firing down on our defenders. If that happened, we would either have to throw them off, after a direct assault uphill, or watch their machine guns cut down our bazooka positions while the armored cars sailed through. Carlo showed me the battery of the eight heavy mortars he had grouped around the base of the huge concrete cross. He had put three platoons of his ex-Paras into the hills to channel Veroso's infantry into the mortars' line of fire.

I asked if he were covering the western flank of the bridge, and Carlo shook his head. He had one small patrol out there, and the recoilless rifles were in reserve at the base of the bridge. He was keeping them there to cover the tiny ditches the earth-movers had dug, in case the armored cars broke through. There was no change at Montijo, the flares still washing the sky in the east and the half-hearted crump of the light artillery. It would have been nice if we had some mines and enough hours to lay them. It would be nice if we had another pilot to get that helicopter gunship back in the air.

"I think that they are coming, Ingles," said Carlo. "They are making a lot of noise over there at Montijo, but they are not attacking in force. To cross the bridge now is their only chance. If Veroso can join up with the tanks . . ." He shrugged and used his walkie-talkie to check again with the lookouts he had posted beyond the bridge tollbooths, our first line of defense. All but one reported no change, but one failed to reply to Carlo's call sign. He tried again, with no success. It was the lookout we had posted two miles up in the hills toward Montijo.

I went across to the jeep Carlo used to get up to the command post. It was military duty, with reinforced brackets to fit a machine gun and a heavy metal base plate, bolted directly to the chassis with retaining nuts to fit a light mortar. One of the ex-sergeants saw what I had in mind and ran off to the mortar battery Carlo had sited. He came back with a spare base for one of the mortars. It slotted neatly into the retaining clips on the jeep, and then he shook his head.

"He says the 81 mm is too heavy for the jeep. The springs will not take the recoil. Forget it," said Carlo. He turned away to try and raise his missing lookout on the radio. On the far side of the river, the RA-LIS guns were firing ranging shots. The tanks must be moving up the old road. We didn't have very long. I radioed back to the embassy and told them it looked as though the big attack was starting. "About time too," replied Chisholm.

Suddenly, from the hill's head, came the angry stutter of automatic fire. One of the platoon leaders radioed in to say that infantry patrols had appeared on both his flanks. Carlo told him to stay put and force any attacks to go round him, down into the low valley covered by our mortars. The other two platoons had each reported their sector quiet when the first shell slammed into one of the tollbooths below us. Two more followed, and we looked back up the road for the flash, but the armored cars were firing from cover. Ahead of us, the automatic fire had thickened into solid ripples of sound, broken by the thud of grenades. The other two platoons had also come under fire. Back at Montijo, the fighting had clearly died away and the RA-LIS guns were firing almost constantly. I tried looking for tracer bullets from the sky, but it looked as though our gunships had been grounded.

The old sergeant who had helped me with the mortar plate was firing short, economical bursts into the valley, hoping to draw fire so we would know when Veroso's infantry were in range of our mortars. We had no night-sights to check their movements. Carlo was shouting into his walkie-talkie, trying to make himself heard to the bazooka positions, who still could not see the armored cars that were shelling the tollbooths. There was nothing for me to do at the command post, so I went back down the hill to the motor bike and drove the few hundred yards up to the bazookas. Joao was there to grin at me as we sheltered in the culvert beside the tollbooths. He pointed down the road.

"They're just behind the shoulder of the hill down there, firing from cover. They must have a man spotting for them, but they're too far for the bazookas to worry them. We're keeping their heads down, that's all." Joao gestured across the wide road to a gully, where one of our machine guns was methodically spraying the shoulder of the hill down the road. He said we had a weak platoon of about twenty men somewhere up on the ridge above us, ready to hold off any of Veroso's infantry who might break through to try and command the road.

By this time, our ears were sullen and raw from the firing. I could no longer tell which direction the firing was coming from, but I was nerving myself to scamper across the road behind the tollbooths to check on the men holding the ridge above us, when Joao's hand on my arm held me back. He pointed down the road and I could make out movement. One of the men at the bazookas rolled onto his back and fired a flare high into the air, and as we looked down the road we saw three heavy trucks creeping out from behind the far hill in line abreast. They stopped, still well out of bazooka range, and began to reverse toward us. Behind them we saw the blunt silhouettes of the armored cars. They were going to use the heavy trucks as cover to get the armored cars near enough to make a dash.

We tried firing bursts low at their tires and we saw the trucks sag, but they still came on, a yard or so between the heavy bodies but enough for the armored cars to fire through. Across the road, one shell hit our machine gun post in the gully and as the flare fell away, we saw the tiny shapes of infantrymen hanging on to the armored cars. As soon as the trucks were stopped the infantry could use them as cover and pick off our bazookas before the armored cars were close enough to be hit.

I gathered four men and loaded us all down with cartridge belts and a GP machine gun, and we squirmed out of the culvert toward the scrub that covered the hills on our flank. We had to get forward, up to the point where the heavy trucks were so we could fire down on the infantry. We made about two hundred yards, and I stuck my head over a tiny fold in the ground. The trucks were still coming slowly on, the tires shot out and moving lamely on their rims. Every armored car was crawling with men. Then the flare died away. There was a tap on my ankle and little Joao, panting like a dog, lay below me pointing to the bazooka he had hauled up from the culvert. It was loaded with one shell, and he had two more on his back. That made about a hundred and ten pounds to drag along the hill under fire. I looked dubiously at the two spare shells. We would have time to fire one, maybe two, but then they would take us out with grenades.

The position we were in could have been worse. The fold in the ground gave some cover, and there was a tiny gully ten yards to our left. If we could fire one shell and then scurry to the second position, we might get off two rounds, perhaps the third. There were five armored cars below us, still crawling slowly behind the limping trucks. They had another thirty yards to go before they passed us. The road was too wide to try and block it by hitting the heavy trucks. We would have to take the cars. I squinted across the road to the ridge where we had a weak platoon. They had the height to fire down above the trucks and pick off the infantry, but the ridge remained silent. I hoped to hell they were old soldiers just holding their fire.

I ducked back down to Joao and the bazooka and sent the other three men off higher up the hill to site the machine gun. Joao and I dragged the bazooka to the edge of the fold in the ground and sighted in on the road just below and behind us. We could hear the straining engines of the trucks, and the flash when the armored cars fired was like red lightning on both sides of the road. I settled the bazooka into my shoulder as Joao readied the two spare shells. The rubber rim on the sight was cool on my cheek as I saw the nose of the first truck lurch into view. I was about thirty yards from it, perhaps twenty feet higher. It groaned past, sparks flicking from the rims of its wheels, and then the first of the armored cars nosed into my sight, squat and low on its huge tires, its silhouette spiky with crouching men. I sighted for the joint between turret and body and fired and ducked back, not even looking to see what damage had been done.

In cover, Joao reloaded for me and we sprint-crawled to the tiny gully. The armored car was blazing and lighting the whole road, and men were falling and jumping off the other cars as our machine gun chattered into them. My second shell was low, going into the next armored car just above the bulbous wheels and exploding underneath, blowing the heavy machine over onto its side. There was a rattle in my ear as rock chips pattered on the bazooka barrel; the machine guns on the other armored cars were spraying the rocks above them.

I ducked back as Joao reloaded for me. He slapped my shoulder to say it was done and squirmed off up the hill, biting the pin from a grenade with his teeth. I risked a look over the rim of my gully. Two of the heavy trucks had stalled, slewed across the road. It looked as though their drivers had been hurt when the first armored car exploded. Our machine gun was still chattering away above me, and the troops who had ridden in on the armored cars had all ducked behind the far side of the stalled trucks. The three armored cars still unharmed were nosing around the trucks, game for a last charge on the bridge. I looked down the road, and four more armored cars were moving up in support. I ducked back again as the infantry in cover began methodically to spray the side of my hill.

One bazooka shell left, and seven armored cars. But we had more bazookas down by the tollbooth. I would have to wait until all seven had passed me and try and block the road by disabling the last one—if the infantry didn't get me first. I couldn't hear our machine gun any more, but a sudden explosive light told me that Joao was still dropping his grenades into the road. Bullets were slamming into the rim of my gully—they had a good idea of where I was. I started to crawl back to the fold in the ground from which I had first fired, when the noise of constant firing exploded into a new ferocity. Across the road, at the ridge's rim, I saw the twinkling darts of gun muzzles. Our weak platoon had come into action, firing down into the unguarded backs of Veroso's battered infantry as they sheltered behind the trucks.

Up the road, the four fresh armored cars were racing down toward the firefight, their machine guns aiming at the rim of the ridge. The three armored cars that had run through our gauntlet were accelerating toward the tollbooths, getting out of my range. The first of the fresh cars slowed to negotiate the gap between the stalled trucks and the edge of the road as the demoralized infantrymen scurried in all directions for cover. I broke cover and nursed the bazooka into my cheek again, sighting on the gap by the stalled truck. The armored car braked to make the bend, entered my sights, and I fired.

I ducked down again, knowing I had missed, and began to squirm across the hill, trying to find our machine gun post that had fallen silent only moments ago. The gun might still be unharmed. I looked back at the road and saw it jammed. My miss had been good enough. I had seen no flash because the shell had gone into the front tire. The wheel had gone and the shock had driven the other front wheel into the ditch. The other wheels were spinning without purchase, the machine gun still firing and the cannon still trained on the tollbooths, but the road was blocked.

Down by the tollbooths, one of the armored cars was burning, but two seemed to have got through our first defense line. I looked at the walkie-talkie on my belt, but even if Carlo could hear me through the firing, my eardrums were still too stunned to hear him. On the ridge, our platoon was still firing down into the road, zeroing in on the three fresh armored cars that were nosing for a way through the tangled trucks and wrecked cars. It looked as though no more cars were coming, and if they did, I had nothing to stop them. I looked above me for the silent machine gun and crawled higher. When I found it, the gun was dismounted and the three men dead. I tried to clear the bolt but it stayed jammed. I took an FN rifle from one of the dead ex-Paras and squirmed across to a nest of rocks and began putting single shots into the tires of the fresh armored cars. It didn't do much good. They were designed to take rifle fire, but there wasn't much else I could do.

There was enough light from the burning cars to try and sight in on the tiny slits through which the drivers saw the road. I remembered, irrelevantly, an old instructor I had known who had been with the 51st Highlanders on the retreat to Dunkerque. They had slowed a Panzer advance by rapid rifle fire at the drivers' slits. The slits had been closed and the tanks had driven off the causeway into the canals. Where I was, there were no canals.

At last I saw what the armored cars were trying to do. They had jockeyed into a hollowed-square position, with enough covered space between them for what was left of their infantry to regroup. One of the armored car turrets opened, and before I could cover it a figure dived out of the hatch, rolled off the flank of the car and onto the ground. I was trying to draw a bead on what little I could see of him when I realized the armored cars were slowly reversing back up the road, the infantry huddled between them. They were pulling back, still firing and looking after their foot soldiers. They were good troops. I put down the rifle and suddenly there was silence.

Our old paratroops up on the ridge had seen the attackers pull back, and they had stopped firing. Down by the tollbooths, one armored car was still blazing, and there was no firing coming from the other two. Either they had been stopped or they had surrendered. I hadn't heard the crack of the recoilless, but with my ears still ringing from the blasts of the bazooka, I wasn't surprised. I called Carlo on the walkie-talkie, but I couldn't even hear static. I turned the set over and saw where something had ripped out its back. I threw the radio aside and began to crawl the long way back to the tollbooths, the FN rifle bumping on my back with each movement.

I was about halfway when I heard the shrill whistle of shells, and had rolled into the ditch when they exploded far behind me, back near the hill shoulder from which the armored cars had launched their charge. RA-LIS must have held off the tanks on the other road, if they could spare artillery to help us. Five shells went over, and then they stopped. Veroso must have got the message by now.

In the culvert by the burned-out tollbooths, Joao was sitting with a flask of brandy, his eyes sullen and distant on the burning wreck of the armored car. He had laid out the three men of our bazooka crew neatly, crossing their arms over their chests, and he had put their soft hats over their faces. Silently he handed me the brandy. I raised the flask to three dead men and drank deep. It tasted flat and still, as though it were water.

Silently, we trailed across the road and down toward the bridge where the crew from the two armored cars were sitting, their hands on their heads, guarded by some of our Paras. The prisoners had been given cigarettes, which they puffed nervously, squinting their eyes against the smoke. One of the guards tossed Joao a packet of SD filters and Joao handed me one, lit one, and put two behind his ears as we started up the hill toward the huge cross and Carlo's command post.

Carlo still wasn't convinced it was over. The three patrols were still out in the hills, still ready to funnel the attackers down into the valley that his mortars covered. The eight barrels were still smoking, and down in the valley I could see the twinkling red of the fires their shells had started.

"He's a good man, that old sergeant," said Carlo, gesturing at the man who had helped with the base plates on the jeep. "They had a battalion moving up through that valley and the mortars were getting too hot to use. He pissed on them to cool the barrels. Said they did it all the time in Angola."

Above our heads, a helicopter clattered across, very high, drifting south to see where Veroso's men were retreating to. Dawn would be coming soon. Carlo told us about RA-LIS and the tanks. They hadn't pressed the attack. Maybe they had wanted to know that the bridge had been taken first, maybe they had heard about the loss of the rest of the armored cars at Santarem. Carlo checked his platoon commanders for casualties. We had fourteen dead and thirty wounded, out of two hundred. We had about forty prisoners. We took their belts and boots and let them go. It was over.

"Funny thing," said Carlo. "When the mortar barrels were hot I couldn't piss at all. Now I feel like I'm carrying ten liters." He walked away from the huge cross and urinated onto the ground. I could hear the splashes. My ears had started to readjust.

I radioed back to the embassy. There had been a long meeting in Washington. Kissinger had been informed of the extreme displeasure of Her Majesty's Government and of the equal displeasure of our German allies. Kissinger had explained that it was all a matter of too much zeal by junior officers and inexperienced diplomats, acting without authority. And at no time would the policy of the United States Government stoop so low as to . . . the Resident related all this. I heard Chisholm's voice in the background saying, "It's all right. Their navy's turned back for Cadiz."

I turned off all the radios, curled up, and slept. Dawn was sending a glow of light to the east where the flares had been. My mouth still tasted of Joao's brandy.

# 22

It was about 10:00 A.M. when Carlo drove me down to the refugee camp where Otto had been held overnight. He had been given a bed and a meal and a doctor for his arm, and he looked rested. I must have looked as though we had lost because Otto's face smiled as I walked into the hut. Not his eyes, just his face.

"You lost, Otto. We're sending you back to Moscow to explain."

His face stopped smiling. "Lost?" he repeated.

"Lost. Stopped in its tracks. Dr. Kissinger says the Americans were not involved apart from an incautious junior officer or two. Lopes Veroso was arrested by his own troops this morning. It's all over, Otto. The coup failed. Portugal is not going to go American, and you and I did a good enough job last week to make sure it won't go Communist." I flopped into a chair opposite him. I wanted to shower and I wanted to sleep. Maybe I could sleep in a shower. Otto was silent. That was okay.

"Last piece of news, Otto. Three members of the executive committee of the Portuguese Communist Party have been arrested and are to face a party trial. For cooperating with you and the Yankees. For obeying Moscow's orders. You'll get a great welcome in Moscow, Otto. I just hope you remember your Russian. There's only one thing left."

I stood up and went and sat on the arm of his chair. Carlo lounged by the door, his tommy gun in the crook of his arm. Otto stared straight ahead into space.

"Where is she, Otto?" He said nothing, so I tapped him lightly on the elbow. He fell off the chair onto the floor. It was the elbow where I'd shot him. I tapped it again. "The girl, Otto. The girl or your arm."

The blood was running down his wrist again before he said that Thayer had her. I said we would get him on a flight to Moscow as soon as we could. He said he'd rather not go to Moscow. Carlo spat.

"You want a deal, Otto? Not much you can offer us, is there? One failed coup, Otto, and the training techniques you learned twenty years ago. No chance. Moscow here we come."

"There is a deal—the American deal. I know the agreement. In return for giving them Portugal, the Americans would let us . . . that's my deal, Maddox. I'll tell you what we get in return."

"Not enough, Otto. We'll find out soon enough. The Americans are feeling very uncomfortable about losing in Portugal. They'll probably tell us themselves. You're probably their problem, anyway. Tell me about the American deal and I'll hand you over to Major Thayer."

237

He agreed—he had little choice. I tried calling Major Thayer at the embassy, but Otto shouted another number at me.

"You won't find him at the embassy. He'll be at the staff college annex near Tancos. That was the operations HQ."

I handed him the phone and told him to get Thayer on the line. The phone rang and rang and finally it was answered. Otto asked for Thayer and waited. He took three long minutes to come to the phone. They spoke in German, Otto reporting what had happened to the plane and the guns. Then he gave me the phone.

"I'll do you a straight swap, Thayer. Otto for the girl. Otherwise we give Otto to the Portuguese and let them put him on trial. It will all come out in court. Otto. You. The deal you made."

I didn't believe it. Chisholm would want to do it but London wouldn't let it happen. It's one thing to humiliate your strongest ally in private—it's another to put them in the dock for an international show trial. But Thayer's own position was too weak to let him take that chance. If the State Department was regretting the actions of its over-zealous juniors, then Thayer was going to be the scapegoat anyway. Still, he tried.

"She's my daughter, Dave. And nobody's going to believe that Otto is anything but German."

"Don't bother, Thayer. We've also got the pilot of the plane that came down with him, and we've got the party cards of some other playmates. And half the Communist Party wants to get into the witness box and testify what detente did to them. I'll give you ninety minutes. We can do the exchange at Guincho, just like you planned. Otherwise Otto goes on trial."

I put the phone down and radioed the embassy. If I were lucky, Chisholm and the Resident would be asleep. I could report I was giving Otto to the Yanks—they wouldn't get woken up for that. But I'd have delivered the message in time. The exchange would be made before Chisholm could stop it. One of the junior attachés took the message. Sure enough, Chisholm and the Resident were resting.

Carlo drove while I sat in the back with Otto. We had

bandaged his elbow again and given him a sling. They moved the bulldozers to let us drive back across the bridge. I asked Carlo why he hadn't removed the equipment.

"You saw the ditches we made across the road—they'll have to be repaired. That's for my friends in the construction business. They can do the repairs. That was my deal, Ingles. So I leave the equipment in place. Meanwhile I'll put some planks over the ditches to let cars through—they can pay me an extra toll fee."

"It's not much recompense, Carlo, for what you and Joao did."

"There'll be more. We've got our own political party now. That's a license to print money. My villas, my investments—they can all go ahead. Tourists come back, there'll be business for the whores again. A lot of building to be done. A lot of new armored cars to be bought for the army. Can you do one thing for me?"

"Name it."

"Does Britain make armored cars, personnel carriers?" I said we made good ones. "Okay—make me the Portuguese agent," grinned Carlo. "The official agent in Portugal. Maybe for helicopters too."

I said I'd do my best and nudged Otto. "What about your business, Otto. Who'll get that?"

"The first man to walk through the door and take over the desk. How should I know?"

I radioed Joao and told him Otto's office address. In the glove compartment of the car I found a sheet of blank paper and told Otto to sign it at the bottom. It was a left-handed signature, so odd that nobody would query it—if they ever asked to see it. Joao could fill in a transfer agreement above the signature. Then he'd take over the business. Carlo began to sing, and the traffic on the roads was starting to move again. It was a nice day.

We drove past the restaurants that dominated each bay of the coast road, and Carlo pointed ahead to the modernized fort in the next bay. "That's the place." He changed down and we crawled around the bend. There was an American car standing alone at the far end of the car park with a man waiting beside it. Carlo drove toward it.

Carlo climbed out and crouched behind the door, his tommy gun resting on his hip. Thayer was unarmed. I pushed Otto out and stood beside him.

"Marianne is unconscious. The guards gave her an injection," said Thayer. "You'll have to come and get her." He paused. "I'm sorry," he called.

I put Otto back in the car and locked the door. We shouted to Thayer to move back from the car, and Carlo and I crouch-sprinted to both sides of the big Yank car. Carlo kept his gun on Thayer while I checked the car. She was lying curled up on the back seat, a rug over her. I opened the door and eased her into my arms and carried her back to our car. I put Marianne down on the ground and covered Otto with my gun while he slowly climbed out and began to walk across to Thayer.

"You've forgotten something, Otto. The deal. What was it?"

He turned slowly and looked back to see if Thayer was in hearing distance. "Angola," he said softly. "They got Portugal and they let us take Angola. The Americans have stopped arming their guerrillas. Our MPLA are going to be allowed to win." He started to turn back to Thayer, then he stopped.

"Maddox, remember you once quoted Engels at me?" I nodded. "You got the quotation wrong. 'History is a cruel goddess and drives her chariot over heaps of slain.' That's how it goes. I wanted to tell you that."

" 'The owl of Minerva spread her wings with her coming of dusk,' Otto. That's Hegel and I don't understand it either."

He gave me a clenched fist salute and began to limp his way to Thayer's car.

The rifle cracked once, sharply, and I rolled under the car, dragging Marianne's body after me. It fired again and I saw Otto clutch his chest with his good hand and spin to the ground. Beyond him, Thayer was slumped across the hood of his car. There was a third shot and his body jerked and rolled off onto the ground. The shot had come from the dunes between the car park and the sea. Carlo had the spot covered, and I sprinted back for the shelter of the little wall of the car park.

Carlo glanced at me and I nodded. He sprayed the top of the

dunes as I broke cover and ran diagonally to the rise of the ground. I looked back. Marianne was under the car, Carlo was in cover. Thayer and Otto lay dead. I inched forward between two hillocks in the sand and looked down at the beach.

The green Bedford truck had its rear door open and the Resident was pouring from a thermos flask. Chisholm was putting the rifle into the back of the vehicle. I stood up and waved to Carlo. He started to pull Marianne from under the car, and I plodded through the sand to the van.

"It's only coffee, I'm afraid," the Resident smiled. He must have slept in his clothes, but he still looked immaculate. Even his shoes were polished and free from sand. "It's tidier this way, Maddox. Just two more casualties of the coup. No questions, no embarrassments."

"I don't think he needed the second shot," said Chisholm. "Had to make sure, though. You know these bloody Yanks. Get up and shoot you in the back soon as look at you. Pity about old Otto. Do you want sugar, Maddox?" asked Chisholm, blowing on his coffee to cool it. The Resident handed me a cup.

"It's Angolan coffee, you know. Probably the last we'll get for some time, from what we hear," said the Resident.

"Why the last?" I said.

"Washington told our ambassador last night. That was the deal. The Russians gave Portugal to the Americans and in return the Yanks would let them have Angola. Nasty little deal. Typical," said Chisholm.

"That's what Otto told me," I said. "Angola. That was my deal with him. He could live if he told me what the deal was. The alternative was going on trial here. It was the thought of being exposed as a Communist who betrayed other Communists that made him tell me. He was all right, Otto."

"We'll have to pull you out, of course," said Chisholm. "The fat man can take over. We've had to bring him in from Madrid. His son is in hospital here, and it made sense. Your face is getting too well known here. There'll be some leave, of course. A few weeks before we send you off again. You'll be going to Angola, Maddox."

241

"Angola?"

"Well, you seem to thrive in this Portuguese environment, and we can't let the Russians have Angola. Too close to Rhodesia and South Africa and all that. You know the policy, Maddox, freedom for the blacks but not for Communism. We've got no networks left there, of course, so we thought of sending you in with some mercenaries. Recruiting has already started. We're rather hoping you could persuade some of your Angolan network here to go back with you."

I shook my head. "They've all settled down. Got businesses here, a future in politics. They won't leave. I'm not sure I will, Chisholm. You didn't have to kill them. You know that, don't you? They could have lived."

"The Yanks wanted it that way. They asked us to tidy up, as a favor. Could hardly refuse when they put it like that. You need some leave, Maddox. A couple of months in the sun with a girl or two. Relax. Forget it."

"I want to see this girl of yours, Maddox," the Resident said, rising to take my arm. Chisholm was going to come too but the Resident waved him back, not even bothering to look to see that Chisholm stayed. Nobody disobeyed the Resident.

I guided him back through the dunes. Carlo was leaning against the car, the tommy gun on his hip. He had put Marianne in the back seat. Still unconscious, but very pale and lovely. A tan would suit her. I tucked the rug more closely around her while Carlo chatted with the Resident. I turned back to them.

"Carlo wants the agency to sell our arms to the Portuguese. He deserves it—he's the man who held the bridge last night."

The Resident nodded. "I'm sure something can be arranged. And now your leave, Maddox. I have a place in the Algarve, between Lagos and Sagres. Why not spend your leave there with your young lady? There's a small boat and it's very quiet. You need the rest. We'll know where to reach you."

I thanked him and walked back over the dune to Chisholm and asked him for some expenses. He silently handed me 5,000 escudos and stuck out his hand. I took the money and ignored his hand and walked back to the Resident.

242

Carlo was carrying Marianne back to her father's car. The Resident handed me its keys.

"It's easier this way. Carlo keeps his car, you drop Thayer's ugly vehicle in Lisbon and then use your car to drive on down to the coast. The villa is open, but I will warn the maid of your arrival."

I shook the Resident's hand and embraced Carlo. "Always the Beira will find me, Ingles." He pulled a card from his pocket and gave it to me. "My agent in the Algarve. You go and see him, anything you need."

Before I climbed into the big car I checked the trunk. Marianne's case was already inside. She was still asleep on the back seat. Thayer hadn't been given a chance to tell me when she'd wake up. I drove back on the coast road to Lisbon to pick up my clothes from the hotel. And her pills. We were going to need them.